VOLUME III : EIGHTEENTH-CENTURY PROSE

EDITED BY D. W. JEFFERSON

57009067

THE PELICAN BOOK OF ENGLISH PROSE

GENERAL EDITOR : KENNETH ALLOTT

VOLUME III

Eighteenth-Century Prose

· 1700–1780 ·

EDITED BY D. W. JEFFERSON

PENGUIN BOOKS

Penguin Books Ltd, Harmondsworth, Middlesex

u.s.a.: Penguin Books Inc., 3300 Clipper Mill Road, Baltimore 11, Md

canada: Penguin Books (Canada) Ltd, 178 Norseman Street,
Toronto 18, Ontario

australia: Penguin Books Pty Ltd, 762 Whitehorse Road,
Mitcham, Victoria

south africa: Penguin Books (S.A.) Pty Ltd, Gibraltar House,
Regent Road, Sea Point, Cape Town

—

First published 1956

Made and printed in Great Britain
by The Whitefriars Press Ltd
London and Tonbridge

CONTENTS

CONTENTS

2. THE MOVEMENT OF IDEAS:
REFLECTION, ARGUMENT, EXHORTATION, SATIRE

CONTENTS

3. THE WORLD OF IMAGINATION, FEELING AND COMIC INVENTION: FICTION, HISTORICAL AND OCCASIONAL WRITING

CONTENTS

GENERAL INTRODUCTION

The Pelican Book of English Prose has the aim of bringing into focus for the ordinary reader nearly three hundred and fifty years of English prose: so that he may see for himself its variety and continuity in successive ages, the many purposes for which it has been employed (including the humbler ones), the prose styles thought expressive at different times, and the ruling interests and attitudes of particular periods with their associated changes of tone in the conduct of prose. This has involved some planning. An anthology is judged practically by what we can do with it. If it is to be read intelligently or used for study, not merely dipped into idly, it needs to support the reader's interest by a certain coherence and consistency of approach: that is to say, its contents must be properly arranged and introduced. The present anthology contains about 425,000 words of text exclusive of editorial matter and includes some three hundred writers who were at work between 1550 and 1880. These initial and terminal dates are plainly convenient: before 1550 prose cannot be read easily by the general reader without a glossary (and it will not be read, one suspects, with a glossary except by the serious student); after 1880 considerations of copyright become troublesome and begin to influence an editor's choice. The preliminary disposition of the material is in five volumes in chronological sequence, as follows:

I Elizabethan and Jacobean prose (1550–1620)
II Seventeenth-Century prose (1620–1700)
III Eighteenth-Century prose (1700–80)
IV Prose of the Romantic Period (1780–1830)
V Victorian prose (1830–80)

Each volume is self-contained and independently edited, but

the unity of the whole anthology is preserved by a 'horizontal' classification which cuts across the 'vertical' chronological division just described. The anthology, then, is sub-divided both chronologically and, within each volume, by an arrangement of subject-matter in accordance with the following scheme:

1. The Picture of the Age: Scene, Personality, Event
2. The Movement of Ideas: Reflection, Argument, Exhortation, Satire
3. The World of Imagination, Feeling and Comic Invention: Fiction, Historical and Occasional Writing
4. The Criticism of the Arts

The editors of the separate volumes have found this scheme, which took its final form only after several revisions, sufficiently flexible; and it is hoped that it may provide a useful framework for the reader and enable him to grasp more rapidly the distinguishing characteristics of prose in each period. It was the general editor's task to see that the agreed scheme was followed and to act as a clearing-house for the suggestions and criticisms of his colleagues. The sharing among six editors of the task of reading and selecting pieces for the five volumes of the anthology has probably been an advantage. It has meant a wider and more accurate coverage of the enormous area of English prose between 1550 and 1880; and it has allowed particular sections of prose to be undertaken by editors whose interests are centred in the periods for which they are responsible. The disunity that might have resulted from the arrangement has been carefully guarded against: both by the adoption of the agreed scheme and by other means of ensuring a common approach which have still to be described.

Some of these means were mechanical. It was decided that a substantial proportion of the passages in each volume, usually selected from the more important writers, should be long enough to furnish material for an hour's discussion if the anthology should be used as a textbook. It was also thought desirable that the introductory essays to the five volumes should be mainly concerned with the discrimination of prose styles, and that they should all contain frequent references to the authors and extracts introduced. Again, it was proposed that in each volume passages should be chosen where possible to shed light on each other, and it was agreed that the value of the whole work would partly depend on the number of the relationships of this kind it was possible to establish. A good deal of effort lies behind whatever success has been achieved. For example, a dozen passages in Volume II bear on any discussion of political and theological attitudes in the Great Rebellion, Volumes III and IV have some nicely mixed specimens of political writing and also groups of passages which touch on marriage and the position of women, Volume I gives us Nashe and Gabriel Harvey on Nashe, Volume V Dickens and Walter Bagehot on Dickens. There are also links between the volumes – it is not an accident that a passage by Carlyle in Volume V should refer to an incident in Mungo Park's African travels which is reproduced in Volume IV. Some of these correspondences lie on the surface, as in the examples chosen, but many are more esoteric and will not be apparent until the anthology is actively used. In each volume the order of the passages in the first section, 'The Picture of the Age', is chronological, but the order in the other three sections – for the sake of these correspondences – offers what F. T. Palgrave calls 'gradations of feeling or subject'. Such gradations may or may not combine with a modified chronological plan.

More important than any of these means of ensuring singleness of approach has been the community of feeling among the editors about what an anthology of prose should be called on to illustrate. *The Pelican Book of English Prose* is not a collection of the best passages of English prose, or even, exclusively, of the best passages of the authors included in it – a collection on either principle would produce an effect less representative than the one aimed at. A common objection to prose anthologies is that their editors do not choose passages typical of the authors represented because they put an undue weight on 'fine writing'. From some anthologies one would naturally conclude that historians reserved all their energies for depicting battle-scenes, or that Lyly, Sir Thomas Browne and Landor were considerably more important as writers of prose than Hooker, Dryden and Gibbon. In contradistinction our working-hypothesis has been that prose should not be too self-conscious, that the writers of the best English prose usually had more on their minds than the problems of style, and that much respectable prose in every age is unmindful of the schoolmaster's ferula.[1] Consequently, in compiling this anthology, we have been guided by the following principles:

1. To choose passages primarily for the interest of their subject-matter (on the assumption, which has been justified, that such passages will inevitably illustrate all the prominent varieties of prose style).

2. To choose from a particular author not his most detachable pieces of fine writing, but passages which are typical of his normal manner when he is writing well.

3. To illustrate sparingly the 'purple passages' of English prose.

4. To include some prose at a pedestrian level of achievement for its documentary value (more particularly in the first section of each volume).

The editors consider that these methods of selection give a

[1]. The degree of self-conscious organization that is 'natural' varies, of course, from age to age, and, in any age, according to literary kind (for example, a declamatory style is more natural in a pulpit or from the hustings than in a diary or private letter).

more accurate cross-section of English prose than is obtained from most anthologies,[1] and that the loss in serious prose-artistry is negligible. Nothing that has been said should be taken to imply a settled antipathy to ornate prose, but it is fair to admit that the editors are suspicious of its self-conscious varieties after the Restoration (while recognizing with Newman that some 'verbiage' may be the natural expression of a generous 'fullness of mind').

The Text. Modernization has been rejected and passages are reproduced with the spelling and punctuation of the copy-texts (except for the silent correction of misprints and the conservative emendation of misleading punctuation). Thus Elizabethan prose retains its 'dramatic' or haphazard pointing except in special instances, and Keats's difficulties with spelling are left to appear. The only passages given in a modernized form are those first printed long after their original composition, e.g. an Elizabethan diary first published in the middle of the nineteenth century. Some unfamiliar words and phrases, which are naturally more frequent in Volumes I and II, are glossed briefly in footnotes where the context seems to require it – this is a matter that has been left to the individual editor's discretion – but no attempt has been made to supply a sense for all unusual words or to explain the many allusions.

The source of each passage is given at its foot, and the abbreviation of titles has been indicated (wherever possible the extended title has been preserved if of interest). First editions have usually been employed, but many passages included in the anthology were added by their authors to editions later

1. *The London Book of Prose* (1932), compiled by Professor Dobrée and Sir Herbert Read, is an obvious exception. Its excellence sets a standard for this kind of work.

than the first, or were revised through several editions, so that the preferred form of a passage may be found, for example, in a fifth edition. On the other hand, the unrevised version of a passage has sometimes been preferred by an editor for its freshness and unfamiliarity. The apparent anomalies in the choice of copy-texts are mostly explicable on such grounds, but there were a few occasions when a first edition would have been used if it had been available. The use of certain copyright material is acknowledged in a note at the end of each volume.

K. A.

INTRODUCTION

It is usual, and conveniently easy, to relate some of the main characteristics of early eighteenth-century prose to social and cultural changes belonging partly to the previous period, such as the growth of scientific discussion (calling for what Sprat, in the well-known passage in his *History of the Royal Society*, described as a 'close, naked, natural way of Speaking') and the rise of a philosophy in sympathy with the scientists' zeal for clarification and for getting down to bedrock. The development, a little later, of the newspaper and periodical journalism generally was another factor making for the utilitarian virtues in prose. At another level simplicity, along with 'naturalness' and 'ease', were now being preferred to ostentation and affectation, as marks of good manners, whether in life or in letters. It was Addison's function, through the immense vogue of his essays, to make current a style embodying these values. Professor James Sutherland, in a most admirable essay [1] on eighteenth-century prose, remarks that Addison's style 'comes near to being the unhurried conversation of an eighteenth-century gentleman', and that it descends from Dryden and the Restoration 'mob of gentlemen who wrote with ease'. This colloquial quality is present in much of the philosophical writing, notably in that of Mandeville and Berkeley. Not only did eighteenth-century philosophy use a language which ordinary educated men could understand, but its tone is often expressive of human contact with the reader. Berkeley's best passages of disciplined explanation are admirably alive: behind the thoroughness with which everything is made more than doubly clear we feel the personal conviction and patience of the teacher who has something good to give. Literary criticism

1. In *Essays on the Eighteenth Century Presented to David Nichol Smith* (1945).

stressed the virtue of simplicity. There had been a reaction against the old ingenious kinds of wit in poetry, in favour of wit based on nature and common experience, and this gave rise to generalizations applicable also to prose. Addison refers (in *Spectator* 62, 11 May 1711) to, 'that beautiful Simplicity, which we so much admire in the Compositions of the Ancients; and which no Body deviates from, but those who want Strength of Genius to shine in its own natural Beauties.' He then introduces the analogy of architecture, the classical style being praised for its beautiful simplicity, the Gothic criticized for trying to make up for the lack of it with 'all the Extravagances of an irregular Fancy'. Swift insisted strongly on simplicity in preaching, expressing considerable animus against the pedantry or coxcombry of those who trespassed against it. Speaking of 'the frequent use of obscure *Terms*, which by the Women are called *Hard Words*, and by the better sort of Vulgar, *Fine Language*', he says that he knows of no more 'universal, inexcusable, and unnecessary Mistake'; and later in the same work, the *Letter to a Young Gentleman* (1721), he condemns a 'quaint, terse, florid Style, rounded into Periods and Cadencies, commonly without either Propriety or Meaning'. Lord Chesterfield's letters to his son, so full of warnings against every form of ill-breeding, whether of the low or the conceited kind, are written in a simple, sensible style which well exemplifies the taste and attitudes he tried to inculcate.

It is very helpful for us that our study of eighteenth-century prose can begin in this way, with the simplest of conceptions, that of simplicity itself, as the dominant emphasis, and with such palpable, readily-grasped historical phenomena as science, common-sense philosophy, journalism, the new social tone in manners and conversation, and the anti-Gothic and anti-metaphysical tendencies in criticism to turn to for 'background'. It is helpful, but only if we regard it as a beginning. It should not serve us for long. The more interested we become in any one of the major figures of the early part of the century the less content we shall be to fit him into this pattern; though, perhaps, our dissatisfaction will be least acute in the case of Addison. Defoe, Swift, Berkeley are all great individual artists, full of personality and idiosyncrasy; they compel us to re-fashion our generalizations. Addison is more a great institution than a great artist. Professor Sutherland says of him that 'he gave to Englishmen an example of good prose that any writer could imitate without losing his own identity; he has a sort of neutral quality that allowed his imitators to develop their own personal idiom. If one must have a model, Addison could hardly be bettered; he will lead to no eccentricities or affectations, he has good manners without being mannered, and he is well within the range of the average mind.' But in Addison the quality of simplicity easily becomes insipidity. The reader who encounters him before making the acquaintance of other writers of this century (his impeccable moral outlook, innocuous humour and unathletic mind, together with the convenient length of the essay as a literary form, have made him an inevitable 'set author') may begin with rather a poor idea of what Augustan prose can give him. No serious harm would be done if Addison were a little neglected in our time. But his position in history, as a popular exponent of the taste and learning of his age, as well as in the sphere of prose style, is unchallengeable.

Words like 'plain' and 'simple' are unsatisfactory when we are trying to do justice to a great writer like Defoe. They may be difficult to avoid, but they have associations which must be fought against. The 'matter-of-factness' of Defoe's autobiographical narrators, for example, may often be regarded as a kind of unconscious rhetoric. One of the great qualities of Crusoe is that he is far more heroic than he realizes (he takes the island experience in his stride, as an episode among others), so that when he tells us at the end of his story the precise details to the last threepence of his financial position and the exact date of his final arrival in England where, at the age of seventy-two, he now intends to settle down, the effect is one of style, of a kind of understatement. And the habit of methodical attention to detail oddly enhances Moll Flanders' telling of the peculiarly hair-raising incident of the robbing of the little girl.[1] The listing of the streets through which she made her way is, in a sense, mere routine; it adds to verisimilitude for a London reader, we may say; but how it contributes to our impression of an experience stamped upon the memory with an awful obsessive particularity! Moll knows, in her own way, that it was a horrible occurrence (she continually refers to the devil), but her mention of so intimate a concrete detail as her pretence of mending the child's clog conveys a shudder which is quite outside her own imaginative range. Defoe's novels abound in passages in themselves unvarnished enough, but full of implications of which the narrator is imperfectly aware. One of his idiosyncrasies in the more toughly factual books, is an unexpected feeling for his subject-matter, which gives excitement to the prose, an effect that owes nothing to conscious rhetoric. In the early part of *The Plan of the English Commerce* (1728), where he claims that English workmen are superior to all others it is through making the phrases of common speech vibrate that he conveys his gratification.[2] 'Matter-of-fact' is another of the drab expressions one ought to keep out of one's vocabulary when speaking of Defoe; but the difficulty is to find words with a similar meaning, without the drabness.

In our reading of eighteenth-century prose we are confronted from the outset with a variety of distinct styles or levels of writing. Addison and Defoe are both conversational, but very different in social tone. From the point of view of the polite, Defoe was 'outside the circumference of wit'. He belonged to an inferior cultural group, he addressed himself to

1. See p. 213.   2. See p. 113.

members of the trading classes and Dissenters. It is interesting to find writers like Tom Brown and Ned Ward still active in this century, also 'low' but not in Defoe's way: their peculiar sprightliness and fustian take us back to Elizabethan pamphleteers like Nashe and Dekker. Skill in manipulating more than one style – a particular style for a particular purpose, or one style in combination or contrast with another – is an important part of the equipment of some of the more sophisticated writers, notably Swift and Fielding. The great Augustan wits were critically and satirically interested in style. Just as Pope pillories absurd styles of poetry in the *Art of Sinking in Poetry*, so Swift's specimens of 'genteel conversation' expose the colloquial insipidities and barbarities of the period, and some of his *jeux d'esprit* like *A Meditation upon a Broomstick* (1710) shows his gifts of parody in other directions. In the *Drapier's Letters* (1724) something like parody is used with great strategic effect. Writing in the character of a simple tradesman (thus identifying himself more nearly with the everyday victims of Wood's Halfpence) he adopts tradesman's English; he pretends to be a Defoe. The vocabulary and tone of the argument are superficially those of the common man, but with an awful joy we see them manipulated and terrifically heightened by a master of verbal impacts and controlled dialectic.[1] No adequate indication can be given here of the unrivalled wealth of Swift's resources as a prose writer.[2]

Fielding combines some of Swift's stylistic virtuosity with a relaxed and urbane temperament and an easy tone which remind us more of Dryden. Like earlier masters of the novel, such as Cervantes, he was fond of varying the interest by using inserted narratives related by personages in the main story;

1. See p. 136.
2. A fuller discussion of them will be found in my essay on Swift in *A Guide to English Literature*, Volume IV (Pelican Book: in the press).

and this provides the opportunity for changes of style which he turns to useful account. For example, when Mr Wilson in *Joseph Andrews* (1742) tells his life story, there is a change from the novelist's habitual lightness and wit to the sober, straightforward idiom of the penitent's autobiography (the same form as we find in Defoe's novels, but more 'educated'). This enables Fielding to testify, in an oblique way, to a serious appreciation of moral values. We know that the heartfelt description of conjugal virtue and happiness with which Mr Wilson ends his story tallies with Fielding's own idea of the good life. But it was not his practice as a novelist (except in his latest work: *Amelia* is more openly serious) to write from a solemn, moral standpoint, and it is only under cover of his secondary narrator that he conveys these attitudes. It is clear that, like many people, he sometimes found this naughty world highly amusing, and sometimes less so; but, on the whole, he preferred to leave the reader guessing how strongly he really felt about the serious things, and his art provides beautifully for tactical evasions. A neat example of this is Mr Allworthy's little sermon to the supposed mother (unmarried) of Tom Jones. Again, moral and religious teachings with which ultimately the novelist was in sympathy, are put on record, impeccably formulated, and uttered by an entirely good character. But the sermonizing idiom and the slight flavour of comedy which always accompanies Mr Allworthy's moral pronouncements (he is a 'model' character charmingly oversimplified, the embodiment of abstract rightness habitually deceived concerning matters of fact) serve to distance the sentiments and keep the novelist out of it. The speech is an artificial 'set piece': it serves Fielding's purpose and suits his humour to give the situation a formalized, non-naturalistic quality. He often does this, and the effect, in novels so full of rude life and elementary human nature, is amusing. There is a pleasing specimen of the set-piece type of speech in *Joseph*

Andrews, where the hero, languishing in pain, addresses a rhapsodical soliloquy to his virtuous sister, the 'most adorable Pamela'.[1] The humorous effect of the idiom is to link the honest, plebeian hero in our minds with heroes in a more courtly tradition. His letter to Pamela in an earlier chapter is in a much homelier style. It is in keeping with Fielding's playful equivocation between different aspects of Joseph that he should turn out later to be a gentleman after all!

With the writers of the middle of our period and later, there is, on the whole, an increase in conscious refinement and artistry in prose. The colloquial quality of Dryden and Addison is inherited by Fielding and Sterne, but they embellish it, and in Sterne especially an elaborate personal manner is developed. Writers like Goldsmith and the historians, Robertson and Gibbon, cultivate a smoothness of diction and sophistication of phrasing which are very seductive to the modern reader. A more studied architectural treatment of the sentence and the paragraph is associated with the names of Johnson, Gibbon and Burke. But some of the later authors, like Boswell, do not move in this direction. There was no question of conformity to a fashion.

A form of 'refinement' characteristic of the comic novelists is the habit of putting a surface on crude and violent themes. Fielding resorts to mock-heroic in the celebrated churchyard battle in *Tom Jones* (1749), and his description of the sluttish personal appearance of Tishy Snap in the passage where Jonathan Wild pays her a visit of courtship is in another style of verbal artifice.[2] Smollett, in scenes involving physical discomfiture (he is far too much addicted to them), uses an elaborate code of euphemisms. A blow is usually a 'compliment' or a 'salutation'. The following description from *Sir Launcelot Greaves* (1762) is typical: 'The second stroke encountered his pate, which being the hardest part about him,

1. See p. 195.   2. See p. 160.

sustained the shock without damage; but the third, lighting on his ribs, he honoured the giver with immediate prostration.' It may be suggested that Smollett's vocabulary incurs the reproach levelled, in Fowler's *Modern English Usage*, against 'polysyllabic' and kindred types of verbal humour. In general, it could be claimed as a defence of Smollett that he knew how to manage a polished and somewhat latinized diction with discretion and adroitness, and that the stylistic offences which Fowler had in mind were mainly those of later writers less sure in their taste. Some readers may feel, and there are passages which support this, that the euphemistic technique of Smollett and others is a means of providing a polite reading public with a little refined brutality. On the other hand, its function may sometimes be to give an acceptable flavour to the honest satirical treatment of social horrors. Was it not Dickens's method often to make unpleasant things comic, so that we enjoy their exposure and do not want to forget them?

No contrast could be steeper or more instructive than that provided by the polite and witty manner of Fielding and Smollett set against the awful directness of Richardson. No comic euphemism relieves the description in *Clarissa* (1747–8) of the women hovering over the death-bed of Mrs Sinclair.[1] Richardson's puritanical seriousness has no use for distancing, whether of solemn ideas or of appalling realities, and the realism of his language has a kind of strength which none of his contemporaries can match; a strength which, however, he was not artist enough to use with the fullest effect. His idiom is that of a less polite world: we are surprised when Clarissa confesses to being 'struck all of a heap'. But this makes possible a style of description which renders the full monstrosity of the Harlowe household and of Clarissa's situation. Mr Solmes, her unlovely suitor, she describes as

1. See p. 220.

'sitting asquat' and again as 'hemming up for a speech, rising and beginning to set his splay feet . . . in an approaching posture.' Of her sister she says, 'poor Bella has, you know, a plump high-fed face,' and 'My sister sat swelling'; and when Bella sneers at her for being their grandfather's favourite it is with expressions like, 'How did he use to hang, till he slabbered again, poor doting old man! on your silver tongue!' It would be difficult to find a book in which the hideousness possible in ordinary family relationships (Clarissa's brother and sister are just ordinary, mean, unattractive people, made monstrous by special circumstances) is so pungently conveyed. In discussions either of the novels or of the prose style of this period, Richardson is in many respects a figure apart.

To return to more refined levels: one of the best-known features of Augustan prose is the use of antithetical or similar groupings of words, and these become commoner as the period advances, especially among the more 'architectural' writers. They may be regarded as the natural expression of certain eighteenth-century mental habits.

A good deal of Addison's social outlook, which was essentially reconciliatory, is summed up in his own phrases about making 'instruction agreeable' and 'diversion useful' and of enlivening morality with wit and tempering wit with morality. The novels and plays are full of contrasting pairs of characters, such as Sheridan's Charles and Joseph Surface, calculated to bring the more elementary antitheses into play. Titles like *Nature and Art* (a novel by Mrs Inchbald) point to the same habit. What with Tom Jones and Blifil, Squire Allworthy and Squire Western, and Thwackum and Square with their opposed philosophies, Fielding's novel continually runs into antithetical situations, and the patterns are sometimes reproduced agreeably in the prose:

Master *Blifil* fell very short of his Companion in the amiable Quality of Mercy; but he as greatly exceeded him in one of a much higher

Kind, namely, in Justice: In which he followed both the Precepts and Example of *Thwackum* and *Square*; for though they would both make frequent Use of the Word *Mercy*, yet it was plain that in reality *Square* held it to be inconsistent with the Rule of Right; and *Thwackum* was for doing Justice, and leaving Mercy to Heaven. The two Gentlemen did indeed somewhat differ in Opinion concerning the Objects of this sublime Virtue; by which *Thwackum* would probably have destroyed one half of Mankind, and *Square* the other half.

Goldsmith's prose, which is not sufficiently praised by modern readers, is continually embellished by antithetical and other verbal patterns. This may be illustrated from *The Vicar of Wakefield* (1766), which is still a schoolroom classic and therefore known to everybody. When the Vicar's daughters are about to meet the Squire (of whom they are told that there is scarce a farmer's daughter within ten miles round 'but what had found him successful and faithless') they are clearly full of pleasure at the prospect of making a conquest, nor is their mother 'less pleased and confident of their allurements and virtue.' The Vicar, preaching to the wretches in prison, refers in elegantly poised phase to 'those shackles, that tyranny has imposed or crime made necessary.' The whole of this sermon,[1] with its unexceptionable propriety of feeling and diction, contrasting with the rude squalor of the setting, is a beautiful example of the set piece, similar in function to Mr Allworthy's discourse. Commenting on the conditions of patronage in France, Goldsmith writes that the nobleman has 'a most pleasing way of satisfying the vanity of an author, without indulging his avarice'. Behind the well-shaped phrase is the author's pleasure in giving neat definition to the situation, which may mean the discovery of ambiguities or other piquancies.

Control of diction, felicity of phrasing, beauty of surface:

1. See p. 91.

these are the qualities which distinguish the prose artists of this period, especially the later part. It has often been noted that the eighteenth-century vocabulary, especially in the field of social and moral values, was admirably solid and well-defined, so that it was natural even for writers of commonplace mind to handle human situations with a precision and smoothness which might well arouse envy to-day. And a great artist could use the conventional phrases expressively and pointedly. Jane Austen, who is not in this period but brings some of its values to their perfection, provides some fine specimens. When she says of Jane Fairfax that, 'living constantly with right-minded and well-informed people, her heart and understanding had received every advantage of discipline and culture', how admirably she evokes a civilized order no longer with us! All her key words have since lost the clarity and strength which they had for her.

One of the functions of this conventional vocabulary was to keep the expression of certain kinds of feeling within limits. The vocabulary of religion is interesting in this context. There were, of course, a number of different levels. With the 'enthusiasts', Wesley and Whitfield, at one extreme, we move away from Augustan uses of language. They are outside the Augustan way of life. More Augustan is the relaxed idiom of Shaftesbury's Deism: 'This however I am persuaded of, that nothing beside ill Humour can give us dreadful or ill Thoughts of a Supreme Manager. Nothing can persuade us of Sullenness or Sourness in such a Being, beside the actual fore-feeling of somewhat of this kind within our-selves . . .' Boswell was not of Shaftesbury's school, but he expresses himself similarly in a letter to his friend Temple, after referring to a terrible fit of melancholy, partly religious, from which he has just recovered: 'I view Deity as I ought to do . . . Is it not incredible that we should think worse of the character of *God* than of that of a sensible worthy *man?*' Nearer the centre, away from these extremes of evangelical intensity and easy good-humour, is an idiom within which serious piety is regulated by the principles of social decorum and good sense. In some writers the distancing turn of phrase may convey a dignified reverence, a spirit of religious reserve, accompanied by – if indeed they are distinguishable from – 'classical' restraint and decency of manners. This we find in Dr Johnson. On all deeply-felt themes, whether his medium is prose or verse, Johnson is all the more powerful when he has recourse to a language seemingly frigid, as if he deliberately disdained emotional 'appeal'. But where piety takes a lighter form, it may nevertheless please by the propriety of the phrasing. The author's attitudes are such as duty requires, and the politeness of the language has the virtues that politeness always has, including that of modesty: there is no violent assertion of personal feeling. But such language could be the cover for mere conformity. It lent itself to stylistic play. Dr Primrose's graceful phrases ('The Author of our religion everywhere professes himself the wretch's friend') are near the border-line of parody. And in sceptics like Gibbon the cool phrases, with a slight flavour of something else here and there, are the ideal vehicle for quiet, sustained insult:

The innumerable miracles of which the tombs of the martyrs were the perpetual theatre revealed to the pious believer the actual state and constitution of the invisible world; and his religious speculations appeared to be founded on the firm basis of fact and experience. Whatever might be the condition of vulgar souls, in the long interval between the dissolution and the resurrection of their bodies, it was evident that the superior spirits of the saints and martyrs did not consume that portion of their existence in silent and inglorious sleep. It was evident (without presuming to determine the place of their habitation or the nature of their felicity) that they enjoyed the lively and active consciousness of their happiness, their virtue and their powers; and that they had already secured the possession of their eternal reward.

Gibbon is the great master of all these refinements in prose. The *Decline and Fall of the Roman Empire* (1776–88), one of the most entertaining as well as one of the most impressive books in the language, is full of superb antitheses and witty juxtapositions:

She was doomed to weep over the death of one of her sons, and over the life of the other.

Like the modesty affected by Augustus, the state maintained by Diocletian was a theatrical representation; but it must be confessed that, of the two comedies, the former was of a much more liberal and manly character than the latter.

Such was the reign of a monster whose life disgraced human nature, and whose reign accused the patience of the Romans.

No one could apply a suavely distancing vocabulary more effectively:

... but when he exercised his skill in the school of gladiators, or in his own palace, his wretched antagonists were frequently honoured with a mortal wound from the hand of Commodus, and obliged to seal their flattery with their blood.

But it is not easy to say anything fresh about Gibbon's style after Mr G. M. Young's brilliant analysis of it.

In approaching Dr Johnson's prose we must agree to come to terms with certain excesses. When he says that at St Andrews 'we were gratified by every mode of kindness, and entertained with all the elegance of lettered hospitality' and that the road beyond Aberdeen 'grew more stony, and continued naked of vegetable decoration,' there is little point in raising issues about cumbersome, latinized diction or overelaborate structure. These are eccentricities to be cherished, the expression of personality incorrigible and unabashed. But there are many passages where the Johnsonian style is handled with admirable finesse. Johnson sometimes enjoys the incongruity between his subject and the language he applies to it. In the celebrated account of Dryden's essays he is clearly conscious that the style he is using is the opposite to the style he is describing:

They have not the formality of a settled style, in which the first half of the sentence betrays the other. The clauses are never balanced, nor the periods modelled: every word seems to drop by chance, though it falls into its proper place. Nothing is cold or languid; the whole is airy, animated and vigorous; what is little is gay; what is great is splendid . . . Though all is easy, nothing is feeble; though all seems careless, there is nothing harsh . . .

The passage about Shenstone's achievement as a gardener contains one of his best constructed paragraphs, a fine specimen of symmetry and measured amplitude.[1] The orotundities have been developed out of proportion to the slender theme, in a spirit of amused indulgence. He manages to convey the recognition that if Shenstone is a lightweight he, Johnson, is perhaps inclined towards the opposite extreme. The curmudgeonly attitude is suggested ('sullen and surly speculator') only to be withheld.

Brief mention only can be made of other aspects of the prose of this period. It is appropriate that it should be rich in the more informal kinds of writing: letters, diaries, and that combination of the two, the epistolary journal, of which Swift, Sterne and Gray left notable specimens. When the literary style is soundly based on the speech-habits of educated people, the principles of good writing still operate even when authors are relaxed and in *déshabille*. And in this environment personal idiosyncrasy, far from being inhibited by 'convention' (a word too often associated with restrictions), seems through a sense of style to achieve its freest and happiest expression. It is also a notable age of parliamentary oratory, though records of speeches only gradually become available and are, for a long time, incomplete. The relation between political

1. See p. 34.

oratory, with its special exigencies, and prose composed for other purposes, is a subject which cannot be developed here. The speeches of Chatham are not as well known as they should be. They would greatly enliven the schoolboy's and under-graduate's initiation into this period of English history.

The dramatists need not detain us: Vanbrugh and Farquhar, who are on the borderline between two centuries, may be more appropriately discussed in relation to the earlier and better period of drama. Their successors, though often amus-ing, made no remarkable contribution. An exception may be made for Gay, whose uses of language in *The Beggar's Opera* are the subject of a brilliant though difficult essay by Professor William Empson.[1] It might be claimed that the most truly dramatic uses of prose in this period are not in plays but in the novels of Richardson and Sterne.

A final question concerns the relation between this period and that which follows. Are there any features in eighteenth-century prose to which it would be helpful to apply the term 'Romantic'?

There is no clear line of demarcation between 'Augustan' and 'Romantic' qualities, and indeed these words are largely terms of convenience. In some of the tirades and invectives of Chatham, 'Junius' and others, a note is discernible to which neither epithet is appropriate. We might call it 'Regency', though these compositions are earlier than the period so called. In the heat or insolence of debate the orotundity coarsens slightly or wit overreaches itself, though before suggesting the presence of a strain of vulgarity we must remember their immeasurable superiority to even the best political prose of our own age. What epithet shall we apply to the Burke of the *Reflections on the French Revolution* (1791)? Here we have the most florid development of the 'architectural' manner, florid in a way not typical of the

1. In *Some Versions of Pastoral* (1936).

eighteenth century, and with an emotional effect based on appeals to nature and the past. If a more unrestrained treatment of moving scenes, a raised emotional temperature, such as in the novel we associate with Dickens and Charlotte Brontë, is a product of Romanticism, then Richardson's strange passages of tension and stress herald this development. If we apply this label to the somewhat archaic rhetoric of the dialogue in Scott's mediaeval novels, then Horace Walpole and others of the 'Gothic' school of fiction are implicated. There are passages in mid-century criticism, in works opposed to the moribund neo-classical spirit, to which the term may with some justification be applied; for example, Young's remarks on originality and genius[1] which, though open to question, are fresh and poetical in tone, and Morgann's splendid panegyric on Shakespeare,[2] which looks ahead to, and is perhaps not inferior to, De Quincey.

D. W. JEFFERSON

1. See p. 243.   2. See p. 255.

THE PICTURE OF THE AGE: SCENE, PERSONALITY, EVENT

A London Street

(c. 1700)

Here a sooty Chimney-sweeper takes the Wall of a grave *Alderman*, and a *Broom-man* justles the *Parson* of the Parish. There a fat greasie *Porter* runs a Trunk full-butt upon you, while another salutes your Antlers with a Flasket of *Eggs* and *Butter. Turn out there you Country Putt,* says a *Bully* with a Sword two Yards long jarring at his *Heels*, and throws him into the Kennel. By and by comes a *Christning*, with the *Reader* screwing up his Mouth to deliver the Service *a-la-mode de Paris*, and afterwards talks immoderately nice and dull with the Gossips, and the *Midwife* strutting in the Front, and young Original Sin as fine as Fippence, followed with the Vocal Musick of *Kitchen stuff ha' you Maids*, and a damned *Trumpeter* calling in the Rabble to see a Calf with six Legs and a Topknot. There goes a Funeral with the Men of Rosemary after it, licking their Lips after three hits of White, Sack and Claret at the House of Mourning, and the *Sexton* walking before, as big and bluff as a *Beef-eater* at a Coronation. Here's a *Poet* scampers for't as fast as his Legs will carry him, and at his heels a brace of *Bandog Bailiffs*, with open Mouths ready to devour him and all the Nine Muses: And there an *Evidence* ready to spue up his *false Oaths* at the sight of the common Executioner.

Thomas Brown
Amusements Serious and Comical (1700)
Text from *Works . . .*, Vol. III (1708)

Beau Nash Transforms Bath

(1705-6)

STILL however, the amusements of this place were neither elegant, nor conducted with delicacy. General society among people of rank or fortune was by no means established. The nobility still preserved a tincture of *Gothic* haughtiness, and refused to keep company with the gentry at any of the public entertainments of the place. Smoking in the rooms was permitted; gentlemen and ladies appeared in a disrespectful manner at public entertainments in aprons and boots. With an eagerness common to those, whose pleasures come but seldom, they generally continued them too long, and thus they were rendered disgusting by too free an enjoyment. If the company liked each other they danced till morning, if any person lost at cards, he insisted on continuing the game till luck should turn. The lodgings for visitants were paltry, though expensive, the dining-rooms and other chambers were floored with boards coloured brown with soot and small-beer, to hide the dirt; the walls were covered with unpainted wainscot; the furniture corresponded with the meanness of the architecture; a few oak chairs, a small looking glass, with a fender and tongs, composed the magnificence of these temporary habitations. The city was in itself mean and contemptible, no elegant buildings, no open streets, nor uniform squares. The Pump-house was without any director; the chairmen permitted no gentlemen or ladies to walk home by night without insulting them; and to add to all this, one of the greatest Physicians of his age conceived a design of ruining the city, by writing against the efficacy of the waters. It was from a resentment of some affronts he had received there, that he took this resolution; and accordingly published a pamphlet, by which he said, *he would cast a toad into the spring.*

In this situation of things it was, that Mr. *Nash* first came into that city, and hearing the threat of this Physician, he humorously assured the people, that if they would give him leave, he would charm away the poison of the Doctor's toad, as they usually charmed the venom of the Tarantula, by music. He therefore was immediately empowered to set up the force of a band of music, against the poison of the Doctor's reptile; the company very sensibly encreased; *Nash* triumphed and the sovereignty of the city was decreed to him by every rank of people.

We are now to behold this gentleman as arrived at a new dignity for which nature seemed to have formed him; we are to see him directing pleasures, which none had better learned to share; placed over rebellious and refractory subjects that were to be ruled only by the force of his address, and governing such as had been long accustomed to govern others. We see a kingdom beginning with him, and sending off *Tunbridge* as one of its colonies.

But to talk more simply, when we talk at best of trifles. None could possibly conceive a person more fit to fill this employment than *Nash*: He had some wit, as I have said once or twice before; but it was of that sort which is rather happy than permanent. Once a week he might say a good thing, this the little ones about him took care to divulge; or if they happened to forget the joke, he usually remembered to repeat it himself. In a long intercourse with the world he had acquired an impenetrable assurance; and the freedom with which he was received by the Great, furnished him with vivacity which could be commanded at any time, and which some mistook for wit. His former intercourse among people of fashion in town, had let him into most of the characters of the nobility; and he was acquainted with many of their private intrigues. He understood rank and precedence, with the utmost exactness; was fond of shew and finery himself, and generally set a pattern of it to others. These were his favourite talents, and he was the favourite of such as had no other.

But to balance these which some may consider as foibles, he was charitable himself, and generally shamed his betters into a similitude of sentiment, if they were not naturally so before. He was fond of advising those young men, who, by youth and too much money, are taught to look upon extravagance as a virtue. He was an enemy to rudeness in others, though in the latter part of his life he did not much seem to encourage a dislike of it by his own example. None talked with more humanity of the foibles of others, when absent, than he, nor kept those secrets with which he was entrusted more inviolably. But above all (if moralists will allow it among the number of his virtues) tho' he gamed high, he always played very fairly. These were his qualifications. Some of the nobility regarded him as an inoffensive, useful companion, the size of whose understanding was, in general, level with their own; but their little imitators admired him as a person of fine sense, and great good breeding. Thus people became fond of ranking him in the number of their acquaintance, told over his jests, and Beau *Nash* at length became the fashionable companion.

His first care when made Master of the Ceremonies, or King of *Bath*, as it is called, was to promote a music subscription, of one guinea each, for a band which was to consist of six performers, who were to receive a guinea a week each for their trouble. He allowed also two guineas a week for lighting and sweeping the rooms, for which he accounted to the subscribers by receipt.

The Pump-house was immediately put under the care of an officer, by the name of the *Pumper*; for which he paid the corporation an annual rent. A row of new houses was begun on the south side of the gravel walks, before which a handsome pavement was then made for the company to walk on. Not less than seventeen or eighteen hundred pounds was raised this year, and in the beginning of 1706, by subscription, and laid out in repairing the roads near the city. The streets began to be better paved, cleaned and lighted, the licenses of the Chairmen were repressed, and by an act of parliament procured on this occasion, the invalids, who came to drink or bathe, were exempted from all manner of toll, as often as they should go out of the city for recreation.

The houses and streets now began to improve, and ornaments were lavished upon them even to profusion. But in the midst of this splendour the company still were obliged to assemble in a booth to drink tea and chocolate, or to game. Mr. *Nash* undertook to remedy this inconvenience. By his direction, one *Thomas Harrison* erected a handsome Assembly-house for these purposes. A better band of music was also procured, and the former subscription of one guinea, was raised to two. *Harrison* had three guineas a week for the room and candles, and the music two guineas a man. The money Mr. *Nash* received and accounted for with the utmost exactness and punctuality. To this house were also added gardens for people of rank and fashion to walk in; and the beauty of the suburbs continued to encrease, notwithstanding the opposition that was made by the corporation, who at that time, looked upon every useful improvement particularly without the walls, as dangerous to the inhabitants within.

Oliver Goldsmith
Life of Richard Nash Esq. (1762)

Chairmen] bearers of Sedan-chairs

LETTERS TO PRUE

(1708)

I

Aug.28, 1708.

DEAR PRUE

THE afternoon coach shall bring you ten pounds. Your letter shows you are passionately in love with me. But we must take our portion of life as it runs without repining and I consider that good nature added to that beautiful form God has given you would make an happiness too great for human life. Your most obliged husband, and most humble sernt.

RICH. STEELE

2

Sept.13, 1708.

DEAR PRUE

I WRITE to you in obedience to what you ordered me; but there are not words to express the tenderness I have for you. Love is too harsh a word for it; but if you knew how my Heart akes when you speak an unkind word to me, and springs with joy when you smile upon me, I am sure you would place your glory rather in preserving my happiness like a good wife, than tormenting me like a peevish beauty. Good Prue, write me word you shall be overjoyed at my return to you, and pity the aukward figure I make when I pretend to resist you, by complying always with the reasonable demands of your enamoured Husband,

RICH. STEELE

P.S. I am Mrs. Binns's servant.

3

Oct.8, 1708.

DEAR PRUE

THIS brings you a quarter of a pound of bohee, and as much of green tea, both which I hope you will find good. To-morrow morning your favourite, Mr. Addison and I, shall set out for Hampton Court; he to meet some great men there; I to see you, who am but what you make me. Yours, With the utmost fondness

RICH. STEELE

Sir Richard Steele
Epistolary Correspondence . . .,
ed. J. Nicholls (1787), Vol. I

ALEXANDER SELKIRK

(1709)

. . . IMMEDIATELY our Pinnace return'd from the shore, and brought abundance of Craw-fish, with a Man cloth'd in Goat-Skins, who look'd wilder than the first Owners of them. He had been on the Island four Years and four Months, being left there by Capt. *Stradling* in the *Cinque-Ports*; his Name was *Alexander Selkirk* a *Scotch* Man, who had been Master of the *Cinque-Ports*, a Ship that came here last with Capt. *Dampier*, who told me that this was the best Man in her; so I immediately agreed with him to be a Mate on board our Ship . . . He told us that he was born at *Largo* in the County of *Fife* in *Scotland*, and was bred a Sailor from his Youth. The reason of his being left here was a difference betwixt him and his Captain; which, together with the Ships being leaky, made him willing rather to stay here, than to go along with him at first; and when he was at last willing, the Captain would not receive him. He had been in the Island before to wood and water, when two of the Ships Company were left upon it for six Months till the Ship return'd, being chas'd thence by two *French South-Sea* Ships.

He had with him his Clothes and Bedding, with a Firelock, some Powder, Bullets, and Tobacco, a Hatchet, a Knife, a Kettle, a Bible, some practical Pieces, and his Mathematical Instruments and Books. He diverted and provided for himself as well as he could; but for the first eight months had much ado to bear up against Melancholy, and the Terror of being left alone in such a desolate place. He built two Hutts with Piemento Trees, cover'd them with long Grass, and lin'd them with the Skins of Goats, which he kill'd with his Gun as he wanted, so long as his Powder lasted, which was but a pound; and that being near spent, he got fire by rubbing two sticks of Piemento Wood together upon his knee. In the lesser Hutt, at some distance from the other, he dress'd his Victuals, and in the larger he slept, and employ'd himself in reading, singing Psalms, and praying; so that he said he was a better Christian while in this solitude than ever he was before or than, he was afraid, he should ever be again. At first he never eat any thing till Hunger constrain'd him, partly for grief and partly for want of Bread and Salt; nor did he go to bed till he could watch no longer: the Piemento Wood, which burnt very clear, serv'd him both for Firing and Candle, and refresh'd him with its fragrant Smell.

He might have had Fish enough, but could not eat 'em for want of Salt, because they occasion'd a looseness; except Crawfish, which are there as large as our Lobsters, and very good: These he sometimes boil'd, and at other times broil'd, as he did his Goats Flesh, of which he made very good Broth, for they are not so rank as ours: he kept an Account of 500 that he killed while there, and caught as many more, which he mark'd on the Ear and let go. When his Powder fail'd, he

took them by speed of foot; for his way of living and continual Exercise of walking and running, clear'd him of all
gross Humours, so that he ran with wonderful Swiftness thro
the Woods and up the Rocks and Hills, as we perceiv'd when
we employ'd him to catch Goats for us. We had a Bull-Dog,
which we sent with several of our nimblest Runners, to help
him in catching Goats; but he distanc'd and tir'd both the
Dog and the Men, catch'd the Goats, and brought 'em to us
on his back. He told us that his Agility in pursuing a Goat had
once like to have cost him his Life; he pursu'd it with so much
Eagerness that he catch'd hold of it on the brink of a Precipice,
of which he was not aware, the Bushes having hid it from
him; so that he fell with the Goat down the said Precipice a
great height, and was so stun'd and bruis'd with the Fall, that
he narrowly escap'd with his Life, and when he came to his
Senses, found the Goat dead under him. He lay there about
24 hours, and was scarce able to crawl to his Hutt, which was
about a mile distant, or to stir abroad again in ten days.

He came at last to relish his Meat well enough without Salt
or Bread, and in the Season had plenty of good Turnips,
which had been sow'd there by Capt. *Dampier's* Men, and
have now overspread some Acres of Ground. He had enough
of good Cabbage from the Cabbage-Trees, and season'd his
Meat with the Fruit of the Piemento Trees, which is the same
as the *Jamaica* Pepper, and smells deliciously. He found there
also a black Pepper called Malagita, which is very good to
expel Wind, and against Griping of the Guts.

He soon wore out all his Shoes and Clothes by running
thro the Woods; and at last being forc'd to shift without
them his Feet became so hard, that he ran every where without Annoyance: and it was some time before he could wear
Shoes after we found him; for not being us'd to any so long,
his Feet swell'd when he came first to wear 'em again.

After he had conquer'd his Melancholy, he diverted

himself sometimes by cutting his Name on the Trees, and the Time of his being left and Continuance there. He was at first much pester'd with Cats and Rats, that had bred in great numbers from some of each Species which had got ashore from Ships that put in there to wood and water. The Rats gnaw'd his Feet and Clothes while asleep, which oblig'd him to cherish the Cats with his Goats-flesh; by which many of them became so tame, that they would lie about him in hundreds, and soon delivered him from the Rats. He likewise tam'd some Kids, and to divert himself would now and then sing and dance with them and his Cats: so that by the Care of Providence and Vigour of his Youth, being now but about 30 years old, he came at last to conquer all the Inconveniences of his Solitude, and to be very easy. When his Clothes wore out, he made himself a Coat and Cap of Goat-Skins, which he stitch'd together with little Thongs of the same, that he cut with his Knife. He had no other Needle but a Nail; and when his Knife was wore to the back, he made others as well as he could of some Iron Hoops that were left ashore, which he beat thin and ground upon Stones. Having some linen Cloth by him, he sow'd himself Shirts with a Nail, and stitch'd 'em with the Worsted of his old Stockings, which he pull'd out on purpose. He had his last Shirt on when we found him in the Island.

At his coming on board us, he had so much forgot his Language for want of Use, that we could scarce understand him, for he seem'd to speak his words by halves. We offer'd him a Dram, but he would not touch it, having drank nothing but Water since his being there, and 'twas some time before he could relish our Victuals.

Woodes Rogers

A Cruising Voyage round the World . . . (1712)

THE SPECTATOR AND ITS PUBLIC

(1711)

IT is with much Satisfaction that I hear this great City inquiring Day by Day after these my Papers, and receiving my Morning Lectures with a becoming Seriousness and Attention. My Publisher tells me, that there are already Three thousand of them distributed every Day: So that if I allow Twenty Readers to every Paper, which I look upon as a modest Computation, I may reckon about Threescore thousand Disciples in *London* and *Westminster*, who I hope will take care to distinguish themselves from the thoughtless Herd of their ignorant and unattentive Brethren. Since I have raised to myself so great an Audience, I shall spare no Pains to make their Instruction agreeable, and their Diversion useful. For which Reasons I shall endeavour to enliven Morality with Wit, and to temper Wit with Morality, that my Readers may, if possible, both Ways find their Account in the Speculation of the Day. And to the End that their Virtue and Discretion may not be short transient intermittent Starts of Thought, I have resolved to refresh their Memories from Day to Day, till I have recovered them out of that desperate State of Vice and Folly into which the Age is fallen. The Mind that lies fallow but a single Day, sprouts up in Follies that are only to be killed by a constant and assiduous Culture. It was said of *Socrates*, that he brought Philosophy down from Heaven, to inhabit among Men; and I shall be ambitious to have it said of me, that I have brought Philosophy out of Closets and Libraries, Schools and Colleges, to dwell in Clubs and Assemblies, at Tea-Tables and in Coffee-Houses.

I would therefore in a very particular Manner recommend these my Speculations to all well regulated Families, that set apart an Hour in every Morning for Tea and Bread and

Butter; and would earnestly advise them for their Good to order this Paper to be punctually served up, and to be looked upon as a Part of the Tea Equipage.

Joseph Addison
The Spectator (12 March, 1711)

THE CORONATION OF GEORGE I

(1714)

I WENT thither with Lady *Bristol*, who had still a greater Mind to be a Lady of the Bedchamber than I had; she told me I was to be one, but durst not then tell me she had heard it from the *Princess* herself. When we came from the *Hall* into the *Abbey* (for we saw every Part of the Ceremony), the Peeresses' Places were so full, that we and several other Ladies went to the Bishops' Benches at the Side of the Altar. I sat next the Pulpit Stairs on the back Bench, and several Ladies coming by me to go nearer the Altar, at last my Lady *Northampton* came pulling my Lady *Nottingham* by the Hand, which Last took my Place from me, and I was forced to mount the Pulpit Stairs. I thought this rude, but did not suppose there had been any Design in it, though we had both been talked of for being Governess to the young Princesses, and she, I believe, had really solicited for it, and apprehended I had done so too, notwithstanding I had never thought of it. However, her Illbreeding got me the best Place in the *Abbey*, for I saw all the Ceremony, which few besides did, and I own I never was so affected with Joy in all my Life; it brought Tears into my Eyes, and I hope I shall never forget the Blessing of seeing our holy Religion thus preserved, as well as our Liberties and Properties.

My Lady *Nottingham*, when the Litany was to be sung,

broke from behind the Rest of the Company, where she was placed, and kneeled down before them all (though none of the Rest did), facing the *King*, and repeating the Litany. Everybody stared at her, and I could read in their Countenances that they thought she overdid her High Church Part. But to return to my Place. The Lords that were over against me, seeing me thus mounted, said to my Lord, that they hoped I would preach; to which he answered that he believed I had Zeal enough for it, but that he did not know that I could preach; to which my Lord *Nottingham* answered, 'No, my Lord? Indeed you must pardon me. She can, and has preached for these last four Years such Doctrines as, had she been prosecuted in any Court for them, you yourself could not defend her.' This he said with such an Air, that my Lord spoke of it to me. That, joined to what my Lady *Nottingham* had done that Day, and some other little Passages that had happened, opened my Eyes, and showed me how that Family maligned me, and helped to persuade me that it was impossible the *Princess* could think of me.

At the Coronation, my Lord *Bolingbroke* for the first Time saw the *King*. He had attempted it before without Success. The *King* seeing a Face he did not know, asked his Name, when he did him Homage; and he (Lord *B*.) hearing it as he went down the Steps from the Throne, turned round and bowed three Times down to the very Ground. The Ladies, not walking in the Procession, had no gold Medals.

One may easily conclude this was not a Day of real Joy to the Jacobites. However, they were all there, looking as cheerful as they could, but very peevish with Everybody that spoke to them. My Lady *Dorchester* stood underneath me; and when the *Archbishop* went round the Throne, demanding the Consent of the People, she turned about to me, and said, 'Does the old Fool think that Anybody here will say no to his Question, when there are so many drawn Swords?' However, there was no Remedy but Patience, and so Everybody was pleased, or pretended to be so.

Mary, Countess Cowper
Diary ... *1714–20*, ed. Spencer Cowper (1864)

JACOBITISM AT OXFORD

1715)

MAY 28 (Sat.). This being the Duke of Brunswick, commonly called King George's Birth-Day, some of the Bells were jambled in Oxford, by the care of some of the Whiggish, Fanatical Crew; but as I did not observe the Day in the least my self, so it was little taken notice of (unless by way of ridicule) by other honest People, who are for K. James IIId. who is the undoubted King of these Kingdoms, & 'tis heartily wish'd by them that he may be restored.

This Day I saw one Ward with Dr. Charlett, who, it seems, hath printed several Things. He is a Clergy Man. I must inquire about him.

May 29 (Sun.) This Morning preached at St. Marie's Mr. Faringdon of Queen's upon Ezra 9. 13, 14. Some Things were well observed relating to the Restauration, but then others against K. James IIId. were as bad; nor was his Complement upon the Duke of Brunswick, now in Possession of the Throne, any better. He concluded with observing that he did not doubt but every Day's Experience would be a sufficient Evidence of the said Prince's wise Administration & of his Firmness & affection to the Church of England. Dr. Charlett sate Vice-Chancellor, & ordered the Sermon to be printed.

In the Afternoon preached Mr. Newlin of Magd. Coll. upon Psal. 127. 1. & made a very good Sermon, much better than the former, upon the Restauration also; but did not say one Word of K. George.

Last night a good Part of the Presbyterian Meeting House in Oxford was pull'd down. There was such a Concourse of People going up and down & putting a stop to the least Sign of rejoycing as can not be described. But then the Rejoycing this Day (notwithstanding Sunday) was so very great and publick in Oxford as hath now been known hardly since the Restauration. There was not an House next the Street but was illuminated. For if any disrespect was shewn the Windows were certainly broke. The People run up and down crying King James the 3d, the true King, no Usurper, the Duke of Ormond, &c. & Healths were every where drank suitable to the Occasion, & every one at the same time Drank to a new Restauration, which I heartily wish may speedily happen. In the Evening they pulled a good Part of the Quakers and Anabaptists Meeting Houses down. This Rejoycing hath caused great Consternation at Court. The Heads of Houses have represented that it was begun by the Whiggs, who met at the Kings Head Tavern on Saturday Night under the Denomination of the Constitution Club, & being about to carry on extravagant Designs, they were prevented by an Honest Party that were in an adjoyning Room, & forced to sneak away. Some of these Fanatical Persons Shot off Guns in some Places, & had like to have kill'd many. Two or three were wounded. . . .

June 5 (Whitsunday). This Morning preached at St. Marie's Mr. Clarke of Merton upon Acts ii. 33.

K. George being inform'd of the Proceedings of the Cavaliers at Oxford on Saturday & Sunday (May 28, 29) he is very angry, & by his Order Townshend one of the Secretaries of State hath sent rattling Letters to Dr. Charlett, Provicechanc. & the Mayor. Dr. Charlett shew'd me his this Morning. This Ld. Townshend says his Majesty (for so they will stile this silly Usurper) hath been fully assur'd that the Riots both Nights were began by Scholars, & that Scholars promoted them, & that he, Dr. Charlett, was so far from discountenancing them that he did not endeavour in the least to suppress them. He likewise observes that his Majesty was as well inform'd that the other Magistrates were not less remiss on those Occasions.

The Heads have had several Meetings upon this Affair, & they have drawn up a Programma, (for they are obliged to do something) to prevent the like hereafter, & this Morning very early old Sherwin the Yeoman Beadle was sent to London to represent the Truth of the Matter.

Thomas Hearne
Remarks and Collections . . ., Vol. V
(Oxford Historical Society, 1901)

MUG-HOUSE POLITICS

(1716)

Friday, July 20. Went to the coffee-house and at the Gill House met with some company that asked me to go with them to the Mug-House in Salisbury Court and I went with them to see the manner of it. I like the design of this institution very well. It is to encourage the friends to King George and keep up the spirit of loyalty and the public spirit among them. They have a president who proposes the healths. Between every health some of the company sing a song that is composed against the Tories and Jacobites. There is something in their manner of singing, which is generally attended with a chorus at the end of each stanza of the song, which has an effect upon those that hear it, something like the drums and trumpets in an army, to raise the courage and spirits of the soldiers. Methought it put me into a very brisk intrepid state to hear them huzza and clap hands and sing together. There is something I believe mechanical in this. It puts the spirits into a hurry and makes them have a swifter motion, as we put spirit into a dull horse by spurring it and hurrying it. I am persuaded these mug-houses are of service to the Government to keep up the public spirit and animate its friends, and I believe in time it will gain over the populace and make King George become popular.

There was a mob gathered about the door and we heard that there were some of the Bridewell boys come to attack us. This came to the ears of the society at the Roebuck and they sent some of their members to inquire into our circumstances and offer their assistance if we needed it and others came from the Tavistock Mug-House, so that our room was quite full. But we were not attacked and I came off very peaceably. The worst of it is I find some of the members of these societies are apt to be too flushed with their strength and attack persons whom they suspect before they are insulted themselves. However, I believe they do service to the Government in keeping its friends in countenance and dispiriting its enemies. There were several gentlemen among them but many as I guess only prentices and ordinary tradesmen. However, we are all upon a level there and those that can entertain the company with the most songs is the most taken notice of, his health being always drunk after he has sung a song. But between every song the public state health is drunk, which the President composes, who is elected new every night.

To bed between 11 and 12.

Sir Dudley Ryder

Diary . . . 1715-16, ed. William Matthews (1939)

COUNTRY HOUSES

Sir John Vanbrugh to Brigadier General Watkins: an extract from a letter (26 August, 1721)

COU'D you See how busy I have been, ever Since I writ to you last, you wou'd easily forgive my being so long before I did it again. I return'd but last night from the North (for here you must know we are in the South,) where I have been near three weeks finding a vast deal to do, both at Delavals and Lumley Castle. Since it is not easy, to go there often, I resolv'd to do all the Service I cou'd while I was there now.

The Admiral is very Gallant in his operations, not being dispos'd to starve the Design at all. So that he is like to have, a very fine Dwelling for himself, now, and his Nephew &c hereafter.

Lumley Castle is a Noble thing; and well deserves the Favours Lord Lumley designs to bestow upon it; In order to which, I stay'd there near a Week, to form a General Design for the whole, Which consists, in altering the House both for State, Beauty and Convenience, And making the Courts Gardens and Offices Suitable to it; All which I believe may be done, for a Sum, that can never ly very heavy upon the Family. If I had had good weather in this Expedition, I shou'd have been well enough diverted in it; there being many more Valuable and Agreeable things and Places to be Seen, than in the Tame Sneaking South of England.

I am going for three or four days again to Castle Howard, where I must Spend a Week or ten days, to do what is necessary there. My Lord Carlisle going on with his Works as usual; by which the Seat is wonderfully improv'd this last Year. Two Years more, tho' they won't compleat all the Building, will so Beautify the Outworks, of Gardens, Park &c, That I think no Place I ever Saw, will dispute with it, for a Delightfull Dwelling in generall, let the Criticks fish out

what particular faults they please in the Architecture. Here are
Several Gentlemen in these Parts of the World, that are
possess'd with the Spirit of Building, And Seem dispos'd to
do it, in so good a Manner, that were they to establish here a
sort of a Board of Works to conduct their Affairs, I do verily
believe, they wou'd sooner make Hawksmr. a Commissioner
of it, than that excellent Architect, Ripley.

Sir John Vanbrugh

Complete Works . . ., ed. Bonamy Dobrée and
Geoffrey Webb, Vol. IV (1928)

THE CLOTH MARKET AT LEEDS

THE Market it self is worth describing, tho' no Description
can come up to the Thing it self; however, take a Sketch of it
with its Customs and Usages as follows:

The Street is a large, broad, fair and well-built Street, beginning, as I have said, at the Bridge, and ascending gently to
the North.

Early in the Morning, there are Tressels placed in two Rows
in the Street, sometimes two Rows on a Side, but always one
Row at least; then there are Boards laid cross those Tressels,
so that the Boards lie like long Counters on either Side, from
one end of the Street to the other.

The Clothiers come early in the Morning with their Cloth;
and as few Clothiers bring more than one Piece, the Market
being so frequent, they go into the Inns and Publick-Houses
with it, and there set it down.

At seven a Clock in the Morning, the Clothiers being supposed to be all come by that time, even in the Winter, but the
Hour is varied as the Seasons advance (in the Summer earlier,
in the Depth of Winter a little later) I take it, at a Medium,

and as it was when I was there, at six or seven, I say, the Market Bell rings; it would surprize a Stranger to see in how few Minutes, without hurry or noise, and not the least disorder, the whole Market is fill'd; all the Boards upon the Tressels are covered with Cloth, close to one another as the Pieces can lie long ways by one another, and behind every Piece of Cloth, the Clothier standing to sell it.

This indeed is not so difficult, when we consider that the whole Quantity is brought into the Market as soon as one Piece, because as the Clothiers stand ready in the Inns and Shops just behind, and that there is a Clothier to every Piece, they have no more to do, but, like a Regiment drawn up in Line, every one takes up his Piece, and has about five Steps to march to lay it upon the first Row of Boards, and perhaps ten to the second Row; so that upon the Market Bell ringing, in half a quarter of an Hour the whole Market is fill'd, the Rows of Boards cover'd, and the Clothiers stand ready.

As soon as the Bell has done Ringing, the Merchants and Factors, and Buyers of all Sorts, come down, and coming along the Spaces between the Rows of Boards, they walk up the Rows, and down as their Occasions direct. Some of them have their foreign Letters of Orders, with Patterns seal'd on them, in Rows, in their Hands; and with those they match Colours, holding them to the Cloths as they think they agree to; when they see any Cloths to their Colours, or that suit their occasions, they reach over to the Clothier and whisper, and in the fewest Words imaginable the Price is stated; one asks, the other bids; and 'tis agree, or not agree, in a Moment.

The Merchants and Buyers generally walk down and up twice on each Side of the Rows, and in little more than an Hour all the Business is done; in less than half an Hour you will perceive the Cloths begin to move off, the Clothier taking it up upon his Shoulder to carry it to the Merchant's House, and by half an hour after eight a Clock the Market

Bell rings again; immediately the Buyers disappear, the Cloth is all sold, or if here and there a Piece happens not to be bought, 'tis carried back into the Inn, and, in a quarter of an Hour, there is not a Piece of Cloth to be seen in the Market.

Thus, you see, Ten or Twenty thousand Pounds value in Cloth, and sometimes much more, bought and sold in little more than an Hour, and the Laws of the Market the most strictly observed as ever I saw done in any Market in *England*; for,

1. Before the Market Bell rings, no Man shews a Piece of Cloth, nor can the Clothiers sell any but in open Market.

2. After the Market Bell rings again, no Body stays a Moment in the Market, but carries his Cloth back if it be not sold.

3. And that which is most admirable is, 'tis all managed with the most profound Silence, and you cannot hear a Word spoken in the whole Market, I mean, by the Persons buying and selling; 'tis all done in whisper.

The reason of this Silence, is chiefly because the Clothiers stand so near to one another; and 'tis always reasonable that one should not know what another does, for that would be discovering their Business, and exposing it to one another.

If a Merchant has bidden a Clothier a Price, and he will not take it, he may go after him to his House, and tell him he has considered of it, and is willing to let him have it; but they are not to make any new Agreement for it, so as to remove the Market from the Street to the Merchant's House.

By nine a Clock the Boards are taken down, the Tressels are removed, and the Street cleared, so that you see no Market or Goods any more than if there had been nothing to do; and this is done twice a Week.

Daniel Defoe

A Tour thro' Great Britain . . ., Vol. III (1727)

An Encounter with a Highwayman

John Byrom to his wife: an extract from a letter (18 *January*, 1728)

My dear love: This day se'nnight I set out from London along with Mr. Collier in the Cambridge coach; we got well hither on Thursday night, and I lay in College in a room which my tutor Mr. Hooper has put me into. I begin to wonder how I lived here formerly, for the manner of living here at present does not suit my constitution at present, and I am afraid of being ill, as I was when I was here last, but I shall take what care I can to escape it. I have sent by this post for my boots, in order to ride back again, for I don't like a coach no more than you. We were half a dozen of us cooped up, and two days a coming. It was very tedious, only indeed we met with an adventure that served to talk the time away upon; for about half a mile or less of Epping, a highwayman in a red rug upon a black horse came out of the bushes up to the coach, and presenting a pistol, first at the coachman and then at the corporation within, with a volley of oaths demanded our money – with a brace of balls amongst us if we did'nt make haste. We had two women in the coach, who were so frightened that though they got out their money, they had not strength to offer it; one of the gentlemen who rode backwards flung a guinea into his hat; Mr. Collier, who sat backwards over against me, threw another; I thought we should be well off if he insisted on no more, but as that seemed to be more than he deserved, I consulted my silver pocket and presented him with five or six shillings of white metal which forsooth affronted him, and he cursed me, and swore he would have gold from me, but not being hasty enough in producing it, he turned to the fourth man, an honest bricklayer of Lynn – "What! must I wait for you?" – *He* came over to my opinion, and tendered him 5s. and some ha'pences; and then

I expected a visit from him on my side the coach. It happened that Mr. Collier's guinea fell upon the road, upon which he made the coachman light and take it him up, and then came round to the other side, from whence he rid into the wood without calling for any second payments, and so we drove on to Epping.

This is the first collector of the highway that I ever had the honour to converse with in all my travels; and, considering the defenceless situation we were in, we came off pretty well, though I must own I never grudged to part with an ounce of silver so much in my life; but being in that enchanted vehicle, there was no help for't.

John Byrom
Private Journal and Literary Remains . . ., Vol. I
(The Chetham Society, 1854)

'THE BEGGAR'S OPERA'

Pope remembers the First Night in 1728

DR. SWIFT had been observing once to Mr. Gay, what an odd pretty sort of a thing a Newgate Pastoral might make. Gay was inclined to try at such a thing, for some time, but afterwards thought it would be better to write a Comedy on the same plan. This was what gave rise to the Beggar's Opera. He began on it, and when first he mentioned it to Swift, the Doctor did not much like the project. As he carried it on, he showed what he wrote to both of us; and we now and then gave a correction, or a word or two of advice; but it was wholly of his own writing. When it was done, neither of us thought it would succeed. We showed it to Congreve, who, after reading it over, said, "It would either take greatly, or be damned confoundedly." – We were all at the first night of it, in great uncertainty of the event, till we were very much encouraged by our hearing the Duke of Argyle, who sat in the next box to us, say, "it will do – it must do! – I see it in the eyes of them." – This was a good while before the first act was over, and so gave us ease soon; for the duke (beside his own good taste) has as particular a knack as any one now living in discovering the taste of the public. He was quite right in this, as usual: the good-nature of the audience appeared stronger and stronger every act, and ended in a clamour of applause. . . .

Joseph Spence
Anecdotes, Observations, and Characters of Books
and Men . . ., ed. S. W. Singer (1820)

FRIENDS IN INFIRMITY

Alexander Pope to Jonathan Swift: an extract from a letter
(19 December, 1734)

I AM truly sorry for any Complaint you have, and it is in regard to the Weakness of your Eyes that I write (as well as print) in Folio. You will think (I know you will, for you have all the Candor of a good Understanding) that the thing which Men of our Age feel the most, is the Friendship of our Equals; and that therefore whatever affects those who are stepped a few Years before us, cannot but sensibly affect us who are to follow. It troubles me to hear you complain of your Memory, and if I am in any part of my Constitution younger than you, it will be in my remembering every thing that has pleased me in you, longer than perhaps you will. The two Summers we passed together dwells always on my Mind, like a Vision which gave me a Glimpse of a better Life and better Company than this World otherwise afforded. I am now an Individual upon whom no other depends, and may go where I will, if the wretched Carcase I am annexed to did not hinder me. I rambled by very easy Journies this Year to Lord *Bathurst* and Lord *Peterborow*, who, upon every Occasion, commemorate, love, and wish for you. I now pass my Days between *Dawley*, *London*, and this Place, not studious nor idle, rather polishing old Works than hewing out new. I redeem now and then a Paper that has been abandoned several years; and of this sort you will soon see one, which I inscribe to our old Friend *Arbuthnot*.

Thus far I had written, and thinking to finish my Letter the same Evening, was prevented by Company, and the next Morning found myself in a Fever, highly disordered, and so continued in Bed for five Days, and in my Chamber till now; but so well recovered as to hope to go abroad To-morrow, even by the Advice of Dr. *Arbuthnot*. He himself, poor Man, is much broke, though not worse than for these two last Months he has been. He took extremely kind your Letter. I wish to God we could once meet again before that Separation, which yet I would be glad to believe, shall re-unite us: But he who made us, not for ours but his Purposes, knows only whether it be for the better or the worse, that the Affections of this Life should or should not continue into the other; and doubtless it is as it should be. Yet I am sure that while I am here, and the thing that I am, I shall be imperfect without the Communication of such Friends as you; you are to me like a Limb lost and buried in another Country. Though we seem quite divided, every accident makes me feel you were once a Part of me.

Alexander Pope

Dean Swift's Literary Correspondence . . . (1741)

Storming the House of Lords

Lady Mary Wortley Montagu to the Countess of Pomfret:
an extract from a letter (March, 1739)

... HERE is no news to be sent you from this place, which
has been for this fortnight and still continues overwhelmed
with politicks, and which are of so mysterious a nature, one
ought to have some of the gifts of Lilly or Partridge to be able
to write about them; and I leave all those dissertations to
those distinguished mortals who are endowed with the talent
of divination; though I am at present the only one of my sex
who seems to be of that opinion, the ladies having shown their
zeal and appetite for knowledge in a most glorious manner.
At the last warm debate in the House of Lords, it was unan-
imously resolved there should be no crowd of unnecessary
auditors; consequently the fair sex were excluded, and the
gallery destined to the sole use of the House of Commons.
Notwithstanding which determination, a tribe of dames
resolved to shew on this occasion that neither men nor laws
could resist them. These heroines were Lady Huntingdon,
the Duchess of Queensberry, the Duchess of Ancaster, Lady
Westmoreland, Lady Cobham, Lady Charlotte Edwin, Lady
Archibald Hamilton and her daughter, Mrs. Scott, and Mrs.
Pendarvis, and Lady Frances Saunderson. I am thus particular
in their names, since I look upon them to be the boldest
assertors, and most resigned sufferers for liberty, I ever read
of. They presented themselves at the door at nine o'clock in
the morning, where Sir William Saunderson respectfully informed them the Chancellor had made an order against their
admittance. The Duchess of Queensberry, as head of the
squadron, pished at the ill-breeding of a mere lawyer, and
desired him to let them up stairs privately. After some modest
refusals, he swore by G— he would not let them in. Her

26

grace, with a noble warmth, answered, by G— they would come in in spite of the Chancellor and the whole House. This being reported, the Peers resolved to starve them out; an order was made that the doors should not be opened till they had raised their siege. These Amazons now showed themselves qualified for the duty even of foot soldiers; they stood there till five in the afternoon, without either sustenance or evacuation, every now and then playing volleys of thumps, kicks, and raps against the door, with so much violence that the speakers in the House were scarce heard. When the Lords were not to be conquered by this, the two Duchesses (very well apprized of the use of stratagems in war) commanded a dead silence of half an hour; and the Chancellor, who thought this a certain proof of their absence, (the Commons also being very impatient to enter,) gave order for the opening of the door; upon which they all rushed in, pushed aside their competitors, and placed themselves in the front rows of the gallery. They stayed there till after eleven, when the House rose; and during the debate gave applause, and showed marks of dislike, not only by smiles and winks (which have always been allowed in these cases), but by noisy laughs and apparent contempts; which is supposed the true reason why poor Lord Hervey spoke miserably. I beg your pardon, dear madam, for this long relation; but 'tis impossible to be short on so copious a subject; and you must own this action very well worthy of record, and I think not to be paralleled in history, ancient or modern. I look so little in my own eyes (who was at that time ingloriously sitting over a tea-table), I hardly dare subscribe myself even,

Yours.

Lady Mary Wortley Montagu
Letters and Works . . ., ed. Lord Wharncliffe
(1837), Vol. II

SIR ROBERT WALPOLE

No man ever was blessed with a clearer head, a truer or quicker judgment, or a deeper insight into mankind; he knew the strength and weakness of everybody he had to deal with, and how to make his advantage of both; he had more warmth of affection and friendship for some particular people than one could have believed it possible for any one who had been so long raking in the dirt of mankind to be capable of feeling for so worthless a species of animals. One should naturally have imagined that the contempt and distrust he must have had for the species in gross, would have given him at least an indifference and distrust towards every particular. Whether his negligence of his enemies, and never stretching his power to gratify his resentment of the sharpest injury, was policy or constitution, I shall not determine: but I do not believe anybody who knows these times will deny that no Minister ever was more outraged, or less apparently revengeful. Some of his friends, who were not unforgiving themselves, nor very apt to see imaginary faults in him, have condemned this easiness in his temper as a weakness that has often exposed him to new injuries, and given encouragement to his adversaries to insult him with impunity....

In all occurrences, and at all times, and in all difficulties, he was constantly present and cheerful; he had very little of what is generally called insinuation, and with which people are apt to be taken for the present, without being gained; but no man ever knew better among those he had to deal with who was to be had, on what terms, by what methods, and how the acquisition would answer. He was not one of those projecting systematical great geniuses who are always thinking in theory, and are above common practice: he had been too long conversant in business not to know that in the fluctuation of human affairs and variety of accidents to which the best concerted schemes are liable, they must often be disappointed who build on the certainty of the most probable events; and therefore seldom turned his thoughts to the provisional warding off future evils which might or might not happen; or the scheming of remote advantages, subject to so many intervening crosses; but always applied himself to the present occurrence, studying and generally hitting upon the properest method to improve what was favourable, and the best expedient to extricate himself out of what was difficult. There never was any minister to whom access was so easy and so frequent, nor whose answers were more explicit. He knew how to oblige when he bestowed, and not to shock when he denied; to govern without oppressing, and conquer without triumph. He pursued his ambition without curbing his pleasures, and his pleasures without neglecting his business; he did the latter with ease, and indulged himself in the other without giving scandal or offence. In private life, and to all who had any dependence upon him, he was kind and indulgent; he was generous without ostentation, and an economist without penuriousness; not insolent in success, nor irresolute in distress; faithful to his friends, and not inveterate to his foes.

John, Baron Hervey

Memoirs of the Reign of George the Second . . . ,
ed. J. W. Croker (1848), Vol. I

RECRUITING ARRANGEMENTS FOR ANSON'S EXPEDITION

(1740)

AND at last, on the 28th of *June* 1740, the Duke of *Newcastle*, Principal Secretary of State, delivered to him his Majesty's instructions, dated *January* 31, 1739, with an additional instruction from the Lords Justices, dated *June* 19, 1740. On the receipt of these, Mr. *Anson* immediately repaired to *Spithead*, with a resolution to sail with the first fair wind, flattering himself that all his difficulties were now at an end. For though he knew by the musters that his squadron wanted three hundred seamen of their complement, (a deficiency which, with all his assiduity, he had not been able to get supplied) yet, as Sir *Charles Wager* informed him, that an order from the board of Admiralty was dispatched to Sir *John Norris* to spare him the numbers which he wanted, he doubted not of his complying therewith. But on his arrival at *Portsmouth*, he found himself greatly mistaken, and disappointed in this persuasion: for on his application, Sir *John Norris* told him, he could spare him none, for he wanted men for his own fleet. This occasioned an inevitable and a very considerable delay; for it was the end of *July* before this deficiency was by any means supplied, and all that was then done was extremely short of his necessities and expectation. For Admiral *Balchen*, who succeeded to the command at *Spithead*, after Sir *John Norris* had sailed to the westward, instead of three hundred able sailors, which Mr. *Anson* wanted of his complement, ordered on board the squadron a hundred and seventy men only; of which thirty-two were from the hospital and sick quarters, thirty-seven from the *Salisbury*, with three Officers of Colonel *Lowther's* regiment, and ninety-eight marines, and these were all that were ever granted to make up the forementioned deficiency.

But the Commodore's mortification did not end here. It has been already observed, that it was at first intended that Colonel *Bland's* regiment, and three independent companies of a hundred men each, should embark as land-forces on board the squadron. But this disposition was now changed, and all the land-forces that were to be allowed, were five hundred invalids to be collected from the out-pensioners of *Chelsea* college. As these out-pensioners consist of soldiers, who from their age, wounds, or other infirmities, are incapable of service in marching regiments, Mr. *Anson* was greatly chagrined at having such a decrepid detachment allotted him; for he was fully persuaded that the greatest part of them would perish long before they arrived at the scene of action, since the delays he had already encountered, necessarily confined his passage round Cape *Horn* to the most rigorous season of the year. Sir *Charles Wager* too joined in opinion with the Commodore, the invalids were no ways proper for this service, and solicited strenuously to have them exchanged; but he was told that persons, who were supposed to be better judges of soldiers than he or Mr. *Anson*, thought them the properest men that could be employed on this occasion. And upon this determination they were ordered on board the squadron on the 5th of *August*: But instead of five-hundred, there came on board no more than two hundred and fifty-nine; for all those who had limbs and strength to walk out of *Portsmouth* deserted, leaving behind them only such as were literally invalids, most of them being sixty years of age, and some of them upwards of seventy. Indeed it is difficult to conceive a more moving scene than the embarkation of these unhappy veterans: They were themselves extremely averse to the service they were engaged in, and fully apprized of all the disasters they were afterwards exposed to; the apprehensions of which were strongly mark'd by the concern that appeared in their countenances, which was mixed with no small degree of indignation, to be thus hurried from their repose into a fatiguing employ, to which neither the strength of their bodies, nor the vigour of their minds, were any ways proportioned, and where, without seeing the face of an enemy, or in the least promoting the success of the enterprize, they would in all probability uselessly perish

by lingring and painful diseases; and this too, after they had
spent the activity and strength of their youth in their Country's
service.

Richard Walter (compiler)

*A Voyage round the World . . . by
George Anson Esq. . . . (1748)*

A VISIT TO NEWCASTLE

(1743)

Mon. 31 – We set out early in the morning, and in the evening
came to Newcastle.

Nov. 2, *Wed*. – The following advertisement was published:

FOR THE BENEFIT OF MR. ESTE,

By the Edinburgh Company of Comedians, on *Friday*,
November 4, will be acted a Comedy called

THE CONSCIOUS LOVERS;
To which will be added a Farce, called,

TRICK UPON TRICK, or METHODISM DISPLAYED.

On *Friday* a vast multitude of spectators were assembled in
the Moot Hall to see this. It was believed there could not be
less than fifteen hundred people, some hundreds of whom sat
on rows of seats built upon the stage. Soon after the comedians had begun the first act of the play, on a sudden all those
seats fell down at once, the supporters of them breaking like a
rotten stick. The people were thrown one upon another,
about five foot forward, but not one of them hurt. After a
short time the rest of the spectators were quiet, and the actors
went on. In the middle of the second act all the shilling seats

gave a crack and sunk several inches down. A great noise and shrieking followed; and as many as could readily get to the door went out and returned no more. Notwithstanding this, when the noise was over, the actors went on with the play. In the beginning of the third act the entire stage suddenly sunk about six inches. The players retired with great precipitation; yet in a while they began again. At the latter end of the third act all the sixpenny seats, without any kind of notice, fell to the ground. There was now a cry on every side, it being supposed that many were crushed in pieces; but, upon inquiry, not a single person (such was the mercy of God!) was either killed or dangerously hurt. Two or three hundred remaining still in the hall, Mr. Este (who was to act the Methodist) came upon the stage and told them, for all this, he was resolved the farce should be acted. While he was speaking the stage sunk six inches more; on which he ran back in the utmost confusion, and the people as fast as they could out of the door, none staying to look behind him.

Which is most surprising – that those players acted this farce the next week, or that some hundreds of people came again to see it?

Sun. 6. – We had an useful practical sermon at St. Nicholas's church in the morning, and another at St. Andrew's in the afternoon. At five I preached to a willing multitude, on the Prodigal Son. How many of these were lost, and now are found!

In the following week I endeavoured to speak severally to each member of the society. The numbers I found neither to rise nor fall; but many had increased in the knowledge and love of God.

Sunday the 13th, and the following days, I preached and regulated the societies at Painshaw, Tanfield, Horsley, and Plessey.

Thur. 17. – I preached at the Spen on Christ Jesus our

'wisdom, righteousness, sanctification, and redemption.' I have seldom seen an audience so greatly moved since the time of my first preaching at Bristol. Men, women, and children wept and groaned and trembled exceedingly; many could not contain themselves in these bounds, but cried with a loud and bitter cry. It was the same at the meeting of the society, and likewise in the morning, while I was showing the happiness of those 'whose iniquities are forgiven, and whose sins are covered.' I afterwards spake with twelve or fourteen of them severally; and found good ground to believe that God had given them to 'taste of the good word, and of the powers of the world to come.'

Sun. 20. – After preaching at Newcastle morning and evening, I earnestly exhorted the society to beware of speaking evil of each other, and of censuring those who followed not with us.

Mon. 21. – I besought them, in my farewell sermon, to 'forget the things which are behind, and press on to the prize of their high calling.'

John Wesley

An Extract of the Reverend Mr. John Wesley's Journal from October 27, 1743 to November 17, 1746 (1753). Text from complete Journal . . ., ed. N. Curnock (1909), Vol. III

SHENSTONE THE GARDENER

(1745)

Now was excited his delight in rural pleasures, and his ambition of rural elegance; he began from this time to point his prospects, to diversify his surface, to entangle his walks, and to wind his waters, which he did with such judgement and such fancy as made his little domain the envy of the great, and the admiration of the skilful: a place to be visited by travellers, and copied by designers. Whether to plant a walk in undulating curves, and to place a bench at every turn where there is an object to catch the view; to make water run where it will be heard, and to stagnate where it will be seen; to leave intervals where the eye will be pleased, and to thicken the plantation where there is something to be hidden, demands any great powers of mind, I will not enquire: perhaps a sullen and surly speculator may think such performances rather the sport than the business of human reason. But it must be at least confessed that to embellish the form of nature is an innocent amusement; and some praise must be allowed by the most supercilious observer to him who does best what such multitudes are contending to do well.

This praise was the praise of Shenstone; but, like all other modes of felicity, it was not enjoyed without its abatements. Lyttelton was his neighbour and his rival, whose empire, spacious and opulent, looked with disdain on the *petty State* that *appeared behind it*. For a while the inhabitants of Hagley affected to tell their acquaintance of the little fellow that was trying to make himself admired; but when by degrees the Leasowes forced themselves into notice, they took care to defeat the curiosity which they could not suppress, by conducting their visitants perversely to inconvenient points of view, and introducing them at the wrong end of a walk to detect a deception; injuries of which Shenstone would heavily complain. Where there is emulation there will be vanity, and where there is vanity there will be folly.

The pleasure of Shenstone was all in his eye; he valued what he valued merely for its looks; nothing raised his indignation more than to ask if there were any fishes in his water.

His house was mean, and he did not improve it; his care was of his grounds. When he came home from his walks he might find his floors flooded by a shower through the broken roof; but could spare no money for its reparation.

In time his expences brought clamours about him, that overpowered the lamb's bleat and the linnet's song; and his groves were haunted by beings very different from fawns and fairies. He spent his estate in adorning it, and his death was probably hastened by his anxieties. He was a lamp that spent its oil in blazing. It is said that if he had lived a little longer he would have been assisted by a pension: such bounty could not have been ever more properly bestowed; but that it was ever asked is not certain: it is too certain that it never was enjoyed.

Samuel Johnson

The Lives of the most eminent English Poets . . . (1779–81).
Text from the third edition (1783), Vol. IV

AN OXFORD COLLEGE

(1752)

THE College of St. Mary Magdalen was founded in the fifteenth century by Wainfleet Bishop of Winchester; and now consists of a president, forty fellows, and a number of inferior students. It is esteemed one of the largest and most wealthy of our academical corporations, which may be compared to the Benedictine abbeys of Catholic countries; and I have loosely heard that the estates belonging to Magdalen College, which are leased by those indulgent landlords at small quit-rents and occasional fines, might be raised, in the hands of private avarice, to an annual revenue of nearly thirty thousand pounds. Our colleges are supposed to be schools of science, as well as of education; nor is it unreasonable to expect that a body of literary men, devoted to a life of celibacy, exempt from the care of their own subsistence, and amply provided with books, should devote their leisure to the prosecution of study, and that some effects of their studies should be manifested to the world. The shelves of their library groan under the weight of the Benedictine folios, of the editions of the fathers, and the collections of the middle ages, which have issued from the single abbey of St. Germain de Préz at Paris. A composition of genius must be the offspring of one mind; but such works of industry, as may be divided among many hands, and must be continued during many years, are the peculiar province of a laborious community. If I inquire into the manufactures of the monks of Magdalen, if I extend the inquiry to the other colleges of Oxford and Cambridge, a silent blush, or a scornful frown, will be the only reply. The fellows or monks of my time were decent easy men, who supinely enjoyed the gifts of the founder; their days were filled by a series of uniform employments; the chapel and the hall, the coffee-house and the common room, till they retired, weary and well satisfied, to a long slumber. From the toil of reading, or thinking, or writing, they had absolved their conscience; and the first shoots of learning and ingenuity withered on the ground, without yielding any fruits to the owners or the public. As a gentleman-commoner, I was admitted to the society of the fellows, and fondly expected that some questions of literature would be the amusing and instructive topics of their discourse. Their conversation stagnated in a round of college business, Tory politics, personal anecdotes, and private scandal: their dull and deep potations excused the brisk intemperance of youth: and their constitutional toasts were not expressive of the most lively loyalty for the house of Hanover. A general election was now approaching: the great Oxfordshire contest already blazed with all the malevolence of party zeal. Magdalen College was devoutly attached to the old interest! and the names of Wenman and Dashwood were more frequently pronounced, than those of Cicero and Chrysostom.

The example of the senior fellows could not inspire the under-graduates with a liberal spirit or studious emulation; and I cannot describe, as I never knew, the discipline of college.

Edward Gibbon

'Memoirs of my Life and Writings' from *Miscellaneous Works...*, ed. Lord Sheffield (1796), Vol. I

KITTEN OVERBOARD

(1754)

Thursday, July 11. ... A most tragical incident fell out this day at sea. While the ship was under sail, but making, as will appear, no great way, a kitten, one of four of the feline in-habitants of the cabin, fell from the window into the water: an alarm was immediately given to the captain, who was then upon deck, and received it with the utmost concern and many bitter oaths. He immediately gave orders to the steersman in favour of the poor thing, as he called it; the sails were instantly slackened, and all hands, as the phrase is, employed to recover the poor animal. I was, I own, extremely surprised at all this; less, indeed, at the captain's extreme tenderness, than at his conceiving any possibility of success; for, if puss had had nine thousand, instead of nine lives, I concluded they had been all lost. The boatswain, however, had more sanguine hopes; for, having stript himself of his jacket, breeches, and shirt, he leapt boldly into the water, and to my great astonishment, in a few minutes, returned to the ship, bearing the motionless animal in his mouth. Nor was this, I observed, a matter of such great difficulty as it appeared to my ignorance, and pos-sibly may seem to that of my fresh-water reader: the kitten was now exposed to air and sun on the deck, where its life, of which it retained no symptoms, was despaired of by all.

The captain's humanity, if I may so call it, did not so totally destroy his philosophy, as to make him yield himself up to affliction on this melancholy occasion. Having felt his loss like a man, he resolved to shew he could bear it like one; and having declared, he had rather have lost a cask of rum or brandy, betook himself to threshing at backgammon with the Portuguese friar, in which innocent amusement they had passed about two-thirds of their time.

But as I have, perhaps, a little too wantonly endeavoured to raise the tender passions of my readers, in this narrative, I should think myself unpardonable if I concluded it, without giving them the satisfaction of hearing that the kitten at last recovered, to the great joy of the good captain; but to the great disappointment of some of the sailors, who asserted that the drowning a cat was the very surest way of raising a favourable wind: a supposition of which, though we have heard several plausible accounts, we will not presume to assign the true original reason.

Henry Fielding
The Journal of a Voyage to Lisbon (1755)

THE FUNERAL OF GEORGE II

Horace Walpole to George Montagu: an extract from a letter
(13 November, 1760)

Do you know I had the curiosity to go to the burying t'other night; I had never seen a royal funeral. Nay, I walked as a rag of quality, which I found would be, and so it was, the easiest way of seeing it. It is absolutely a noble sight. The Prince's Chamber hung with purple and a quantity of silver lamps, the coffin under a canopy of purple velvet, and six vast chandeliers of silver on high stands had a very good effect:

the ambassador from Tripoli and his son were carried to see that chamber. The procession through a line of foot-guards, every seventh man bearing a torch, the horse-guards lining the outside, their officers with drawn sabres and crape sashes, on horseback, the drums muffled, the fifes, bells tolling and minute guns, all this was very solemn. But the charm was the entrance of the Abbey, where we were received by the Dean and chapter in rich copes, the choir and almsmen all bearing torches; the whole Abbey so illuminated, that one saw it to greater advantage than by day; the tombs, long aisles, and fretted roof all appearing distinctly, and with the happiest chiaroscuro. There wanted nothing but incense, and little chapels here and there with priests saying mass for the repose of the defunct – yet one could not complain of its not being Catholic enough. I had been in dread of being coupled with some boy of ten years old – but the heralds were not very accurate, and I walked with George Grenville, taller and older enough to keep me in countenance. When we came to the chapel of Henry VII all solemnity and decorum ceased – no order was observed, people sat or stood where they could or would, the yeomen of the guard were crying out for help, oppressed by the immense weight of the coffin, the Bishop read sadly, and blundered in the prayers, the fine chapter, *Man that is born of a woman*, was chanted not read, and the anthem, besides being unmeasurably tedious, would have served as well for a nuptial. The real serious part was the figure of the Duke of Cumberland, heightened by a thousand melancholy circumstances. He had a dark brown adonis, and a cloak of black cloth with a train of five yards. Attending the funeral of a father, how little reason soever he had to love him, could not be pleasant. His leg extremely bad, yet forced to stand upon it near two hours, his face bloated and distorted with his late paralytic stroke, which has affected too one of his eyes, and placed over the mouth of the vault, into which in all probability he must himself so soon descend – think how unpleasant a situation! He bore it all with a firm and unaffected countenance. This grave scene was fully contrasted by the burlesque Duke of Newcastle – he fell into a fit of crying the moment he came into the chapel and flung himself back in a stall, the Archbishop hovering over him with a smelling bottle – but in two minutes his curiosity got the better of his hypocrisy and he ran about the chapel with his glass to spy who was or was not there, spying with one hand and mopping his eyes with t'other. Then returned the fear of catching cold, and the Duke of Cumberland, who was sinking with heat, felt himself weighed down, and turning round, found it was the Duke of Newcastle standing upon his train to avoid the chill of the marble. It was very theatric to look down into the vault, where the coffin lay, attended by mourners with lights. Clavering, the Groom of the Bedchamber, refused to sit up with the body, and was dismissed by the King's order.

I have nothing more to tell you but a trifle, a very trifle – the King of Prussia has totally defeated Marshal Daun. This which would have been prodigious news a month ago, is nothing today; it only takes its turn among the questions, 'Who is to be Groom of the Bedchamber?' 'What is Sir T. Robinson to have?' I have been at Leicester Fields today; the crowd was immoderate; I don't believe it will continue so. Good night.

Horace Walpole

Letters ... to George Montagu, Esq. (1818). Text from
The Yale Edition of Horace Walpole's Correspondence,
ed. W. S. Lewis, Vol. IX (1941)

A TRIP TO GREENWICH

(1763)

ON Saturday, July 30, Dr. Johnson and I took a sculler at the Temple-stairs, and set out for Greenwich. I asked him if he really thought a knowledge of the Greek and Latin languages an essential requisite to a good education. JOHNSON. 'Most certainly, Sir; for those who know them have a very great advantage over those who do not. Nay, Sir, it is wonderful what a difference learning makes upon people even in the common intercourse of life, which does not appear to be much connected with it.' 'And yet, (said I) people go through the world very well, and carry on the business of life to good advantage, without learning.' JOHNSON. 'Why, Sir, that may be true in cases where learning cannot possibly be of any use; for instance, this boy rows us as well without learning, as if he could sing the song of Orpheus to the Argonauts, who were the first sailors.' He then called to the boy, 'What would you give, my lad, to know about the Argonauts?' 'Sir, (said the boy,) I would give what I have.' Johnson was much pleased with his answer, and we gave him a double fare. Dr. Johnson then turning to me, 'Sir, (said he) a desire of knowledge is the natural feeling of mankind; and every human being, whose mind is not debauched, will be willing to give all that he has to get knowledge.'

We landed at the Old Swan, and walked to Billingsgate, where we took oars, and moved smoothly along the silver Thames. It was a very fine day. We were entertained with the immense number and variety of ships that were lying at anchor, and with the beautiful country on each side of the river.

I talked of preaching, and of the great success which those called Methodists have. JOHNSON. 'Sir, it is owing to their expressing themselves in a plain and familiar manner, which is the only way to do good to the common people, and which clergymen of genius and learning ought to do from a principle of duty, when it is suited to their congregations; a practice, for which they will be praised by men of sense. To insist against drunkenness as a crime, because it debases Reason, the noblest faculty of man, would be of no service to the common people: but to tell them that they may die in a fit of drunkenness, and shew them how dreadful that would be, cannot fail to make a deep impression. Sir, when your Scotch clergy give up their homely manner, religion will soon decay in that country.' Let this observation, as Johnson meant it, be ever remembered.

I was much pleased to find myself with Johnson at Greenwich, which he celebrates in his 'London' as a favourite scene. I had the poem in my pocket, and read the lines aloud with enthusiasm:

> 'On Thames's banks in silent thought we stood,
> Where Greenwich smiles upon the silver flood:
> Pleas'd with the seat which gave ELIZA birth,
> We kneel, and kiss the consecrated earth.'

He remarked that the structure of Greenwich hospital was too magnificent for a place of charity, and that its parts were too much detached to make one great whole . . . .

We walked in the evening in Greenwich Park. He asked me, I suppose, by way of trying my disposition, 'Is not this very fine?' Having no exquisite relish of the beauties of Nature, and being more delighted with 'the busy hum of men,' I answered, 'Yes, Sir; but not equal to Fleet-street.' JOHNSON. 'You are right, Sir.'

James Boswell
The Life of Samuel Johnson, LL.D. (1791)

MONTPELLIER
(1763)

THE weather was extremely hot when we entered Montpellier, and put up at the *Cheval Blanc*, counted the best *auberge* in the place, tho' in fact it is a most wretched hovel, the habitation of darkness, dirt, and imposition. Here I was obliged to pay four livres a meal for every person in my family, and two livres a night for every bed, though all in the same room: one would imagine that the further we advance to the southward the living is the dearer, though in fact every article of housekeeping is cheaper in Languedoc than many other provinces of France. This imposition is owing to the concourse of English who come hither, and, like simple birds of passage, allow themselves to be plucked by the people of the country, who know their weak side, and make their attacks accordingly. They affect to believe, that all the travellers of our country are grand seigneurs, immensely rich and incredibly generous; and we are silly enough to encourage this opinion, by submitting quietly to the most ridiculous extortion, as well as by committing acts of the most absurd extravagance. This folly of the English, together with a concourse of people from different quarters, who come hither for the re-establishment of their health, has rendered Montpellier one of the dearest places in the South of France. The city, which is but small, stands upon a rising ground fronting the Mediterranean, which is about three leagues to the southward: on the other side is an agreeable plain, extending about the same distance towards the mountains of the Cevennes. The town is reckoned well built, and what the French call *bien percée*; yet the streets are in general narrow, and the houses dark. The air is counted salutary in catarrhous consumptions, from its dryness and elasticity: but too sharp in cases of pulmonary imposthumes.

It was at Montpellier that we saw for the first time any signs of that gaiety and mirth for which the people of this country are celebrated. In all other places through which we passed since our departure from Lyons, we saw nothing but marks of poverty and chagrin. We entered Montpellier on a Sunday, when the people were all dressed in their best apparel. The streets were crowded; and a great number of the better sort of both sexes sat upon stone seats at their doors, conversing with great mirth and familiarity. These conversations lasted the greatest part of the night; and many of them were improved with musick both vocal and instrumental: next day we were visited by the English residing in the place, who always pay this mark of respect to new comers. They consist of four or five families, among whom I could pass the winter very agreeably, if the state of my health and other reasons did not call me away.

Tobias Smollett
Travels through France and Italy (1766)

THE REPEAL OF THE STAMP ACT

Mrs. Elizabeth Montagu to Mrs. Elizabeth Vesey: an extract from a letter
(22 February, 1766)

THE stamp act was repeal'd by a majority of one hundred and eight, and our friend Mr. Burke spoke divinely, yes divinely, dont misunderstand me, and report he spoke as well as mortal man could do, I tell you he spoke better. The great Commoner praised him highly in the Senate, and all people join in the chorus. Indeed Mr. Burke has every day acquired great praise but yesterday crown'd all. Mr. Pitt did not speak so well as he has done. He described the American planter sitting in his native innocence in his native woods, and how cruel to disturb him there with a stamp duty, but as this duty was not to be levied on men who under the shade of melancholly boughs lose and neglect the creeping hours of time, but affects the litigious man who goes to law, or the mercantile man who sends commodities out to Sea, the pastoral part of the speech, though adorned with quotations from the Georgics, did not greatly move the House. In the House of Lords there will be more opposition to the Ministry, but still the act will be repealed.

Elizabeth Montagu

Mrs. Montagu 'Queen of the Blues' ...
1762–1800, ed. R. Blunt (1923), Vol. I

STERNE AND ELIZA

(1767)

MUNDAY. AP: 15.

worn out with fevers of all kinds but most, by that fever of the heart with wch. I'm eternally wasting, & shall waste till I see Eliza again – dreadful Suffering of 15 Months! – it may be more – great Controuler of Events! surely thou wilt proportion this, to my Strength, and to that of my Eliza. pass'd the whole afternoon in reading her Letters, & reducing them to the order in which they were wrote to me – staid the whole evening at home – no pleasure or Interest in either Society or Diversions – What a change, my dear Girl, hast thou made in me! – but the Truth is, thou hast only turn'd the tide of my passions a new way – they flow, Eliza to thee – & ebb from every other Object in this world – & Reason tells me they do right – for my heart has rated thee at a Price, that all the world is not rich enough to purchase thee from me at. In a high fever all the night.

Ap: 16. and got up so ill, I could not go to Mrs. James as I had promised her – took James's Powder however – & leand the whole day with my head upon My hand; sitting most dejectedly at the Table with my Eliza's Picture before me – sympathizing & soothing me – O my Bramine! my Friend! my Help-mate! – for that, (if I'm a prophet) is the Lot mark'd out for thee, – & such I consider thee now & thence it is, Eliza, I Share so righteously with thee, in all the evil or good which befalls thee – But all our portion is Evil now, & all our hours grief – I look forwards towards the Elysium we have so often and rapturously talk'd of – Cordelia's Spirit will fly to tell thee in some sweet Slumber, the moment the door is opend for thee – & The Bramin of the Vally, shall follow the track wherever it leads him, to get to his Eliza, & invite her to his Cottage. –

5 in the afternoon – I have just been eating my Chick-ing, sitting over my repast upon it, with Tears – a bitter Sause – Eliza! but I could eat it with no other – when Molly spread the Table Cloath, my heart fainted with in me – one solitary plate – one knife – one fork – one Glass! – O Eliza! twas pain-fully distressing, – I gave a thousand pensive penetrating Looks at the Arm chair thou so often graced on these quiet sentimental Repasts – & Sighed & laid down my knife & fork, – took out my handkerchiff, clap'd it across my face, & wept like a child – I shall read the same affecting Acct. of many a sad Dinner wch. Eliza has had no power to taste of, from the same feelings & recollections, how She & her Bramin have eat their bread in peace and Love together.

Laurence Sterne

'The Journal to Eliza' in *Works* . . ., ed. Wilbur
L. Cross (1904), Vol. VIII. Text from *Letters* . . .,
ed. L. P. Curtis (1935)

The Execution of Gibson and Payne

(1768)

Of all publick spectacles, that of a capital execution draws the greatest number of spectators. And I must confess that I myself am never absent from any of them. Nor can I accuse myself of being more hard hearted than other people. On the contrary, I am persuaded that nobody feels more sincerely for the distresses of his fellow-creatures than I do, or would do more to relieve them. When I first attended executions, I was shocked to the greatest degree. I was in a manner convulsed with pity and terror, and for several days, but especially nights after, I was in a very dismal situation. Still, however, I persisted in attending them, and by degrees my sensibility abated; so that I can now see one with great composure, and my mind is not afterwards haunted with frightful thoughts: though for a while a certain degree of gloom remains upon it. I can account for this curiosity in a philosophical manner, when I consider that death is the most aweful object before every man, who ever directs his thoughts seriously towards futurity; and that it is very natural that we should be anxious to see people in that situation which affects us so much. It is true indeed that none of us, who go to see an execution have any idea that we are to be executed and few of us need be under any apprehension whatever of meeting with that fate. But dying publickly at Tyburn, and dying privately in one's bed, are only different modes of the same thing. They are both death; they are both that wonderous, that alarming scene of quitting all that we have ever seen, heard, or known, and at once passing into a state of being totally unknown to us, and in which we cannot tell what may be our situation. Therefore it is that I feel an irresistible impulse to be present at every execution, as I there behold the various effects of the near approach of death, according to the various tempers of the unhappy sufferers, and by studying them I learn to quiet and fortify my own mind.

I shall never forget the last execution I saw at Tyburn, when Mr. Gibson, the attorney, for forgery, and Benjamin Payne, for an highway robbery, were executed. Poor Payne was a thin young lad of twenty, in a mean dress, and a red night-cap, with nothing to discriminate him from the many miserable beings who are penitent and half dead with fear. But Mr. Gibson was indeed an extraordinary man. He came from Newgate in a coach, with some friends attending him. I met the mournful procession in Oxford-road, and I declare that if I had not been told it, I should not have known which was Mr. Gibson. He was drawn backwards, and looked as calm and easy as ever I saw a man in my life. He was dressed in a full suit of black, wore his own hair round and in a natural curl, and a hat. When he came to the place of execution he was allowed to remain a little in the coach. A signal was then given him that it was time to approach the fatal tree. He took leave of his friends, stepped out of the coach, and walked firmly to the cart. He was helped up upon it, as he was pinioned and had not the free use of his arms. When he was upon the cart, he gave his hat to the executioner, who immediately took off Mr. Gibson's cravat, unloosed his shirt neck, and fixed the rope. Mr. Gibson never once altered his countenance. He refreshed his mouth by sucking a sweet orange. He shewed no stupid insensibility; nor did he affect to brave it out like those hardened wretches who boast that they die hard. He appeared to all the spectators a man of sense and reflexion, of a mind naturally sedate and placid. He submitted with a manly and decent resolution to what he knew to be the just punishment of the law. Mr. Moore, the Ordinary of Newgate, discharged his duty with much earnestness, and a fervour for which I and all around me esteemed and loved him. Mr.

Moore seems worthy of his office, which, when justly considered, is a very important one, if administering divine comfort to multitudes of miserable beings, be important. Poor
Payne seemed to rely on that mercy which I trust has not
been refused him—Mr. Gibson seemed truely devout; and,
in short, from first to last, his behaviour was the most perfect
that I ever saw, or indeed could conceive of one in his unhappy
circumstances.

James Boswell

The Publick Advertiser, 26 April, 1768; reprinted
in *The London Magazine,* May, 1783. Text from
Boswell's Column . . ., ed. Margaret Bailey (1951)

GRAY IN THE LAKE DISTRICT

(1769)

OCT: 3. Wd. at S.E., a heavenly day. rose at seven, & walk'd
out under the conduct of my Landlord to *Borrodale.* the grass
was cover'd with a hoar-frost, wch. soon melted, & exhaled
in a thin blewish smoke. cross'd the meadows obliquely,
catching a diversity of views among the hills over the lakes
& islands, & changing prospect at every ten paces, left *Cock-
shut* & Castle-hill (wch. we formerly mounted) behind me, &
drew near the foot of *Walla-crag,* whose bare and rocky brow,
cut perpendicularly down above 400 feet, as I guess, awefully
overlooks the way: our path here tends to the left, & the
ground gently rising, & cover'd with a glade of scattering
trees & bushes on the very margin of the water, opens both
ways the most delicious view, that my eyes ever beheld. behind you are the magnificent heights of *Walla*-crag; opposite
lie the thick hanging woods of Ld. Egremont, & *Newland*-
valley with green & smiling fields embosom'd in the dark
cliffs; to the left the jaws of *Borodale,* with that turbulent chaos

of mountain behind mountain roll'd in confusion; beneath you and stretching far away to the right, the shining purity of the *Lake*, just ruffled by the breeze enough to shew it is alive, reflecting rocks, woods, fields, & inverted tops of mountains, with the white buildings of *Keswick, Crosthwait*-church, & *Skiddaw* for a back-ground at distance. oh Doctor! I never wish'd more for you; & pray think, how the glass played its part in such a spot, wch. is called *Carf-close-reeds*: I chuse to set down these barbarous names, that any body may enquire on the place, & easily find the particular station, that I mean. this scene continues to *Barrow-gate*, & a little farther, passing a brook called *Barrow-beck*, we enter'd *Borodale*. the crags, named *Lodoor-banks* now begin to impend terribly over your way; & more terribly, when you hear, that three years since an immense mass of rock tumbled at once from the brow, & bar'd all access to the dale (for this is the only road) till they could work their way thro' it. luckily no one was passing at the time of this fall; but down the side of the mountain & far into the lake lie dispersed the huge fragments of this ruin in all shapes & in all directions. Something farther we turn'd aside into a coppice, ascending a little in front of *Lodoor* water-fall; the height appears to be about 200 feet, the quantity of water not great, tho' (these three days excepted) it had rain'd daily in the hills for near two months before: but then the stream was nobly broken, leaping from rock to rock, & foaming with fury. on one side a towering crag, that spired up to equal, if not overtop, the neighbouring cliffs (this lay all in shade & darkness) on the other hand a rounder broader projecting hill shag'd with wood & illumined by the sun, wch. glanced sideways on the upper part of the cataract. the force of the water wearing a deep channel in the ground hurries away to join the lake. we descended again, & passed the stream over a rude bridge. soon after we came under *Gowder-crag*, a hill more formidable to the eye & to the apprehension than that of *Lodoor*; the rocks atop, deep-cloven perpendicularly by the rains, hanging loose & nodding forwards, seem just starting from their base in shivers: the whole way down & the road on both sides is strew'd with piles of the fragments strangely thrown across each other & of a dreadful bulk . . .

Thomas Gray

'The Journal in the Lakes' in *Poems* . . ., ed. W.
Mason (1775), Vol. II. Text from *Correspondence*,
ed. P. Toynbee and L. Whibley (1935), Vol. III

JOHNSON IN THE HIGHLANDS

(1773)

OF the hills many may be called with Homer's Ida *abundant in springs*, but few can deserve the epithet which he bestows upon Pelion by *waving their leaves*. They exhibit very little variety; being almost wholly covered with dark heath, and even that seems to be checked in its growth. What is not heath is nakedness, a little diversified by now and then a stream rushing down the steep. An eye accustomed to flowery pastures and waving harvests is astonished and repelled by this wide extent of hopeless sterility. The appearance is that of matter incapable of form or usefulness, dismissed by nature from her care and disinherited of her favours, left in its original elemental state, or quickened only with one sullen power of useless vegetation.

It will very readily occur, that this uniformity of barrenness can afford very little amusement to the traveller; that it is easy to sit at home and conceive rocks and heath, and waterfalls; and that these journeys are useless labours, which neither impregnate the imagination, nor enlarge the understanding. It is true that of far the greater part of things, we must content ourselves with such knowledge as description may exhibit, or analogy supply; but it is true likewise, that these ideas are always incomplete, and that at least, till we have compared them with realities, we do not know them to be just. As we see more, we become possessed of more certainties, and consequently gain more principles of reasoning, and found a wider basis of analogy.

Regions mountainous and wild, thinly inhabited, and little cultivated, make a great part of the earth, and he that has never seen them, must live unacquainted with much of the face of nature, and with one of the great scenes of human existence.

As the day advanced towards noon, we entered a narrow valley not very flowery, but sufficiently verdant. Our guides told us, that the horses could not travel all day without rest or meat, and intreated us to stop here, because no grass would be found in any other place. The request was reasonable and the argument cogent. We therefore willingly dismounted and diverted ourselves as the place gave us opportunity.

I sat down on a bank, such as a writer of Romance might have delighted to feign. I had indeed no trees to whisper over my head, but a clear rivulet streamed at my feet. The day was calm, the air soft, and all was rudeness, silence, and solitude. Before me, and on either side, were high hills, which by hindering the eye from ranging, forced the mind to find entertainment for itself. Whether I spent the hour well I know not; for here I first conceived the thought of this narration.

We were in this place at ease and by choice, and had no evils to suffer or to fear; yet the imaginations excited by the view of an unknown and untravelled wilderness are not such as arise in the artificial solitude of parks and gardens, a flattering notion of self-sufficiency, a placid indulgence of voluntary delusions, a secure expansion of the fancy, or a cool concentration of the mental powers. The phantoms which haunt a desert are want, and misery, and danger; the evils of dereliction rush upon the thoughts; man is made unwillingly acquainted with his own weakness, and meditation shows him only how little he can sustain, and how little he can perform. There were no traces of inhabitants, except perhaps a rude pile of clods called a summer hut, in which a herdsman had rested in the favourable seasons. Whoever had been in the place where I then sat, unprovided with provisions and ignorant of the country, might, at least before the roads were made, have wandered among the rocks, till he had perished with hardship, before he could have found either food or shelter. Yet what are these hillocks to the ridges of Taurus, or these spots of wildness to the desarts of America?

Samuel Johnson
A Journey to the Western Islands of Scotland (1775)

EXPLORING THE SOUTH PACIFIC

(1774)

ON the 30th, at four o'clock in the morning, we perceived the clouds, over the horizon to the South, to be of an unusual snow-white brightness, which we knew announced our approach to field-ice. Soon after, it was seen from the top-mast head; and at eight o'clock, we were close to its edge. It extended East and West, far beyond the reach of our sight. In the situation we were in, just the southern half of our horizon was illuminated, by the rays of light reflected from the ice, to a considerable height. Ninety-seven ice hills were distinctly seen within the field, besides those on the outside; many of them very large, and looking like a ridge of mountains, rising one above another till they were lost in the clouds. The outer, or northern edge of this immense field, was composed of loose or broken ice close packed together; so that it was not possible for anything to enter it. This was about a mile broad; within which was solid ice in one continued compact body. It was rather low and flat, (except the hills) but seemed to increase in height, as you traced it to the South; in which direction it extended beyond our sight. Such mountains of ice as these, were, I believe, never seen in the Greenland Seas; at least, not that I ever heard or read of; so that we cannot draw a comparison between the ice here, and there. It must be allowed that these prodigious ice mountains must add such additional weight to the ice fields which inclose them, as cannot but make a great difference between the navigating this icy sea and that of Greenland.

I will not say it was impossible any where to get farther to the South; but the attempting it would have been a dangerous and rash enterprise, and what, I believe, no man in my situation would have thought of. It was, indeed, *my* opinion, as well as the opinion of most on board, that this ice extended quite to the pole, or perhaps, joined to some land, to which it had been fixed from the earliest time; and that it is here, that is to the South of this parallel, where all the ice we find scattered up and down to the North, is first formed, and afterwards broken off by gales of wind, or other causes, and brought to the North by the currents, which we always found to set in that direction in the high latitudes. As we drew near this ice, some penguins were heard, but none seen; and but few other birds, or any other thing, that could induce us to think any land was near. And yet I think there must be some to the South behind this ice; but if there is, it can afford no better retreat for birds, or any other animals, than the ice itself, with which it must be wholly covered. I, who had ambition not only to go farther than anyone had been before, but as far as it was possible for man to go, was not sorry at meeting with this interruption; as it, in some measure, relieved us; at least shortened the dangers and hardships inseparable from the navigation of the southern polar regions. Since therefore we could not proceed one inch farther to the South, no other reason need be assigned for my tacking, and standing back to the North; being at this time in the latitude of 71° 10′ South, longitude 106° 54′ West. . . .

I now came to a resolution to proceed to the North and to spend the ensuing winter within the Tropic, if I met with no employment before I came there. I was now well satisfied no continent was to be found in this ocean, but what must lie so far to the South as to be wholly inaccessible on account of ice; and that if one should be found in the Southern Atlantic Ocean, it would be necessary to have the whole summer before us to explore it. . . .

James Cook

A Voyage towards the South Pole and
Round the World . . . (1777), Vol. I

A QUARREL AND A RECONCILIATION
(1778)

BOOKS of Travels having been mentioned, Johnson praised Pennant[1] very highly, as he did at Dunvegan, in the Isle of Sky. Dr. Percy, knowing himself to be the heir male of the ancient Percies, and having the warmest and most dutiful attachment to the noble House of Northumberland, could not sit quietly and hear a man praised, who had spoken disrespectfully of Alnwick-Castle and the Duke's pleasure-grounds, especially as he thought meanly of his travels. He therefore opposed Johnson eagerly. JOHNSON. 'Pennant in what he said of Alnwick, has done what he intended; he has made you very angry.' PERCY. 'He has said the garden is *trim*, which is representing it like a citizen's parterre, when the

1. Thomas Pennant (1726–98), traveller and naturalist, author of *A Tour in Scotland* (1771), etc.

truth is, there is a very large extent of fine turf and gravel walks.' JOHNSON. 'According to your own account, Sir, Pennant is right. It *is* trim. Here is grass cut close, and gravel rolled smooth. Is not that trim? The extent is nothing against that; a mile may be as trim as a square yard. Your extent puts me in mind of the citizen's enlarged dinner, two pieces of roast-beef, and two puddings. There is no variety, no mind exerted in laying out the ground, no trees.' PERCY. 'He pretends to give the natural history of Northumberland, and yet takes no notice of the immense number of trees planted there of late.' JOHNSON. 'That, Sir, has nothing to do with the *natural* history; that is *civil* history. A man who gives the natural history of the oak, is not to tell how many oaks have been planted in this place or that. A man who gives the natural history of the cow, is not to tell how many cows are milked at Islington. The animal is the same, whether milked in the Park or at Islington.' PERCY. 'Pennant does not describe well; a carrier who goes along the side of Loch-lomond would describe it better.' JOHNSON. 'I think he describes very well.' PERCY. 'I travelled after him.' JOHNSON. 'And *I* travelled after him.' PERCY. 'But, my good friend, you are shortsighted, and do not see so well as I do.' I wondered at Dr. Percy's venturing thus. Dr. Johnson said nothing at the time; but inflammable particles were collecting for a cloud to burst. In a little while Dr. Percy said something more in disparagement of Pennant. JOHNSON. (pointedly) 'This is the resentment of a narrow mind, because he did not find every thing in Northumberland.' PERCY. (feeling the stroke) 'Sir, you may be as rude as you please.' JOHNSON. 'Hold, Sir! Don't talk of rudeness; remember, Sir, you told me (puffing hard with passion struggling for a vent) I was short-sighted. We have done with civility. We are to be as rude as we please.' PERCY. 'Upon my honour, Sir, I did not mean to be uncivil.' JOHNSON. 'I cannot say so, Sir; for I *did* mean to be uncivil, thinking *you* had been uncivil.' Dr. Percy rose, ran up to him, and taking him by the hand, assured him affectionately that his meaning had been misunderstood; upon which a reconciliation instantly took place. JOHNSON. 'My dear Sir, I am willing you shall *hang* Pennant.' PERCY. (resuming the former subject) 'Pennant complains that the helmet is not hung out to invite to the hall of hospitality. Now I never heard that it was a custom to hang out a *helmet*.' JOHNSON. 'Hang him up, hang him up.' BOSWELL. (humouring the joke) 'Hang out his skull instead of a helmet, and you may drink ale out of it in your hall of Odin, as he is your enemy; that will be truly ancient. *There* will be "Northern Antiquities".' JOHNSON. 'He's a *Whig*, Sir,; a *sad dog* (smiling at his own violent expressions, merely for *political* difference of opinion). But he's the best traveller I ever read; he observes more things than any one else does.'

James Boswell
The Life of Samuel Johnson, LL.D. (1791)
Text from the second edition (1793)

JOHNSON AND THE POOR

SEVERITY towards the poor was, in Dr. Johnson's opinion (as is visible in his Life of Addison particularly), an undoubted and constant attendant or consequence upon whiggism; and he was not contented with giving them relief, he wished to add also indulgence. He loved the poor as I never yet saw any one else do, with an earnest desire to make them happy. – What signifies, says some one, giving halfpence to common beggars? they only lay it out in gin or tobacco. 'And why should they be denied such sweeteners of their existence (says Johnson)? it is surely very savage to refuse them every possible avenue to pleasure, reckoned too coarse for our own acceptance. Life is a pill which none of us can bear to swallow without gilding; yet for the poor we delight in stripping it still barer, and are not ashamed to shew even visible displeasure, if ever the bitter taste is taken from their mouths.' In consequence of these principles he nursed whole nests of people in his house, where the lame, the blind, the sick, and the sorrowful found a sure retreat from all the evils whence his little income could secure them: and commonly spending the middle of the week at our house, he kept his numerous family in Fleet-street upon a settled allowance; but returned to them every Saturday, to give them three good dinners, and his company, before he came back to us on the Monday night – treating them with the same, or perhaps more ceremonious civility, than he would have done by as many people of fashion – making the holy scriptures thus the rule of his conduct, and only expecting salvation as he was able to obey its precepts.

Hester Lynch Piozzi
Anecdotes of the late Samuel Johnson, LL.D... (1786)

GIBBON SUMS UP

(*c.* 1787)

WHEN I contemplate the common lot of mortality, I must acknowledge that I have drawn a high prize in the lottery of life. The far greater part of the globe is overspread with barbarism or slavery: in the civilized world, the most numerous class is condemned to ignorance and poverty; and the double fortune of my birth in a free and enlightened country, in an honourable and wealthy family, is the lucky chance of an unit against millions. The general probability is about three to one, that a new-born infant will not live to complete his fiftieth year. I have now passed that age, and may fairly estimate the present value of my existence in the three-fold division of mind, body and estate.

1. The first and indispensable requisite of happiness is a clear conscience, unsullied by the reproach or remembrance of an unworthy action.

> – Hic murus aheneus esto,
> Nil conscire sibi, nulla pallescere culpa.

I am endowed with a cheerful temper, a moderate sensibility, and a natural disposition to repose rather than to activity: some mischievous appetites and habits have perhaps been corrected by philosophy or time. The love of study, a passion which derives fresh vigour from enjoyment, supplies each day, each hour, with a perpetual source of independent and rational pleasure; and I am not sensible of any decay of the mental faculties. The original soil has been highly improved by cultivation; but it may be questioned, whether some flowers of fancy, some grateful errors, have not been eradicated with the weeds of prejudice. 2. Since I have escaped from the long perils of my childhood, the serious advice of a physician has seldom been requisite. "The madness of superfluous health" I have never known, but my tender constitution has been fortified by time, and the inestimable gift of the sound and peaceful slumbers of infancy may be imputed both to the mind and body. 3. I have already described the merits of my society and situation; but these enjoyments would be tasteless or bitter if their possession were not assured by an annual and adequate supply. According to the scale of Switzerland, I am a rich man; and I am indeed rich, since my income is superior to my expense, and my expense is equal to my wishes. . . .

I am disgusted with the affectation of men of letters, who complain that they have renounced a substance for a shadow, and that their fame (which sometimes is no insupportable weight) affords a poor compensation for envy, censure, and persecution. My own experience, at least, has taught me a very different lesson; twenty happy years have been animated by the labour of my History, and its success has given me a name, a rank, a character, in the world, to which I should not otherwise have been entitled. The freedom of my writings has indeed provoked an implacable tribe; but, as I was safe from the stings, I was soon accustomed to the buzzing of the hornets: my nerves are not tremblingly alive, and my literary temper is so happily framed, that I am less sensible of pain than of pleasure. The rational pride of an author may be offended, rather than flattered, by vague indiscriminate praise; but he cannot, he should not, be indifferent to the fair testimonies of private and public esteem. Even his moral sympathy may be gratified by the idea, that now, in the present hour, he is imparting some degree of amusement or knowledge to his friends in a distant land; that one day his mind will be familiar to the grandchildren of those who are yet unborn. . . .

The present is a fleeting moment, the past is no more; and our prospect of futurity is dark and doubtful. This day may *possibly* be my last: but the laws of probability, so true in general, so fallacious in particular, still allow about fifteen years. I shall soon enter into the period which, as the most agreeable of his long life, was selected by the judgement and experience of the sage Fontenelle. His choice is approved by the eloquent historian of nature, who fixes our moral happiness to the mature season in which our passions are supposed to be calmed, our duties fulfilled, our ambition satisfied, our fame and fortune established on a solid basis. In private conversation, that great and amiable man added the weight of his own experience; and this autumnal felicity might be exemplified in the lives of Voltaire, Hume, and many other men of letters. I am far more inclined to embrace than to dispute this comfortable doctrine. I will not suppose any premature decay of the mind or body; but I must reluctantly observe that two causes, the abbreviation of time, and the failure of hope, will always tinge with a browner shade the evening of life.

Edward Gibbon

'Memoirs of my Life and Writings' from *Miscellaneous Works* . . ., ed. Lord Sheffield (1796) Vol. I

II

THE MOVEMENT OF IDEAS: REFLECTION, ARGUMENT, EXHORTATION, SATIRE

LORD CHESTERFIELD'S VIEWS ON GOOD COMPANY

From a letter to his son, 12 October, 1748

GOOD company is not what respective sets of company are pleased either to call or think themselves, but it is that company which all the people of the place call and acknowledge to be good company, notwithstanding some objections which they may form to some of the individuals who compose it. It consists chiefly (but by no means without exception) of people of considerable birth, rank, and character; for people of neither birth nor rank are frequently, and very justly, admitted into it, if distinguished by any peculiar merit, or eminency in any liberal art or science. Nay, so motley a thing is good company, that many people, without birth, rank, or merit, intrude into it by their own forwardness, and others slide into it by the protection of some considerable person; and some even of indifferent characters and morals make part of it. But, in the main, the good part preponderates, and people of infamous and blasted characters are never admitted. In this fashionable good company, the best manners and the best language of the place are most unquestionably to be learnt; for they establish and give the tone to both, which are therefore called the language and manners of good company, there being no legal tribunal to ascertain either.

A company consisting wholly of people of the first quality

cannot, for that reason, be called good company, in the common acceptation of the phrase, unless they are, into the bargain, the fashionable and accredited company of the place; for people of the very first quality can be as silly, as ill-bred, and as worthless, as people of the meanest degree. On the other hand, a company consisting entirely of people of very low condition, whatever their merit or parts may be, can never be called good company, and consequently should not be much frequented, though by no means despised.

A company wholly composed of men of learning, though greatly to be valued and respected, is not meant by the words *good company*; they cannot have the easy manners and *tournure* of the world, as they do not live in it. If you can bear your part well in such a company, it is extremely right to be in it sometimes, and you will be but more esteemed in other companies for having a place in that; but then do not let it engross you, for, if you do, you will be only considered as one of the *literati* by profession, which is not the way either to shine or rise in the world.

The company of professed wits and poets is extremely inviting to most young men, who, if they have wit themselves, are pleased with it, and, if they have none, are sillily proud of being one of it; but it should be frequented with moderation and judgment, and you should by no means give yourself up to it. A wit is a very unpopular denomination, as it carries terror along with it; and people in general are as much afraid of a live wit in company as a woman is of a gun, which she thinks may go off by itself, and do her a mischief. Their acquaintance is, however, worth seeking, and their company worth frequenting; but not exclusively of others, nor to such a degree as to be considered only as one of that particular set.

But the company which of all others you should most carefully avoid, is that low company which, in every sense of the word, is low indeed – low in rank, low in parts, low in manners, and low in merit. You will, perhaps, be surprised that I should think it necessary to warn you against such company; but yet I do not think it wholly unnecessary, after the many instances which I have seen of men of sense and rank, discredited, vilified, and undone, by keeping such company. Vanity, that source of many of our follies, and of some of our crimes, has sunk many a man into company in every light infinitely below himself, for the sake of being the first man in it; there he dictates, is applauded, admired; and, for the sake of being the *Coryphæus* of that wretched chorus, disgraces and disqualifies himself soon for any better company. Depend upon it, you will sink or rise to the level of the company which you commonly keep; – people will judge of you, and not unreasonably, by that. There is good sense in the Spanish saying, 'Tell me whom you live with, and I will tell you who you are.' Make it therefore your business, wherever you are, to get into that company which everybody of the place allows to be the best company, next to their own: – which is the best definition which I can give you of good company. But here, too, one caution is very necessary, for want of which many young men have been ruined, even in good company. Good company (as I have before observed) is composed of a great variety of fashionable people, whose characters and morals are very different, though their manners are pretty much the same.

Philip Dormer Stanhope, fourth Earl of Chesterfield

Letters . . . to his Son (1774). Text from complete
Letters . . ., ed. Bonamy Dobrée (1932), Vol. IV

PRIDE AND GOOD MANNERS

A MAN of Exalted Pride may so hide it, that no Body shall be able to discover that he has any; and yet receive greater

Satisfaction from that Passion than another, who indulges himself in the Declaration of it before all the World. Good Manners have nothing to do with Virtue or Religion; instead of extinguishing, they rather inflame the Passions. The Man of Sense and Education never exults more in his Pride than when he hides it with the greatest dexterity, and in feasting on the Applause which he is sure all good Judges will pay to his Behaviour; he enjoys a Pleasure altogether unknown to the Short-Sighted, surly Alderman, that shews his Haughtiness glaringly in his Face, pulls off his Hat to no Body, and hardly deigns to speak to an Inferior.

A Man may carefully avoid every thing that in the Eye of the World is esteem'd to be the result of Pride, without mortifying himself, or making the least conquest of his Passion. It is possible that he only sacrifices the insipid outward part of his Pride, which none but silly Ignorant People take delight in, to that part we all feel within, and which the Men of the Highest Spirit and most Exalted Genius feed on with so much extasy in silence. The Pride of Great and Polite Men is no where more conspicuous than in the Debates about Ceremony and Precedency, where they have an Opportunity of giving their Vices the appearance of Virtues, and can make the World believe that it is their care, their Tenderness for the Dignity of their Office, or the Honour of their Masters, what is the result of their own personal Pride and Vanity. This is most manifest in all Negotiations of Ambassadors and Plenipotentiaries, and must be known by all that observe what is transacted at publick Treaties, and it will ever be true, that Men of the best Taste have no Relish in their Pride as long as any Mortal can find out that they are Proud.

Bernard Mandeville

'An Enquiry into the Origin of Moral Virtue' in *The Fable of the Bees* (1714). Text from second edition (1723)

PHILOSOPHY AND GOOD BREEDING

To *philosophize*, in a just Signification, is but To carry *Good-breeding* a step higher. For the Accomplishment of Breeding is, To learn whatever is *decent* in Company, or *beautiful* in Arts; and the Sum of Philosophy is, To learn what is *just* in Society, and *beautiful* in Nature, and the Order of the World.

'Tis not *Wit* merely, but a *Temper* which must form the WELL-BRED MAN. In the same manner, 'tis not *a Head* merely, but *a Heart* and *Resolution* which must compleat the *real* PHILOSOPHER. Both *Characters* aim at what is *excellent*, aspire to *a just Taste*, and carry in view the Model of what is *beautiful* and *becoming*. Accordingly, the respective Conduct and distinct Manners of each Party are regulated: *The one* according to the perfectest Ease, and good Entertainment of COMPANY; *the other* according to the strictest Interest of MANKIND and SOCIETY: *The one* according to a Man's Rank and Quality in his private NATION; *the other* according to his Rank and Dignity in NATURE.

Whether each of these Offices, or social Parts, are in themselves as *convenient* as *becoming*, is the great Question which must some-way be decided. The WELL-BRED MAN has already decided this, in his own Case, and declar'd on the side of what is Handsom: For whatever he practises in this kind, he accounts no more than what he owes purely to himself; without regard to any further Advantage. The *Pretender to* PHILOSOPHY, who either knows not how to determine this Affair, or if he has determin'd, knows not how to pursue his Point, with Constancy, and Firmness, remains in respect of *Philosophy*, what a Clown or Coxcomb is in respect of *Breeding* and *Behaviour*. Thus, according to our Author, the TASTE of Beauty, and the *Relish* of what is decent, just, and amiable, perfects the *Character* of the GENTLEMAN, and the PHILOSOPHER. And the Study of such a TASTE or *Relish* will, as we suppose, be ever the great Employment and Concern of him, who covets as well to be *wise* and *good*, as *agreeable* and *polite*.

Anthony Ashley Cooper, third Earl of Shaftesbury
Characteristicks of Men, Manners, Opinions, Times (1711)
Text from second edition (1714), Vol. III

ALTRUISM AND SELF-LOVE

... MANKIND are by Nature so closely united, there is such a Correspondence between the inward Sensations of one Man and those of another, that Disgrace is as much avoided as bodily Pain, and to be the Object of Esteem and Love as much desired as any external Goods: And in many particular Cases, Persons are carried on to do Good to others, as the End their Affection tends to and rests in; and manifest that they find real Satisfaction and Enjoyment in this Course of Behaviour. There is such a natural Principle of Attraction in Man towards Man, that having trod the same Tract of Land, having breathed in the same Climate, barely having been born in the same artificial District or Division, becomes the Occasion of contracting Acquaintances and Familiarities many Years after; For any thing may serve the Purpose. Thus Relations meerly nominal are sought and invented, not by Governours, but by the lowest of the People; which are found sufficient to hold Mankind together in little Fraternities and Copartnerships: Weak ties indeed, and what may afford Fund enough for Ridicule, if they are absurdly considered as the real Principles of that Union: But they are in Truth meerly the Occasions, as any thing may be of any thing, upon which our Nature carries us on according to its own previous Bent and Bias; which Occasions therefore would be nothing at all were there not this prior Disposition and Bias of Nature. Men are so much one Body, that in a peculiar Manner they feel for each other, Shame, sudden Danger, Resentment, Honour, Prosperity, Distress; one or another, or all of these, from the social Nature in general, from Benevolence, upon the Occasion of natural Relation, Acquaintance, Protection, Dependance; each of these being distinct Cements of Society. And therefore to have no Restraint from, no regard to others in our Behaviour, is the speculative Absurdity of considering ourselves as single and independant, as having nothing in our Nature which has Respect to our Fellow-Creatures, reduced to Action and Practice. And this is the same Absurdity, as to suppose a Hand, or any Part to have no natural Respect to any other, or to the whole Body.

But allowing all this, it may be asked, "Has not Man Dispositions and Principles within which lead him to do Evil to others, as well as to do Good? Whence come the many Miseries else, which Men are the Authors and Instruments of to each other?" These Questions, so far as they relate to the foregoing Discourse, may be answered by asking, Has not Man also Dispositions and Principles within, which lead him to do Evil to himself, as well as Good? Whence come the many Miseries else, Sickness, Pain, and Death, which Men are the Instruments and Authors of to themselves?

It may be thought more easy to answer one of these Questions than the other, but the Answer to both is really the same; that Mankind have ungoverned Passions which they will gratifie at any Rate, as well to the Injury of Others, as in Contradiction to known private Interest...

If it be said, that there are Persons in the World, who are in great Measure without the natural Affections towards their Fellow-Creatures: There are likewise Instances of Persons without the common natural Affections to themselves: But the Nature of Man is not to be judged of by either of these, but by what appears in the common World, in the Bulk of Mankind.

I am afraid it would be thought very strange, if to confirm the Truth of this Account of Humane Nature, and make out the Justness of the foregoing Comparison, it should be added, that from what appears, Men in Fact as much and as often contradict that *Part* of their Nature which respects *Self*, and which leads them to their *own private* Good and Happiness; as they contradict that *Part* of it which respects *Society*, and tends to *publick* Good: That there are as few Persons, who attain the greatest Satisfaction and Enjoyment which they might attain in the present World; as who do the greatest Good to others which they might do: Nay, that there are as few who can be said really and in earnest to aim at one, as at the other. Take a survey of Mankind: The World in general, the Good and Bad, almost without Exception, equally are agreed, that were Religion out of the Case, the Happiness of the present Life would consist in a Manner wholly in Riches, Honours, sensual Gratifications; insomuch that one scarce hears a Reflection made upon Prudence, Life, Conduct, but upon this Supposition. Yet on the contrary, that Persons in the greatest Affluence of Fortune are no happier than such as have only a Competency; that the Cares and Disappointments of Ambition for the most Part far exceed the Satisfactions of it; as also the miserable Intervals of Intemperance and Excess, and the many untimely Deaths occasioned by a dissolute Course of Life: These things are all seen, acknowledged, by every one acknowledged; but are thought no Objections against, though they expressly contradict, this universal Principle, that the Happiness of the present Life consists in one or other of them. Whence is all this Absurdity and Contradiction? Is not the middle Way obvious? Can any Thing be more manifest, than that the Happiness of Life consists in these possessed and enjoyed only to a certain Degree; that to pursue them

beyond this Degree, is always attended with more Inconvenience than Advantage to a Man's self, and often with extream
Misery and Unhappiness. Whence then, I say, is all this
Absurdity and Contradiction? Is it really the Result of Consideration in Mankind, how they may become most easy to
themselves, most free from Care, and enjoy the chief Happiness attainable in this World? Or is it not manifestly owing
either to this, that they have not cool and reasonable Concern
enough for themselves, to consider wherein their chief Happiness in the present Life consists; or else, if they do consider it,
that they will not act conformably to what is the Result of
that Consideration: *i.e.* reasonable Concern for themselves, or
cool Self-love is prevailed over by Passion and Appetite. So
that from what appears, there is no Ground to assert that those
Principles in the Nature of Man, which most directly lead us
to promote the Good of our Fellow-Creatures, are more generally or in a greater Degree violated, than those, which most
directly lead us to promote our own private Good and
Happiness.

Joseph Butler
Fifteen Sermons preached at the Rolls Chapel . . . (1726)
Text from second edition (1729)

THE BENEFITS OF REASON

WHAT you have told me, (said my Master) upon the Subject
of War, doth indeed discover most admirably the Effects of
that Reason you pretend to: However, it is happy that the
Shame is greater than the *Danger*; and that Nature hath left
you utterly uncapable of doing much Mischief: For your
Mouths lying flat with your Faces, you can hardly bite each
other to any Purpose, unless by Consent. Then, as to the

Claws upon your Feet before and behind, they are so short and tender, that one of our *Yahoos* would drive a Dozen of yours before him. And therefore in recounting the Numbers of those who have been killed in Battle, I cannot but think that you have *said the Thing which is not*.

I could not forbear shaking my Head and smiling a little at his Ignorance. And, being no Stranger to the Art of War, I gave him a Description of Cannons, Culverins, Muskets, Carabines, Pistols, Bullets, Powder, Swords, Bayonets, Sieges, Retreats, Attacks, Undermines, Countermines, Bombardments, Sea-fights; Ships sunk with a Thousand Men; twenty Thousand killed on each Side; dying Groans, Limbs flying in the Air: Smoak, Noise, Confusion, trampling to Death under Horses Feet: Flight, Pursuit, Victory; Fields strewed with Carcases left for Food to Dogs, and Wolves, and Birds of Prey; Plundering, Stripping, Ravishing, Burning and Destroying. And, to set forth the Valour of my own dear Countrymen, I assured him, that I had seen them blow up a Hundred Enemies at once in a Siege, and as many in a Ship; and beheld the dead Bodies drop down in Pieces from the Clouds, to the great Diversion of all the Spectators.

I was going on to more Particulars, when my Master commanded me Silence. He said, whoever understood the Nature of *Yahoos* might easily believe it possible for so vile an Animal, to be capable of every Action I had named, if their Strength and Cunning equalled their Malice. But, as my Discourse had increased his Abhorrence of the whole Species, so he found it gave him a Disturbance in his Mind, to which he was wholly a Stranger before. He thought his Ears being used to such abominable Words, might by Degrees admit them with less Detestation. That, although he hated the *Yahoos* of this Country, yet he no more blamed them for their odious Qualities, than he did a *Gnnayh* (a Bird of Prey) for its Cruelty, or a sharp Stone for cutting his Hoof. But, when a Creature pretending to Reason, could be capable of such Enormities, he dreaded lest the Corruption of that Faculty might be worse than Brutality itself. He seemed therefore confident, that instead of Reason, we were only possessed of some Quality fitted to increase our natural Vices; as the Reflection from a troubled Stream returns the Image of an ill-shapen Body, not only *larger*, but more *distorted*.

Jonathan Swift

Travels into Several Remote Nations . . .
by Lemuel Gulliver (1726). Text from
Works . . . (1735), Vol. III

THE SOPHISTS

NEXT Morning, *Alciphron* and *Lysicles* said the Weather was so fine they had a mind to spend the Day abroad, and take a cold Dinner under a Shade in some pleasant part of the Country. Whereupon, after Breakfast, we went down to a Beach about half a mile off; where we walked on the smooth sand, with the Ocean on one hand, and on the other wild broken Rocks, intermixed with shady Trees and Springs of Water, till the Sun began to be uneasy. We then withdrew into a hollow Glade, between two Rocks, where we had no sooner seated ourselves but *Lysicles* addressing himself to *Euphranor*, said: I am now ready to perform what I undertook last Evening, which was to shew, there is nothing in that necessary Connection which some Men imagine between those Principles you contend for, and the public Good. I freely own, that if this Question was to be decided by the authority of Legislators or Philosophers, it must go against us. For those Men generally take it for granted, that Vice is pernicious to the Public; and that Men cannot be kept from Vice but by the Fear of God, and the Sense of a future State; whence they are induced to think the belief of such things necessary to the well-being of humane Kind. This false notion hath prevailed for many ages in the World, and done an infinite deal of mischief, being in truth the cause of religious Establishments, and gaining the protection and encouragement of Laws and Magistrates to the Clergy and their Superstitions. Even some of the wisest among the Ancients, who agreed with our Sect in denying a Providence and the Immortality of the Soul, had nevertheless the weakness to lie under the common prejudice, that Vice was hurtful to Societies of Men. But *England* hath of late produced great Philosophers who have undeceived the world, and proved to a demonstration that private Vices are public Benefits. This Discovery was reserved to our Times, and our Sect hath the glory of it. *CRI[TO]*. It is possible some Men of fine Understanding might in former ages have had a glimpse of this important Truth; but it may be presumed they lived in ignorant times and bigotted countries, which were not ripe for such a discovery. *LYS.* Men of narrow capacities and short sight being able to see no further than one link in a chain of Consequence, are shocked at small evils which attend upon Vice. But those who can enlarge their view, and look through a long series of events, may behold Happiness resulting from Vice, and Good springing out of Evil in a thousand instances. To prove my point I shall not trouble you with Authorities or far-fetched Arguments, but bring you to plain Matter of Fact. Do but take a view of each particular Vice, and trace it through its Effects and Consequences, and then you will clearly perceive the advantage it brings to the Public.

11. Drunkenness, for instance, is by your sober Moralists thought a pernicious Vice; but it is for want of considering the good effects that flow from it. For in the first place it encreases the Malt-Tax, a principal branch of his Majesty's Revenue, and thereby promotes the safety, strength, and glory of the Nation. Secondly, it employs a great number of

hands, the Brewer, the Maltster, the Ploughman, the dealer in Hops, the Smith, the Carpenter, the Brasier, the Joiner, with all other artificers necessary to supply those enumerated, with their respective instruments and utensils. All which advantages are procured from Drunkenness in the vulgar way, by strong Beer. . . . With as much judgment your half-witted folk are accustomed to censure Gaming. And indeed (such is the ignorance and folly of Mankind) a Gamester and a Drunkard are thought no better than public nuisances, when in truth, they do each in their way greatly conduce to the public benefit. If you look only on the surface and first appearance of things, you will no doubt think playing at Cards a very idle and fruitless occupation. But dive deeper, and you shall perceive this idle amusement employs the Card-maker, and he sets the Paper-mills at work, by which the poor Ragman is supported; not to mention the Builders and Workers in wood and iron that are employ'd in erecting and furnishing those Mills. Look still deeper, and you shall find that Candles and Chair-hire employ the industrious and the poor, who by these means come to be relieved by Sharpers and Gentlemen, who wou'd not give one penny in charity. But you will say that many Gentlemen and Ladies are ruined by play, without considering that what one Man loses another gets, and that consequently as many are made as ruined: money changeth hands, and in this circulation the life of business and commerce consists. When money is spent, it is all one to the Public who spends it. Suppose a fool of quality becomes the dupe of a Man of mean birth and circumstance, who has more wit. In this case what harm doth the Public sustain? Poverty is relieved, Ingenuity is rewarded, the Money stays at home, and has a lively circulation, the ingenious Sharper being enabled to set up an equipage and spend handsomely, which cannot be done without employing a world of people. But you will perhaps object, that a Man reduced by play may be put upon desperate courses, hurtful to the Public. Suppose the worst, and that he turns Highwayman, such Men have a short life and a merry. While he lives, he spends, and for one that he robs makes twenty the better for his expence. And when his time is come, a poor Family may be relieved by fifty or a hundred Pounds set upon his Head. A vulgar eye looks on many a Man as an idle or mischievous fellow, whom a true Philosopher, viewing in another light, considers as a Man of pleasant occupation who diverts himself, and benefits the Public: And that with so much ease, that he employs a multitude of Men, and sets an infinite Machine in motion, without knowing the good he does, or even intending to do any: which is peculiar to that Gentleman-like way of doing good by Vice. I was considering Play, and that insensibly led me to the advantages, which attend robbing on the highway. Oh the beautiful and never enough admired connection of Vices! It wou'd take too much time to show how they all hang together, and what an infinite deal of good takes its rise from every one of them. One word for a favourite Vice, and I shall leave you to make out the rest your self, by applying the same way of reasoning to all other vices. A poor Girl, who might not have the spending of half a Crown a week in what you call an honest way, no sooner hath the good fortune to be a kept Mistress, but she employs Milliners, Laundresses, Tire-women, Mercers, and a number of other trades, to the benefit of her Country. It wou'd be endless to trace and pursue every particular Vice through its consequences and effects, and shew the vast advantage they all are of to the Public. The true Springs that actuate the great Machine of Commerce, and make a flourishing State, have been hitherto little understood. Your Moralists and Divines have for so many ages been corrupting the genuine Sense of mankind, and filling their heads with such absurd principles, that it is in the power of few Men to contemplate real life with an unprejudiced

Eye. And fewer still have sufficient Parts and Sagacity to pursue a long train of consequences, relations, and dependences, which must be done in order to form a just and entire notion of the public weal. But, as I said before, our Sect hath produced Men capable of these discoveries, who have displayed them in a full light, and made them public for the benefit of their Country.

111. Oh! Said *Euphranor*, who heard this discourse with great attention, you *Lysicles* are the very Man I wanted, eloquent and ingenious, knowing in the principles of your Sect, and willing to impart them. Pray tell me, do these principles find an easy admission in the World? *LYS*. They do among ingenious Men and People of fashion, though you will sometimes meet with strong prejudices against them in the middle sort, an effect of ordinary Talents and mean Breeding. *EUPH*. I shou'd wonder if Men were not shocked at notions of such a surprising nature, so contrary to all Laws, Education, and Religion. *LYS*. They wou'd be shocked much more if it had not been for the skilful address of our Philosophers, who, considering that most Men are influenced by names rather than things, have introduced a certain polite way of speaking, which lessens much of the abhorrence and prejudice towards Vice. *EUPH*. Explain me this. *LYS*. Thus in our Dialect a vicious Man is a Man of pleasure, a Sharper is one that plays the whole game, a Lady is said to have an affair, a Gentleman to be gallant, a Rogue in business to be one that knows the World. By this means we have no such things as Sots, Debauchees, Whores, Rogues, or the like, in the *beau monde*, who may enjoy their vices without incurring disagreeable Appellations. *EUPH*. Vice then is, it seems, a fine thing with an ugly name. *LYS*. Be assured it is. *EUPH*. It shou'd seem then, that *Plato*'s fearing lest youth might be corrupted, by those Fables which represented the Gods vicious, was an effect of his weakness and ignorance. *LYS*. It was, take my

word for it. *EUPH.* And yet *Plato* had kept good Company, and lived in a Court. And *Cicero* who knew the World well had a profound esteem for him. *CRI.* I tell you, *Euphranor*, that *Plato* and *Tully* might perhaps make a figure in *Athens* or *Rome*: But were they to revive in our days, they wou'd pass but for underbred Pedants, there being at most Coffee-houses in *London*, several able Men who cou'd convince them they knew nothing in, what they are valued so much for, Morals and Politics.

George Berkeley

From the Second Dialogue in *Alciphron,*
or the Minute Philosopher (1732)

OBJECTIONS AGAINST THE ABOLITION
OF CHRISTIANITY

BUT why we should therefore cast off the Name and Title of Christians, although the general Opinion and Resolution be so violent for it, I confess I cannot (with submission) apprehend the Consequence necessary. However, since the Undertakers propose such wonderful Advantages to the Nation by this Project, and advance many plausible Objections against the System of Christianity, I shall briefly consider the Strength of both, fairly allow them their greatest Weight, and offer such Answers as I think most reasonable. After which I will beg leave to shew what Inconveniences may possibly happen by such an Innovation, in the present Posture of our Affairs.

First, One great Advantage proposed by the abolishing of Christianity is, That it would very much enlarge and establish Liberty of Conscience, that great Bulwark of our Nation, and of the Protestant Religion, which is still too much limited by Priest-craft, notwithstanding all the good Intentions of the Legislature, as we have lately found by a severe Instance. For it is confidently reported, that two Young Gentlemen of real Hopes, bright Wit, and profound Judgment, who upon a thorough Examination of Causes and Effects, and by the meer Force of natural Abilities, without the least Tincture of Learning, having made a Discovery, that there was no God, and generously communicating their Thoughts for the good of the Publick; were some time ago by an unparalleled Severity, and upon I know not what obsolete Law, broke for Blasphemy. And as it hath been wisely observed, if Persecution once begins no Man alive knows how far it may reach, or where it will end.

In answer to all which, with deference to wiser Judgments, I think this rather shews the Necessity of a Nominal Religion among us. Great Wits love to be free with the highest Objects, and if they cannot be allowed a God to revile or renounce; they will speak Evil of Dignities, abuse the Government, and reflect upon the Ministry, which I am sure few will deny to be of much more pernicious Consequence, according to the saying of *Tiberius, Deorum Offensa Diis curæ.* As to the particular Fact related, I think it is not fair to argue from one Instance, perhaps another cannot be produced, yet (to the Comfort of all those who may be apprehensive of Persecution) Blasphemy we know is freely spoke a Million of times in every Coffee-House and Tavern, or wherever else good Company meet. It must be allowed indeed that to Break an *English* Free-born Officer only for Blasphemy, was, to speak the gentlest of such an Action, a very high strain of absolute Power. Little can be said in Excuse for the General; Perhaps he was afraid it might give Offence to the Allies, among whom, for ought we know, it may be the Custom of the Country to believe a God. But if he argued, as some have done, upon a mistaken Principle, that an Officer who is guilty of speaking Blasphemy, may sometime or other proceed so far as to raise a Mutiny, the Consequence is by no means to be admitted; For, surely, the Commander of an *English* Army is like to be but ill obey'd, whose Soldiers fear and reverence him as little as they do a Deity.

It is further objected against the Gospel System, that it obliges Men to the Belief of Things too difficult for free Thinkers, and such who have shook off the Prejudices that usually cling to a confined Education. To which I answer, that Men should be cautious how they raise Objections which reflect upon the Wisdom of the Nation. Is not every body freely allowed to believe whatever he pleases, and to publish his Belief to the World whenever he thinks fit, especially if it serves to strengthen the Party which is in the Right. Would any indifferent Foreiner, who should read the Trumpery lately written by *Asgill*, *Tindall*, *Toland*, *Coward*, and Forty more, imagine the Gospel to be our Rule of Faith, and to be confirmed by Parliaments. Does any Man either Believe, or say he believes, or desire to have it thought that he says he Believes one Syllable of the Matter, and is any Man worse received upon that Score, or does he find his want of Nominal Faith a disadvantage to him in the Pursuit of any Civil or Military Employment? What if there be an old dormant Statute or two against him, are they not now obsolete, to a degree, that *Empson* and *Dudley* themselves if they were now alive, would find it impossible to put them in Execution?

It is likewise urged, that there are by Computation in this Kingdom above Ten Thousand Parsons, whose Revenues added to those of my Lords the Bishops, would suffice to maintain at least Two Hundred Young Gentlemen of Wit and Pleasure, and Free-thinking, Enemies to Priest-Craft, narrow Principles, Pedantry, and Prejudices, who might be an Ornament to the Court and Town: And then, again, so great a Number of able (bodied) Divines might be a Recruit to our Fleet and Armies. This indeed appears to be a Consideration of some Weight: But then on the other side, several

Things deserve to be considered likewise: As, First, Whether it may not be thought necessary that in certain Tracts of Country, like what we call Parishes, there should be one Man at least, of Abilities to Read and Write. Then it seems a wrong Computation, that the Revenues of the Church throughout this Island would be large enough to maintain Two Hundred Young Gentlemen, or even half that Number, after the present refined way of Living, that is, to allow each of them such a Rent, as in the modern Form of Speech, would make them Easy. But still there is in this Project a greater Mischief behind; And we ought to beware of the Woman's Folly, who killed the Hen that every Morning laid her a Golden Egg. For, pray what would become of the Race of Men in the next Age, if we had nothing to trust to besides the Scrophulous consumptive Productions furnished by our Men of Wit and Pleasure, when having squandred away their Vigor, Health and Estates, they are forced by some dis-agreeable Marriage to piece up their broken Fortunes, and entail Rottenness and Politeness on their Posterity. Now, here are Ten Thousand Persons reduced by the wise Regula-tions of *Henry* the Eighth, to the necessity of a low Dyet, and moderate Exercise, who are the only great Restorers of our Breed, without which the Nation would in an Age or two become but one great Hospital.

Another Advantage proposed by the Abolishing of Christi-anity, is the clear Gain of one Day in Seven, which is now entirely lost, and consequently the Kingdom one Seventh less considerable in Trade, Business, and Pleasure; besides the Loss to the Publick of so many Stately Structures now in the Hands of the Clergy, which might be converted into Play-houses, Exchanges, Market-houses, common Dormitories, and other Publick Edifices.

I hope I shall be forgiven a hard Word if I call this a perfect Cavil. I readily own there hath been an old Custom time out of mind, for People to assemble in the Churches every *Sunday*, and that shops are still frequently shut, in order as it is conceived, to preserve the Memory of that antient Practice; but how this can prove a hindrance to Business or Pleasure, is hard to imagine. What if the Men of Pleasure are forced one Day in the Week to Game at Home instead of the *Chocolate-House*. Are not the *Taverns* and *Coffee-Houses* open? Can there be a more convenient Season for taking a Dose of Physick? Are fewer Claps got upon *Sundays* than other Days? Is not that the chief Day for Traders to Sum up the Accounts of the Week, and for Lawyers to prepare their Briefs? But I would fain know how it can be pretended that the Churches are misapplied. Where are more Appointments and Rendevouzes of Gallantry? Where more Care to appear in the foremost Box with greater Advantage of Dress? Where more Meetings for Business? Where more Bargains driven of all sorts? And where so many Conveniences or Incitements to Sleep?

Jonathan Swift

'An Argument to prove that the Abolishing of Christianity in England, may . . . be attended with some Inconveniences . . .' in *Miscellanies in Prose and Verse* (1711)

THE WORKINGS OF THE SPIRIT

BUT here, before I can proceed further, a very dangerous Objection must, if possible, be removed: For, it is positively denied by certain Criticks, that the *Spirit* can by any means be introduced into an Assembly of Modern Saints, the Disparity being so great in many material Circumstances, between the Primitive Way of Inspiration, and that which is practised in the present Age. This they pretend to prove from the second Chapter of the *Acts*, where comparing both, it appears; *First*, that *the Apostles were gathered together with one accord in one place*; by which is meant, an universal Agreement in Opinion, and Form of Worship; a Harmony (say they) so far from being found between any two Conventicles among Us, that it is in vain to expect it between any two Heads in the same. Secondly, the *Spirit* instructed the Apostles in the Gift of speaking several Languages; a Knowledge so remote from our Dealers in this Art, that they neither understand Propriety of Words, or Phrases in their own. Lastly, (say these Objectors) The Modern Artists do utterly exclude all Approaches of the *Spirit*, and bar up its antient Way of entring, by covering themselves so close, and so industriously a top. For, they will needs have it as a Point clearly gained, that the *Cloven Tongues* never sat upon the Apostles Heads, while their Hats were on.

Now, the Force of these Objections, seems to consist in the different Acceptation of the Word, *Spirit*: which if it be understood for a supernatural Assistance, approaching from without, the Objectors have Reason, and their Assertions may be allowed; But the *Spirit* we treat of here, proceeding entirely from within, the Arguments of these Adversaries is wholly eluded. And upon the same Account, our Modern Artificers, find it an Expedient of absolute Necessity, to cover their Heads as close as they can, in order to prevent Perspiration, than which nothing is observed to be a greater Spender of Mechanick Light, as we may, perhaps, farther shew in convenient Place.

To proceed therefore upon the *Phænomenon of Spiritual Mechanism*, It is here to be noted, that in forming and working up the *Spirit*, the Assembly has a considerable Share, as well as the Preacher; The Method of this *Arcanum*, is as follows. They violently strain their Eye-balls inward, half closing the Lids; Then, as they sit, they are in a perpetual Motion of *See-saw*, making long Hums at proper Periods, and continuing

the Sound at equal Height, chusing their Time in those
Intermissions, while the Preacher is at Ebb. Neither is this
Practice, in any part of it, so singular or improbable, as not be
traced in distant Regions, from Reading and Observation.
For, first, the *Jauguis*, or enlightned Saints of *India*, see all
their Visions, by help of an acquired straining and pressure of
the Eyes. Secondly, the Art of *See-saw* on a Beam, and swing-
ing by Session upon a Cord, in order to raise artificial Extasies,
hath been derived to Us, from our *Scythian* Ancestors, where
it is practised at this Day, among the Women. Lastly, the
whole Proceeding, as I have here related it, is performed by
the Natives of *Ireland*, with a considerable Improvement;
And it is granted, that this noble Nation, hath of all others,
admitted fewer Corruptions, and degenerated least from the
Purity of the Old *Tartars*. Now it is usual for a Knot of *Irish*,
Men and Women, to abstract themselves from Matter, bind
up all their Senses, grow visionary and spiritual, by Influence
of a short Pipe of Tobacco, handed round the Company;
each preserving the Smoak in his Mouth, till it comes again
to his Turn to take it in fresh: At the same Time, there is a
Consort of a continued gentle Hum, repeated and renewed
by Instinct, as Occasion requires, and they move their Bodies
up and down, to a Degree, that sometimes their Heads and
Points lie parallel to the Horizon. Mean while, you may
observe their Eyes turn'd up in the Posture of one, who
endeavours to keep himself awake; by which, and many
other Symptons among them, it manifestly appears, that the
Reasoning Faculties are all suspended and superseded, that
Imagination hath usurped the Seat, scattering a thousand
Deliriums over the Brain. Returning from this Digression, I
shall describe the Methods, by which the *Spirit* approaches.
The Eyes being disposed according to Art, at first, you can
see nothing, but after a short pause, a small glimmering Light
begins to appear, and dance before you. Then, by frequently

moving your Body up and down, you perceive the Vapors to ascend very fast, till you are perfectly dosed and flustred like one who drinks too much in a Morning. Mean while, the Preacher is also at work; He begins a loud Hum, which pierces you quite thro'; This is immediately returned by the Audience, and you find your self prompted to imitate them, by a meer spontaneous Impulse, without knowing what you do. The *Interstitia* are duly filled up by the Preacher, to prevent too long a Pause, under which the *Spirit* would soon faint and grow languid.

Jonathan Swift

'A Discourse concerning the Mechanical Operation of the Spirit' in *A Tale of a Tub* . . . (1704)

SUPERSTITION

THE universal propensity to believe in invisible, intelligent power, if not an original instinct, being at least a general attendant of human nature, may be considered as a kind of mark or stamp, which the divine workman has set upon his work; and nothing surely can more dignify mankind, than to be thus selected from all the other parts of the creation, and to bear the image or impression of the universal Creator. But consult this image, as it commonly appears in the popular religions of the world. How is the deity disfigured in our representations of him! What caprice, absurdity, and immorality are attributed to him! How much is he degraded even below the character which we should naturally, in common life, attribute to a man of sense and virtue!

What a noble privilege is it of human reason to attain the knowledge of the supreme Being; and, from the visible works of nature, be enabled to infer so sublime a principle as its supreme Creator. But turn the reverse of the medal. Survey most nations and most ages. Examine the religious principles, which have, in fact, prevailed in the world. You will scarcely be persuaded, that they are other than sick men's dreams: Or perhaps will regard them more as the playsome whimsies of monkeys in human shape, than the serious, positive, dogmatical asseverations of a being, who dignifies himself with the name of rational.

Hear the verbal protestations of all men: Nothing they are so certain of as their religious tenets. Examine their lives: You will scarcely think that they repose the smallest confidence in them.

The greatest and truest zeal gives no security against hypocrisy: The most open impiety is attended with a secret dread and compunction.

No theological absurdities so glaring as have not, sometimes, been embraced by men of the greatest and most cultivated understanding. No religious precepts so rigorous as have not been adopted by the most voluptuous and most abandoned of men.

David Hume

'The Natural History of Religion',
in *Four Dissertations* (1757)

THE BEST OF BEINGS

GOOD HUMOUR is not only the best Security against *Enthusiasm*, but the best Foundation of *Piety* and *true Religion*: For if right Thoughts and worthy Apprehensions of the Supreme Being, are fundamental to all true Worship and Adoration; 'tis more than probable, that we shall never miscarry in this respect, except thro' ill Humour only. Nothing beside ill Humour, either natural or forc'd, can bring a Man to think seriously that the World is govern'd by any devilish or malicious Power. I very much question whether any thing, besides ill Humour, can be the Cause of Atheism. For there are so many Arguments to persuade a Man in Humour, that, in the main, all things are kindly and well dispos'd, that one wou'd think it impossible for him to be so far out of conceit with Affairs, as to imagine they all ran at adventures; and that *the World*, as venerable and wise a Face as it carry'd, had neither Sense nor Meaning in it. This however I am persuaded of, that nothing beside ill Humour can give us dreadful or ill Thoughts of a Supreme Manager. Nothing can persuade us of Sullenness or Sourness in such a Being, beside the actual fore-feeling of somewhat of this kind within our-selves: and if we are afraid of bringing good Humour into Religion, or thinking with Freedom and Pleasantness on such a Subject as GOD 'tis because we conceive the Subject so like our-selves, and can hardly have a Notion of *Majesty* and *Greatness*, without *Stateliness* and *Moroseness* accompanying it.

This, however, is the just Reverse of that Character, which we own to be most *divinely Good*, when we see it, as we sometimes do, in Men of highest Power among us. If they pass for truly *Good*, we dare treat them freely, and are sure they will not be displeas'd with this Liberty. They are doubly Gainers by this Goodness of theirs. For the more they are search'd into, and familiarly examin'd, the more their Worth appears; and the Discoverer, charm'd with his Success, esteems and loves more than ever, when he has prov'd this additional Bounty in his Superior, and reflects on that Candor and Generosity he has experienc'd.

Anthony Ashley Cooper, third Earl of Shaftesbury

A Letter Concerning Enthusiasm (1708), in *Characteristicks of Men, Manners, Opinions, Times* (1711)
Text from second edition (1714) Vol. I

'As Flies to Wanton Boys'?

The optimist philosopher answered

HAVING thus dispatched the consideration of particular evils, he comes at last to a general reason for which *evil* may be said to be *our good*. He is of opinion that there is some inconceivable benefit in pain abstractedly considered; that pain however inflicted, or wherever felt, communicates some good to the general system of being, and that every animal is some way or other the better for the pain of every other animal. This opinion he carries so far as to suppose that there passes some principle of union through all animal life, as attraction is communicated to all corporeal nature; and that the evils suffered on this globe, may by some inconceivable means contribute to the felicity of the inhabitants of the remotest planet.

How the origin of evil is brought nearer to human conception by any *inconceivable* means, I am not able to discover. We believed that the present system of creation was right, though we could not explain the adaptation of one part to the other, or for the whole succession of causes and consequences. Where has this enquirer added to the little knowledge that we had before. He has told us of the benefits of evil, which no man feels, and relations between distant parts of the universe, which he cannot himself conceive. There was enough in this question inconceivable before, and we have little advantage from a new inconceivable solution.

I do not mean to reproach this author for not knowing what is equally hidden from learning and from ignorance. The shame is to impose words for ideas upon ourselves or others. To imagine that we are going forward when we are only turning round. To think that there is any difference between him that gives no reason, and him that gives a reason, which by his own confession cannot be conceived.

But that he may not be thought to conceive nothing but things inconceivable, he has at last thought on a way by which human sufferings may produce good effects. He imagines that as we have not only animals for food, but choose some for our diversion, the same privilege may be allowed to some beings above us, *who may deceive, torment, or destroy us for the ends only of their own pleasure or utility.* This he again finds impossible to be conceived, *but that impossibility lessens not the probability of the conjecture, which by analogy is so strongly confirmed.*

I cannot resist the temptation of contemplating this analogy, which I think he might have carried further very much to the advantage of his argument. He might have shewn that these *hunters whose game is man* have many sports analogous to our own. As we drown whelps and kittens, they amuse themselves now and then with sinking a ship, and stand round the fields of *Blenheim* or the walls of *Prague,* as we encircle a cock-pit. As we shoot a bird flying, they take a man in the midst of his business or pleasure, and knock him down with an apoplexy. Some of them, perhaps, are virtuosi, and delight in the operations of an asthma, as a human philosopher in the effects of the air pump. To swell a man with a tympany is as good sport as to blow a frog. Many a merry bout have these frolic beings at the vicissitudes of an ague, and good sport it is to see a man tumble with an epilepsy, and revive and tumble again, and all this he knows not why. As they are wiser and more powerful than we, they have more exquisite diversions, for we have no way of procuring any sport so brisk and so lasting as the paroxysms of the gout and stone which undoubtedly must make high mirth, especially if the play be a little diversified with the blunders and puzzles of the blind and deaf. We know not how far their sphere of observation may extend. Perhaps now and then a merry being may place himself in such a situation as to enjoy at once all the varieties of an epidemical disease, or amuse his leisure with the tossings and contortions of every possible pain exhibited together.

One sport the merry malice of these beings has found means of enjoying to which we have nothing equal or similar. They now and then catch a mortal proud of his parts, and flattered either by the submission of those who court his kindness, or the notice of those who suffer him to court theirs. A head thus prepared for the reception of false opinions, and the projection of vain designs, they easily fill with idle notions, till in time they make their plaything an author: their first diversion commonly begins with an ode or an epistle, then rises perhaps to a political irony, and is at last brought to its height, by a treatise of philosophy. Then begins the poor animal to entangle himself in sophisms, and flounder in absurdity, to talk confidently of the scale of being, and to give solutions which himself confesses impossible to be understood. Sometimes, however, it happens that their pleasure is without much mischief. The author feels no pain, but while they are wondering at the extravagance of his opinion, and pointing him out to one another as a new example of human folly, he is enjoying his own applause, and that of his companions, and perhaps is elevated with the hope of standing at the head of a new sect.

Many of the books which now croud the world, may be justly suspected to be written for the sake of some invisible order of beings, for surely they are of no use to any of the corporeal inhabitants of the world. Of the productions of the last bounteous year, how many can be said to serve any purpose of use or pleasure. The only end of writing is to enable the readers better to enjoy life, or better to endure it: and how will either of those be put more in our power by him who tells us, that we are puppets, of which some creature not much wiser than ourselves manages the wires? That a set of beings unseen and unheard, are hovering about us, trying experiments upon our sensibility, putting us in agonies to see our limbs quiver, torturing us to madness, that they may laugh at our vagaries, sometimes obstructing the bile, that they may see how a man looks when he is yellow: sometimes breaking a traveller's bones to try how he will get home; sometimes wasting a man to a skeleton, and sometimes killing him fat for the greater elegance of his hide.

This is an account of natural evil, which though, like the rest, not quite new, is very entertaining, though I know not how much it may contribute to patience. . . .

Samuel Johnson

*From a review of Soame Jenyns' Free Inquiry into the
Nature and Origin of Evil in The Literary Magazine,
No. XV (1757)*

THE VICAR'S SERMON IN PRISON

BUT though religion is very kind to all men, it has promised peculiar rewards to the unhappy; the sick, the naked, the houseless, the heavy-laden, and the prisoner, have ever most frequent promises in our sacred law. The author of our religion every where professes himself the wretch's friend, and unlike the false ones of this world, bestows all his caresses upon the forlorn. The unthinking have censured this as partiality, as a preference without merit to deserve it. But they never reflect that it is not in the power even of heaven itself to make the offer of unceasing felicity as great a gift to the happy as to the miserable. To the first eternity is but a single blessing, since at most it but encreases what they already possess. To the latter it is a double advantage; for it diminishes their pain here, and rewards them with heavenly bliss hereafter.

But providence is in another respect kinder to the poor than to the rich; for as it thus makes the life after death more desirable, so it smooths the passage there. The wretched have had a long familiarity with every face of terror. The man of sorrows lays himself quietly down, without possessions to regret, and but few ties to stop his departure: he feels only nature's pang in the final separation, and this is no way greater than he has often fainted under before; for after a certain degree of pain, every new breach that death opens in the constitution, nature kindly covers with insensibility. . . .

These are therefore the consolations which the wretched have peculiar to themselves, and in which they are above the rest of mankind; in other respects they are below them. They who would know the miseries of the poor, must see life and endure it. To declaim on the temporal advantages they enjoy, is only repeating what none either believe or practise. The men who have the necessaries of living are not poor, and they who want them must be miserable. Yes, my friends, we must be miserable. No vain efforts of a refined imagination can soothe the wants of nature, can give elastic sweetness to the dank vapour of a dungeon, or ease to the throbbings of a broken heart. Let the philosopher from his couch of softness tell us that we can resist all these. Alas! the effort by which we resist them is still the greatest pain! Death is slight, and any man may sustain it; but torments are dreadful, and these no man can endure.

To us then, my friends, the promises of happiness in heaven should be peculiarly dear; for if our reward be in this life alone, we are then indeed of all men the most miserable. When I look round these gloomy walls, made to terrify, as well as to confine us; this light that only serves to shew the horrors of the place, those shackles that tyranny has imposed, or crime made necessary; when I survey these emaciated looks, and hear those groans, O my friends, what a glorious exchange would heaven be for these! To fly through regions unconfined as air, to bask in the sunshine of eternal bliss, to carrol over endless hymns of praise, to have no master to threaten or insult us, but the form of Goodness himself for ever in our eyes; when I think of these things, death becomes the messenger of very glad tidings; when I think of these things, his sharpest arrow becomes the staff of my support; when I think of these things, what is there in life worth having? when I think of these things, what is there that should not be spurned away? kings in their palaces should groan for such advantages; but we, humbled as we are, should yearn for them.

And shall these things be ours? Ours they will certainly be, if we but try for them; and what is a comfort, we are shut out from many temptations that would retard our pursuit. Only let us try for them, and they will certainly be ours, and what is still a comfort, shortly too; for if we look back on past life, it appears but a very short span, and whatever we may think of the rest of life, it will yet be found of less duration; as we grow older, the days seem to grow shorter, and our intimacy with time ever lessens the perception of his stay. Then let us take comfort now, for we shall soon be at our journey's end; we shall soon lay down the heavy burthen laid by heaven upon us; and though death, the only friend of the wretched, for a little while mocks the weary traveller with the view, and like his horizon, still flies before him; yet the time will certainly and shortly come, when we shall cease from our toil; when the luxurious great ones of the world shall no more tread us to the earth; when we shall think with pleasure on our sufferings below; when we shall be surrounded with all our friends, or such as deserved our friendship; when our bliss shall be unutterable, and still, to crown all, unending.

Oliver Goldsmith

The Vicar of Wakefield (1766). **Text** from second edition (1766)

FORTITUDE

THE cure for the greatest part of human miseries is not radical, but palliative. Infelicity is involved in corporeal nature, and interwoven with our being; all attempts therefore to decline it wholly are useless and vain: the armies of pain send their arrows against us on every side, the choice is only between those which are more or less sharp, or tinged with poison of greater or less malignity; and the strongest armour which reason can supply, will only blunt their points, but cannot repel them.

The great remedy which heaven has put in our hands is patience, by which, though we cannot lessen the torments of the body, we can in a great measure preserve the peace of the mind, and shall suffer only the natural and genuine force of an evil, without heightening its acrimony, or prolonging its effects.

There is indeed nothing more unsuitable to the nature of man in any calamity than rage and turbulence, which, without examining whether they are not sometimes impious, are at least always offensive, and incline others rather to hate and despise than to pity and assist us. If what we suffer has been brought upon us by ourselves, it is observed by an ancient poet, that patience is eminently our duty, since no one should be angry at feeling that which he has deserved.

> *Leniter ex merito quicquid patiare serendum est.*
> Let pain deserv'd without complaint be borne.

And surely, if we are conscious that we have not contributed to our own sufferings, if punishment falls upon innocence, or disappointment happens to industry and prudence, patience, whether more necessary or not, is much easier, since our pain is then without aggravation, and we have not the bitterness of remorse to add to the asperity of misfortune.

In those evils which are allotted to us by providence, such as deformity, privation of any of the senses, or old age, it is always to be remembered, that impatience can have no present effect, but to deprive us of the consolations which our condition admits, by driving away from us those by whose conversation or advice we might be amused or helped; and that with regard to futurity it is yet less to be justified, since, without lessening the pain, it cuts off the hope of that reward, which he by whom it is inflicted will confer upon them that bear it well.

In all evils which admit a remedy, impatience is to be avoided, because it wastes that time and attention in complaints, that, if properly applied, might remove the cause. Turenne, among the acknowledgements which he used to pay in conversation to the memory of those by whom he had been instructed in the art of war, mentioned one with honour who taught him not to spend his time in regretting any mistake which he had made, but to set himself immediately and vigorously to repair it.

Patience and submission are very carefully to be distinguished from cowardice and indolence. We are not to repine, but we may lawfully struggle; for the calamities of life, like the necessities of nature, are calls to labour and exercises of diligence. When we feel any pressures of distress, we are not to conclude that we can only obey the will of heaven by languishing under it, any more than when we perceive the pain of thirst we are to imagine that water is prohibited. Of misfortune it never can be certainly known whether, as proceeding from the hand of GOD, it is an act of favour, or of punishment: but since all the ordinary dispensations of providence are to be interpreted according to the general analogy of things, we may conclude that we have a right to remove one inconvenience as well as another; that we are only to take care lest we purchase ease with guilt; and that our

Maker's purpose, whether of reward or severity, will be answered by the labours which he lays us under the necessity of performing.

This duty is not more difficult in any state than in diseases intensely painful, which may indeed suffer such exacerbations as seem to strain the powers of life to the utmost stretch, and leave very little of the attention vacant to precept or reproof. In this state the nature of man requires some indulgence, and every extravagance but impiety may be easily forgiven him. Yet, lest we should think ourselves too soon entitled to the mournful privileges of irresistible misery, it is proper to reflect, that the utmost anguish which human wit can contrive, or human malice can inflict, has been borne with constancy; and that if the pains of disease be, as I believe they are, sometimes greater than those of artificial torture, they are therefore in their own nature shorter, the vital frame is quickly broken, or the union between soul and body is for a time suspended by insensibility, and we soon cease to feel our maladies when they once become too violent to be borne. I think there is some reason for questioning whether the body and mind are not so proportioned, that the one can bear all that can be inflicted on the other, whether virtue cannot stand its ground as long as life, and whether a soul well principled will not be separated sooner than subdued.

Samuel Johnson

The Rambler (7 July, 1750). Text from
the fourth edition (1756) Vol. I

PHILOSOPHY AND HUMAN NATURE

THE passion for philosophy, like that for religion, seems liable to this inconvenience, that, though it aims at the correction of our manners and extirpation of our vices, it may only serve, by imprudent management, to foster a predominant inclination, and push the mind, with more determined resolution, towards that side, which already *draws* too much, by the biass and propensity of the natural temper. It is certain, that, while we aspire to the magnanimous firmness of the philosophic sage, and endeavour to confine our pleasures altogether within our own minds, we may, at last, render our philosophy like that of EPICTETUS and other *Stoics*, only a more refin'd system of selfishness, and reason ourselves out of all virtue, as well as social enjoyment. While we study with attention the vanity of human life, and turn all our thoughts towards the empty and transitory nature of riches and honours, we are, perhaps, all the while flattering our natural indolence, which, hating the bustle of the world, and drudgery of business, seeks a pretence of reason, to give itself a full and uncontrouled indulgence. There is, however, one species of philosophy, which seems little liable to this inconvenience, and that because it strikes in with no disorderly passion of the human mind, nor can mingle itself with any natural affection or propensity; and that is the ACADEMIC or SCEPTICAL philosophy. The academics talk always of doubt and suspence of judgment, of danger in hasty determinations, of confining to very narrow bounds the enquiries of the understanding, and of renouncing all speculations that lie not within the limits of common life and practice. Nothing, therefore, can be more contrary than such a philosophy to the supine indolence of the mind, its rash arrogance, its lofty pretensions, and its superstitious credulity. Every passion is mortified by it, except the love of truth; and that passion never is, nor can be carried to too high a degree. It is surprising, therefore, that this philosophy, which, in almost every instance, must be harmless and innocent, should be the subject of so much groundless reproach and obloquy. But, perhaps, the very circumstance which renders it so innocent, is what chiefly exposes it to the public hatred and resentment. By flattering no irregular passion, it gains few partizans: By opposing so many vices and follies, it raises to itself abundance of enemies, who stigmatize it as libertine, prophane, and irreligious.

Nor need we fear, that this philosophy, while it endeavours to limit our enquiries to common life, should ever undermine the reasonings of common life, and carry its doubts so far as to destroy all action, as well as speculation. Nature will always maintain her rights, and prevail in the end over any abstract reasoning whatsoever. Though we should conclude, for instance, as in the foregoing section, that, in all reasonings from experience, there is a step taken by the mind, which is not supported by any argument or process of the understanding; there is no danger, that these reasonings, on which almost all knowledge depends, will ever be affected by such a discovery. If the mind be not engaged by argument to make this step, it must be induced by some other principle of equal weight and authority; and that principle will preserve its influence as long as human nature remains the same. What that principle is, may well be worth the pains of enquiry.

Suppose a person, though endowed with the strongest faculties of reason and reflection, to be brought on a sudden into this world; he would, indeed, immediately observe a continual succession of objects, and one event following another; but he would not be able to discover any thing farther. He would not, at first, by any reasoning, be able to reach the idea of cause and effect; since the particular powers, by which all natural operations are performed, never appear to the senses; nor is it reasonable to conclude, merely because one event, in one instance, precedes another, that therefore the one is the cause, and the other the effect. Their conjunction may be arbitrary and casual. There may be no reason to infer the existence of the one from the appearance of the other. And in a word, such a person, without more experience, could never employ his conjecture or reasoning concerning any matter of fact, or be assured of any thing beyond what was immediately present to his memory and senses.

Suppose again, that he has acquired more experience, and has liv'd so long in the world as to have observed similar objects or events to be constantly conjoined together; What is the consequence of this experience? He immediately infers the existence of one object from the appearance of the other. Yet he has not, by all his experience, acquired any idea or knowledge of the secret power, by which the one object produces the other; nor is it, by any process of reasoning, he is engaged to draw this inference. But still he finds himself determin'd to draw it: And though he should be convinced, that his understanding has no part in the operation, he would nevertheless continue in the same course of thinking. There is some other principle, which determines him to form such a conclusion.

The Principle is CUSTOM or HABIT. For wherever the repetition of any particular act or operation produces a propensity to renew the same act or operation, without being impelled by any reasoning or process of the understanding; we always say, that this propensity is the effect of *Custom*. By employing that word, we pretend not to have given the ultimate reason of such a propensity. We only point out a principle of human nature, which is universally acknowledg'd, and which is well known by its effects. Perhaps, we can push our enquiries no farther, or pretend to give the cause of this cause; but must rest contented with it as the ultimate principle, which we can assign, of all our conclusions from experience. It is sufficient satisfaction, that we can go so far; without repining at the narrowness of our faculties, because they will carry us no farther. And it is certain we here advance a very intelligible proposition at least, if not a true one, when we assert, that after the constant conjunction of two objects, heat and flame, for instance, weight and solidity, we are determined by custom alone to expect the one from the appearance of the other. This hypothesis seems even the only one, which explains the difficulty, why we draw from a thousand instances, an inference which we are not able to draw from one instance, that is, in no respect, different from them. Reason is incapable of any such variation. The conclusions which it draws from considering one circle are the same, which it would form upon surveying all the circles in the universe. But no man, having seen only one body move after being impelled by another, could infer, that every other body will move after a like impulse. All inferences from experience, therefore, are effects of custom, not of reasoning.

Custom, then, is the great guide of human life. It is that principle alone, which renders our experience useful to us, and makes us expect for the future, a similar train of events with those which have appeared in the past. Without the influence of custom, we should be entirely ignorant of every matter of fact, beyond what is immediately present to the memory and senses. We should never know how to adjust means to ends, or to employ our natural powers in the production of any effect. There would be an end at once of all action, as well as of the chief part of speculation.

David Hume

Philosophical Essays concerning Human Understanding (1748). Text from *Essays and Treatises . . .*, edition of 1777, Vol. II

REALITY

XXXV. I do not argue against the Existence of any one thing that we can apprehend, either by Sense or Reflexion. That the things I see with mine Eyes and touch with my Hands do exist, really exist, I make not the least Question. The only thing whose Existence we deny, is that which Philosophers call Matter or corporeal Substance. And in doing of this, there is no Damage done to the rest of Mankind, who, I dare say, will never miss it. The Atheist indeed will want the Colour of an empty Name to support his Impiety; and the Philosophers may possibly find, they have lost a great Handle for Trifling and Disputation.

XXXVI. If any Man thinks this detracts from the Existence or Reality of Things, he is very far from understanding what hath been premised in the plainest Terms I could think of. Take here an Abstract of what has been said. There are spiritual Substances, Minds, or humane Souls, which will or excite Ideas in themselves at pleasure: but these are faint, weak, and unsteady in respect of others they perceive by Sense, which being impressed upon them according to certain Rules or Laws of Nature, speak themselves the Effects of a Mind more powerful and wise than humane Spirits. These latter are said to have more *Reality* in them than the former. By which is meant that they are affecting, orderly, and distinct, and that they are not Fictions of the Mind perceiving them. And in this Sense, the Sun that I see by Day is the real Sun, and that which I imagine by Night is the Idea of the former. In the Sense here given of *Reality*, it is evident that every Vegetable, Star, Mineral, and in general each Part of the Mundane System, is as much a *real Being* by our Principles as by any other. Whether others mean any thing by the term *Reality* different from what I do, I intreat them to look into their own Thoughts and see.

XXXVII. It will be urged that thus much at least is true, to wit, that we take away all corporeal Substances. To this my Answer is, That if the Word *Substance* be taken in the vulgar Sense, for a Combination of sensible Qualities, such as Extension, Solidity, Weight, and the like: This we cannot be accused of taking away. But if it be taken in a philosophic Sense, for the support of Accidents or Qualities without the Mind: Then indeed I acknowledge that we take it away, if one may be said to take away that which never had any Existence, not even in the Imagination.

XXXVIII. But, say you, it sounds very harsh to say we eat and drink Ideas, and are clothed with Ideas. I acknowledge it does so, the Word *Idea* not being used in common Discourse to signify the several Combinations of sensible Qualities, which are called *Things*: and it is certain that any Expression which varies from the familiar Use of Language, will seem harsh and ridiculous. But this doth not concern the Truth or the Proposition, which in other Words is no more than to say, we are fed and clothed with those Things which we perceive immediately by our Senses. The Hardness or Softness, the Colour, Taste, Warmth, Figure, and such like Qualities, which combined together constitute the several Sorts of Victuals and Apparel, have been shown to exist only in the Mind that perceives them; and this is all that is meant by calling them *Ideas*; which Word, if it was as ordinarily used as *Thing*, would sound no harsher nor more ridiculous than it. I am not for disputing about the Propriety, but the Truth of the Expression. If therefore you agree with me that we eat and drink, and are clad with the immediate Objects of Sense which cannot exist unperceived or without the Mind: I shall readily grant it is more proper or conformable to Custom, that they should be called Things rather than Ideas.

XXXIX. If it be demanded why I make use of the word *Idea*, and do not rather in Compliance with Custom call them Things. I answer, I do it for two Reasons: First, because the Term *Thing*, in contradistinction to *Idea*, is generally supposed to denote somewhat existing without the Mind: Secondly, because *Thing* hath a more comprehensive Signification than *Idea*, including Spirits, or thinking Things, as well as Ideas.

Since therefore the Objects of Sense exist only in the Mind, and are withal thoughtless and inactive, I chose to mark them by the word *Idea* which implies those Properties.

XL. But say what we can, some one perhaps may be apt to reply, he will still believe his Senses, and never suffer any Arguments, how plausible soever, to prevail over the Certainty of them. Be it so, assert the Evidence of Sense as high as you please, we are willing to do the same. That what I see, hear, and feel doth exist, that is to say, *is perceived by me*, I no more doubt than I do of my own Being. But I do not see how the Testimony of Sense can be alledged as a Proof for the Existence of any thing, which is not perceived by Sense.

George Berkeley
A Treatise concerning the Principles of Human Knowledge (1710)
Text from second edition (1734)

THE PROPER SUBJECTS OF SCIENCE AND ENQUIRY

IT seems to me, that the only objects of the abstract sciences or of demonstration are quantity and number, and that all attempts to extend this more perfect species of knowledge beyond these bounds are mere sophistry and illusion. As the component parts of quantity and number are entirely similar, their relations become intricate and involved; and nothing can be more curious, as well as useful, than to trace, by a variety of mediums, their equality or inequality, through their different appearances. But as all other ideas are clearly distinct and different from each other, we can never advance farther, by our utmost scrutiny, than to observe this diversity, and, by an obvious reflection, pronounce one thing not to be another. Or if there be any difficulty in these decisions, it proceeds entirely from the undeterminate meaning of words, which is corrected by juster definitions. That *the square of the hypothenuse is equal to the squares of the other two sides*, cannot be known, let the terms be ever so exactly defined, without a train of reasoning and enquiry. But to convince us of this proposition, *that where there is no property, there can be no injustice*, it is only necessary to define the terms, and explain injustice to be a violation of property. This proposition is, indeed, nothing but a more imperfect definition. It is the same case with all those pretended syllogistical reasonings, which may be found in every other branch of learning, except the sciences of quantity and number; and these may safely, I think, be pronounced the only proper objects of knowledge and demonstration.

All other enquiries of men regard only matter of fact and existence; and these are evidently incapable of demonstration. Whatever *is* may *not be*. No negation of a fact can involve a contradiction. The non-existence of any being, without exception, is as clear and distinct an idea as its existence. The proposition, which affirms it not to be, however false, is no less conceivable and intelligible, than that which affirms it to be. The case is different with the sciences, properly so called. Every proposition, which is not true, is there confused and unintelligible. That the cube root of 64 is equal to the half of 10, is a false proposition, and can never be distinctly conceived. But that CÆSAR, or the angel GABRIEL, or any being never existed, may be a false proposition, but still is perfectly conceivable, and implies no contradiction.

The existence, therefore, of any being can only be proved by arguments from its cause or its effect; and these arguments are founded entirely on experience. If we reason *a priori*, anything may appear able to produce anything. The falling of a pebble may, for aught we know, extinguish the sun; or the wish of a man control the planets in their orbits. It is only experience, which teaches us the nature and bounds of cause and effect, and enables us to infer the existence of one object from that of another. Such is the foundation of moral reasoning, which forms the greater part of human knowledge, and is the source of all human action and behaviour.

Moral reasonings are either concerning particular or general facts. All deliberations in life regard the former; as also all disquisitions in history, chronology, geography, and astronomy.

The sciences, which treat of general facts, are politics, natural philosophy, physic, chemistry, &c. where the qualities, causes and effects of a whole species of objects are enquired into.

Divinity or Theology, as it proves the existence of a Deity, and the immortality of souls, is composed partly of reasonings concerning particular, partly concerning general facts. It has a foundation in *reason*, so far as it is supported by experience. But its best and most solid foundation is *faith* and divine revelation.

Morals and criticism are not so properly objects of the understanding as of taste and sentiment. Beauty, whether moral or natural, is felt, more properly than perceived. Or if we reason concerning it, and endeavour to fix its standard, we regard a new fact, to wit, the general tastes of mankind, or some such fact, which may be the object of reasoning and enquiry.

When we run over libraries, persuaded of these principles, what havoc must we make? If we take in our hand any volume; of divinity or school metaphysics, for instance; let us ask, *Does it contain any abstract reasoning concerning quantity or number?* No. *Does it contain any experimental reasoning concerning matter of fact and existence?* No. Commit it then to the flames: For it can contain nothing but sophistry and illusion.

David Hume

Philosophical Essays concerning the Human Understanding (1748)
Text from *Essays and Treatises . . .*, edition of 1777, Vol. II

THE ANCIENT PHILOSOPHERS REBUKED

BUT how shall we excuse the supine inattention of the Pagan and philosophic world, to those evidences which were presented by the hand of Omnipotence, not to their reason, but to their senses? During the age of Christ, of his apostles, and of their first disciples, the doctrine which they preached was confirmed by innumerable prodigies. The lame walked, the blind saw, the sick were healed, the dead were raised, dæmons were expelled, and the laws of Nature were frequently suspended for the benefit of the church. But the sages of Greece and Rome turned aside from the awful spectacle, and pursuing the ordinary occupations of life and study, appeared unconscious of any alterations in the moral or physical government of the world. Under the reign of Tiberius, the whole earth, or at least a celebrated province of the Roman empire, was involved in a præternatural darkness of three hours. Even this miraculous event, which ought to have excited the wonder, the curiosity, and the devotion of mankind, passed without notice in an age of science and history. It happened during the lifetime of Seneca and the elder Pliny, who must have experienced the immediate effects, or received the earliest intelligence, of the prodigy. Each of these philosophers, in a laborious work, has recorded all the great phenomena of Nature, earthquakes, meteors, comets, and eclipses, which his indefatigable curiosity could collect. Both the one and the other have omitted to mention the greatest phenomenon to which the mortal eye has been witness since the creation of the globe. A distinct chapter of Pliny is designed for eclipses of an extraordinary nature and unusual duration; but he contents himself with describing the singular defect of light which followed the murder of Cæsar, when, during the greatest part of the year, the orb of the sun appeared pale and without splendour. This season of obscurity, which cannot surely be compared with the præternatural darkness of the Passion, had been already celebrated by most of the poets and historians of that memorable age.

Edward Gibbon

The History of the Decline and Fall of the Roman Empire,
Vol. I (1776). Text from second edition (1782)

THE SCIENTISTS

THIS Academy is not an entire single Building, but a Continuation of several Houses on both Sides of a Street; which growing waste, was purchased and applyed to that Use.

I was received very kindly by the Warden, and went for many Days to the Academy. Every Room hath in it one or more Projectors; and I believe I could not be in fewer than five Hundred Rooms.

The first Man I saw was of a meagre Aspect, with sooty Hands and Face, his Hair and Beard long, ragged and singed in several Places. His Clothes, Shirt, and Skin were all of the same Colour. He had been Eight Years upon a Project for extracting Sun-Beams out of Cucumbers, which were to be put into Vials hermetically sealed, and let out to warm the Air in raw inclement Summers. He told me, he did not doubt in Eight Years more, that he should be able to supply the Governors Gardens with Sun-shine at a reasonable Rate; but he complained that his Stock was low, and intreated me to give him something as an Encouragement to Ingenuity especially since this had been a very dear Season for Cucumbers. I made him a small Present, for my Lord had furnished me with Money on purpose, because he knew their Practice of begging from all who go to see them. . . .

I saw another at work to calcine Ice into Gunpowder; who

likewise shewed me a Treatise he had written concerning the Malleability of Fire, which he intended to publish.

There was a most ingenious Architect who had contrived a new Method for building Houses, by beginning at the Roof, and working downwards to the Foundation; which he justified to me by the like Practice of those two prudent Insects the Bee and the Spider.

There was a Man born blind, who had several Apprentices in his own Condition: Their Employment was to mix Colours for Painters, which their Master taught them to distinguish by feeling and smelling. It was indeed my Misfortune to find them at that Time not very perfect in their Lessons; and the Professor himself happened to be generally mistaken: This Artist is much encouraged and esteemed by the whole Fraternity.

In another Apartment I was highly pleased with a Projector, who had found a Device of plowing the Ground with Hogs, to save the Charges of Plows, Cattle, and Labour. The Method is this: In an Acre of Ground you bury at six Inches Distance, and eight deep, a Quantity of Acorns, Dates, Chesnuts, and other Masts or Vegetables whereof these Animals are fondest; then you drive six Hundred or more of them into the Field, where in a few Days they will root up the whole Ground in search of their Food, and make it fit for sowing, at the same time manuring it with their Dung. It is true, upon Experiment they found the Charge and Trouble very great, and they had little or no Crop. However, it is not doubted that this Invention may be capable of great Improvement.

I went into another Room, where the Walls and Ceiling were all hung round with Cobwebs, except a narrow Passage for the Artist to go in and out. At my Entrance he called aloud to me not to disturb his Webs. He lamented the fatal Mistake the World had been so long in of using Silk-Worms, while we had such plenty of domestick Insects, who infinitely excelled the former, because they understood how to weave as well as spin. And he proposed farther, that by employing Spiders, the Charge of dying Silks would be wholly saved; whereof I was fully convinced when he shewed me a vast Number of Flies most beautifully coloured, wherewith he fed his Spiders; assuring us, that the Webs would take a Tincture from them; and as he had them of all Hues, he hoped to fit every Body's Fancy, as soon as he could find proper Food for the Flies, of certain Gums, Oyls, and other glutinous Matter, to give a Strength and Consistence to the Threads.

Jonathan Swift

*Travels into Several Remote Nations . . .
by Lemuel Gulliver* (1726). Text from
Works . . . (1735), Vol. III

INSECTS

FROM the Head pass we to the Members concerned in their Motion. And here we have a copious Subject, if I was minded to expatiate. I might take notice of the admirable Mechanism in those that creep; the curious Oars in those amphibious Insects that swim and walk; the incomparable Provision made in the Feet of such as walk, or hang upon smooth Surfaces; the great Strength and Spring in the Legs of such as leap; the strong and well-made Feet and Talons of such as dig: and to name no more, the admirable Faculty of such as cannot fly, to convey themselves with Speed and Safety, by the help of their Webs, or some other Artifice, to make their Bodies lighter than the Air: these, and a Multitude of other such like Things as these, I might, I say, take notice of, as great Evidences of the infinite Creator's Wisdom: But lest I should be too tedious, I will confine my Observations to the Legs and Wings only.

And these, at first View, we find to be incomparably fitted up for their intended Service, not to overload the Body, nor in the least to retard it, but to give it the most proper and convenient Motion. What, for Example, can be better contrived, and made for this Service, than the Wings? Distended and strengthened by the finest Bones, and these covered with the finest and lightest Membranes, some of them adorned with neat and beautiful Feathers; and many of them provided with the finest Articulations, and Foldings, for the Wings to be withdrawn, and neatly laid up in their *Vaginæ*, and Cases, and again readily extended for Flight.

And then for the Poising of the Body, and keeping it upright, and steady in Flight, it is an admirable Artifice and Provision for this Purpose; in some, by four Wings; and in such as have but two, by Pointels and Poises placed under the Wings, on each Side the Body.

And lastly, It is an amazing Thing to reflect upon the surprising Minuteness, Art, and Curiosity of the Joynts, the Muscles, the Tendons, the Nerves, necessary to perform all the Motions of the Legs, the Wings, and every other Part. I have already mentioned this in the larger Animals; but to consider, that all these Things concur in minute Animals, even in the smallest Mite; yea, the Animalcules, that (without good Microscopes) escape our Sight; to consider, I say, that those minutest Animals have all the Joints, Bones, Muscles, Tendons, and Nerves, necessary to that brisk and swift Motion that many of them have, is so stupendous a Piece of curious Art, as plainly manifesteth the Power and Wisdom of the infinite Contriver of those inimitable Fineries. But having named those minute Animals, why should I mention only any one Part of their Bodies, when we have, in that little Compass, a whole and compleat Body, as exquisitely formed, and (as far as our Scrutiny can possibly reach) as neatly adorned, as the largest Animal? Let us consider, that there we have Eyes, a Brain, a Mouth, a Stomach, Entrails, and every other Part of an animal Body, as well as Legs and Feet; and that all those Parts have each of them their necessary *Apparatus* of Nerves, of various Muscles, and every other Part that other Insects have; and that all is covered and guarded with a well-made Tegument, beset with Bristles, adorned with neat Imbrications, and many other Fineries. And lastly, Let us consider in how little Compass all Art and Curiosity may lie, even in a Body many times less than a small Grain of Sand, so that the least Drop of Water can contain many of them, and afford them also sufficient Room to dance and frisk about in.

William Derham

Physico-Theology . . . (1712). Text
from fourth edition (1716)

FRIENDSHIP AMONG ANIMALS

Gilbert White to the Hon. Daines Barrington (8 June, 1775)

DEAR SIR, – There is a wonderful spirit of sociality in the brute creation, independent of sexual attachment: the congregation of gregarious birds in the winter is a remarkable instance.

Many horses, though quiet with company, will not stay one minute in a field by themselves: the strongest fences cannot restrain them. My neighbour's horse will not only not stay by himself abroad, but he will not bear to be left alone in a strange stable, without discovering the utmost impatience, and endeavouring to break the rack and manger with his fore feet. He has been known to leap out at a stable-window, through which dung was thrown, after company; and yet, in other respects, is remarkably quiet. Oxen and cows will not fatten by themselves; but will neglect the finest pasture that is not recommended by society. It would be needless to instance in sheep, which constantly flock together.

But this propensity seems not to be confined to animals of the same species; for we know a doe, still alive, that was brought up from a little fawn with a dairy of cows; with them it goes a-field, and with them it returns to the yard. The dogs of the house take no notice of this deer, being used to her; but, if strange dogs come by, a chase ensues; while the master smiles to see his favourite securely leading her pursuers over hedge, or gate, or stile, till she returns to the cows, who, with fierce lowings, and menacing horns, drive the assailants quite out of the pasture.

Even great disparity of kind and size does not always prevent social advances and mutual fellowship. For a very intelligent and observant person has assured me, that in the former part of his life, keeping but one horse, he happened also on a time to have but one solitary hen. These two incongruous animals spent much of their time together, in a lonely orchard, where they saw no creature but each other. By degrees, an apparent regard began to take between these two sequestered individuals. The fowl would approach the quadruped with notes of compacency, rubbing herself gently against his legs; while the horse would look down with satisfaction, and move with the greatest caution and circumspection, lest he should trample on his diminutive companion. Thus, by mutual good offices, each seemed to console the vacant hours of the other: so that Milton, when he puts the following sentiment in the mouth of Adam, seems to be somewhat mistaken:

> ' Much less can bird with beast, or fish with fowl
> So well converse, nor with the ox the ape.'

Gilbert White

*The Natural History and Antiquities
of Selborne* (1789)

THE ENGLISH WORKMAN

TRAVELLING in the North Part of *Britain*, I observed, that, in the Time of their Harvest, they had always an Overseer to keep the Reapers to their Work, and a Bagpipe to encourage them while they were at Work: And one of our Company observing that we had no such merry Doings at our Harvests in *England*; another answer'd him, 'twas true, nor was there any need of it, for that the *English* work'd merrily enough without Musick; adding, our Workmen have good Victuals and good Drink: Let's enquire how these poor People feed, said he; and so we did, when we found that the best of their Provision was a Cake of Oat Bread, which they call a Bannock, and a Draught of Water only; and twice in the Day, the Farmer or Steward gave them every one a Dram of *Glasgow* Brandy, as they call'd it; that is to say, good Malt Spirits.

Upon the whole, it was evident, the poor Men had need enough of Music to encourage them at their Labour; nor would the Music do neither, without the Overseer or Steward being in the Field too, to see that they stood to their Work.

In *England* we see the Farmers in Harvest Time, providing good Beef and Mutton, Pyes, Puddings, and other Provisions to a strange Profusion, feasting their Workmen, rather than feeding them; and giving them good Wages besides: But let any Man see the difference of the Work, these need no Music, the Feast is better than the Fiddle, and the Pudding does more than the Bag-Pipe; *in short* they work with a Vigor and Spirit, not to be seen in other Countries.

I could give like Examples among the Manufacturers; the Spirit and Courage of the Workmen, is seen in the Goodness and Substance of their Manufacture; of which, this must be said, our Manufacture may not be so cheap as the same Kinds made in other Countries; but bring them to the Scale and try their Substance, you will find the *English* Man's Work, according to his Wages, out-weigh the other; as his Beer is strong, so is his Work; and as he gives more Strength of Sinews to his Strokes in the Loom, his Work is firmer and faster, and carries a greater Substance with it, than the same Kinds of Goods, and of the same Denomination made in foreign Parts.

I remember in our former Contests about Commerce, great Noise was made of the *French* imitating our woollen Manufacture, and making them to such Perfection, as to out-do us in foreign Markets; from whence it was inferr'd, that they would in Time supplant our Trade, and carry away the Business from us: The Reason that was given, was, that their Poor could work so much cheaper than ours, that their Goods would be sold cheaper than the *English*, and consequently they would have the first and best of the Market always from us; and had this been fully and fairly made out; had they brought sufficient Evidence of the Facts suggested, the Inference had been good. Now to prove how finely the *French* perform'd, and how good their Cloths were; Patterns were shew'd here of their several Cloths, as finish'd for the *Turky* Trade, by the great Manufactory, as they call it, in *Languedoc*; for it was this Part that was brought for the Support of the Argument; and it is true, that the Patterns were extraordinary, the Cloth well dress'd, the Colours well dy'd; nay to Perfection; and to a superficial Eye, they rather went beyond the *English*, than come short of them.

But when they came to be look'd well into by Clothiers and Workmen who understood it, and whose Business it was; the Deficiency soon discover'd it self; their Cloths appear'd to be slight, thin, without Substance and Proportion, and unfit to do Service in wearing; in a word, they were no Way equal in Goodness to the *English* Manufacture of the same Kind. This was farther prov'd by the *Armenian* Merchants at *Aleppo*, at *Smyrna*, and other Places in *Turky*, where the said Goods were usually sold; where upon bringing the *English* and *French* Cloths to the Scale, there was no Comparison between them; but the *English* always out-weigh'd them forty to fifty Pounds *per* Bale, and sometimes much more; the Consequence of which was,

1. That those *Armenian* Merchants would very seldom buy the *French Cloths*, so long as there were any of the *English Cloths* left at the Market.

2. That when they did buy them, they always had them at a much cheaper Rate.

This is an evident Proof of the *English* manner of performing; and it will hold in many other Cases, perhaps in all Manufacturing Cases: The strong Labour of the *English* Workmen in all their manual Operations is very remarkable in the Works themselves: And I say, it is evident in many other Manufactures, besides that of Broad Cloths; *in a word*, our Workmen, by the meer Vigour and Strength of their Spirits, supported by their strong Feeding, and by their better Wages than in any other Nation, are not used to work slight and superficially, but strong and substantial in every Thing they do; and as they have better Wages for it than other Nations give, and perform their Work accordingly, so their Goods make it evident, for that they fetch a better Price at Market, than any Goods of the same Species, made in any other Country.

It is the same Thing in their several Manufactures of Brass and Iron, and other Hard-ware Works; but expecially, in their building of Ships, in which it is evident, the *Dutch* and *French*, *Swedes* and *Danes*, build cheaper; but the *English* build stronger and firmer; and an *English* Ship will always endure more severity, load heavier, and reign (*as the Seamen call it*) longer, than any foreign built Ship whatever; the Examples are seen every Year, particularly in the Coal Trade, the Loading of which is very heavy, and the Ships swim deep in the

Water, by the Eagerness of the Masters, to carry large Burthens; and yet it is frequently known, that a *New-Castle* or *Ipswich built Colier*, shall reign, (as I say the Seaman call it) forty to fifty Years, and come to a good End at last; that is, be broken up; not founder at Sea, or break her Back upon the Sands, as Ships weaker built, often, nay generally do.

Daniel Defoe

A Plan of the English Commerce (1728)

THE USES OF PARSIMONY

CAPITALS are increased by parsimony, and diminished by prodigality and misconduct.

Whatever a person saves from his revenue he adds to his capital, and either employs it himself in maintaining an additional number of productive hands, or enables some other person to do so, by lending it to him for an interest, that is, for a share of the profits. As the capital of an individual can be increased only by what he saves from his annual revenue or his annual gains, so the capital of a society, which is the same with that of all the individuals who compose it, can be increased only in the same manner.

Parsimony and not industry is the immediate cause of the increase of capital. Industry, indeed, provides the subject which parsimony accumulates. But whatever industry might acquire, if parsimony did not save and store up, the capital would never be the greater.

Parsimony, by increasing the fund which is destined for the maintenance of productive hands, tends to increase the number of those hands whose labour adds to the value of the subject upon which it is bestowed. It tends therefore to increase the exchangeable value of the annual produce of the land and labour of the country. It puts into motion an additional quantity of industry, which gives an additional value to the annual produce.

What is annually saved is as regularly consumed as what is annually spent, and nearly in the same time too; but it is consumed by a different sett of people. That portion of his revenue which a rich man annually spends, is in most cases consumed by idle guests, and menial servants, who leave nothing behind them in return for their consumption. That portion which he annually saves, as for the sake of the profit it is immediately employed as a capital, is consumed in the same manner, and nearly in the same time too, but by a different sett of people, by labourers, manufacturers, and artificers, who re-produce with a profit the value of their annual consumption. His revenue, we shall suppose, is paid him in money. Had he spent the whole, the food, cloathing, and lodging, which the whole could have purchased, would have been distributed among the former sett of people. By saving a part of it, as that part is for the sake of the profit immediately employed as a capital either by himself or by some other person, the food, cloathing, and lodging, which may be purchased with it, are necessarily reserved for the latter. The consumption is the same, but the consumers are different.

By what a frugal man annually saves, he not only affords maintenance to an additional number of productive hands, for that or the ensuing year, but, like the founder of a publick workhouse, he establishes as it were a perpetual fund for the maintenance of an equal number in all times to come. The perpetual allotment and destination of this fund, indeed, is not always guarded by any positive law, by any trust-right or deed of mortmain. It is always guarded, however, by a very powerful principle, the plain and evident interest of every individual to whom any share of it shall ever belong. No part of it can ever afterwards be employed to maintain any but productive hands, without an evident loss to the person who thus perverts it from its proper destination.

The prodigal perverts it in this manner. By not confining his expence within his income, he encroaches upon his capital. Like him who perverts the revenues of some pious foundation to profane purposes, he pays the wages of idleness with those funds which the frugality of his forefathers had, as it were, consecrated to the maintenance of industry. By diminishing the funds destined for the employment of productive labour, he necessarily diminishes, so far as it depends upon him, the quantity of that labour which adds a value to the subject upon which it is bestowed, and, consequently, the value of the annual produce of the land and labour of the whole country, the real wealth and revenue of its inhabitants. If the prodigality of some was not compensated by the frugality of others, the conduct of every prodigal, by feeding the idle with the bread of the industrious, tends not only to beggar himself, but to impoverish his country.

Adam Smith

*An Inquiry into the Nature and Causes
of the Wealth of Nations* (1776), Vol. I

THE GIN LICENSING ACT

From a speech in the House of Lords, 22 February, 1743

THE law before us, my lords, seems to be the effect of that practice of which it is intended likewise to be the cause, and to be dictated by the liquor of which it so effectually promotes the use; for surely it never before was conceived by any man entrusted with the administration of public affairs, to raise taxes by the destruction of the people.

Nothing, my lords, but the destruction of all the most

laborious and useful parts of the nation, can be expected, from the licence which is now proposed to be given not only to drunkenness, but to drunkenness of the most detestable and dangerous kind, to the abuse not only of intoxicating, but of poisonous liquors.

Nothing, my lords, is more absurd than to assert, that the use of spirits will be hindered by the Bill now before us, or indeed that it will not be in a very great degree promoted by it. For what produces all kind of wickedness, but the prospect of impunity on one part, or the solicitation of opportunity on the other; either of these have too frequently been sufficient to overpower the sense of morality, and even of religion; and what is not to be feared from them, when they shall unite their force, and operate together, when temptations shall be increased, and terror taken away?

It is allowed by those who have hitherto disputed on either side of this question, that the people appear obstinately enamoured of this new liquor; it is allowed on both parts, that this liquor corrupts the mind, enervates the body, and destroys vigour and virtue at the same time; that it makes those who drink it too idle and too feeble for work; and, while it impoverishes them by the present expence, disables them from retrieving its ill consequences by subsequent industry.

It might be imagined, my lords, that those who had thus far agreed, would not easily find any occasions of dispute; nor would any man, unacquainted with the motives by which parliamentary debates are too often influenced, suspect that after the pernicious qualities of this liquor, and the general inclination among the people to the immoderate use of it, had been generally admitted, it could be afterwards inquired, whether it ought to be made more common, whether this universal thirst for poison ought to be encouraged by the legislature, and whether a new statute ought to be made to secure drunkards in the gratification of their appetites.

To pretend, my lords, that the design of this Bill is to prevent or diminish the use of spirits, is to trample upon common sense, and to violate the rules of decency as well as of reason. For when did any man hear, that a commodity was prohibited by licensing its sale? or that to offer and refuse is the same action?

It is indeed pleaded, that it will be made dearer by the tax which is proposed, and that the increase of the price will diminish the number of the purchasers; but it is at the same time expected that this tax shall supply the expence of a war on the continent: it is asserted therefore, that the consumption of spirits will be hindered, and yet that it will be such as may be expected to furnish, from a very small tax, a revenue sufficient for the support of armies, for the re-establishment of the Austrian family, and the repressing of the attempts of France.

Surely, my lords, these expectations are not very consistent, nor can it be imagined that they are both formed in the same head, though they may be expressed by the same mouth. It is however some recommendation of a statesman, when of his assertions one can be found reasonable or true; and this praise cannot be denied to our present ministers; for though it is undoubtedly false, that this tax will lessen the consumption of spirits, it is certainly true, that it will produce a very large revenue, a revenue that will not fail but with the people from whose debaucheries it arises.

Our ministers will therefore have the same honour with their predecessors, of having given rise to a new fund, not indeed for the payment of our debts, but for much more valuable purposes, for the exaltation of our hearts under oppression, for the elevation of our spirits amidst miscarriages and disappointments, and for the cheerful support of those debts which we have lost hopes of paying. They are resolved, my lords, that the nation, which nothing can make wise, shall, while they are at its head, at least be merry; and since public happiness is the end of government, they seem to imagine that they shall deserve applause by an expedient which will enable every man to lay his cares asleep, to drown sorrow, and lose in the delights of drunkenness both the public miseries and his own.

Philip Dormer Stanhope, fourth Earl of Chesterfield
The Parliamentary History of England . . .
to the year 1803 . . ., Vol. XII

GIN, TAR-WATER AND THE SPLEEN

THE soul of man was supposed by many ancient sages, to be thrust into the human body as into a prison, for punishment of past offences. But the worst prison is the body of an indolent Epicure, whose blood is inflamed by fermented liquors and high sauces, or render'd putrid, sharp and corrosive, by a stagnation of the animal juices through sloth and indolence; whose membranes are irritated by pungent salts; whose mind is agitated by painful oscillations of the nervous system, and whose nerves are mutually affected by the irregular passions of his mind. This ferment in the animal œconomy darkens and confounds the intellect. It produceth vain terrours and vain conceits, and stimulates the soul with mad desires, which, not being natural, nothing in nature can satisfy. No wonder, therefore, there are so many fine persons of both sexes, shining themselves, and shone on by fortune, who are inwardly miserable and sick of life.

The hardness of stubbed vulgar constitutions, renders them insensible of a thousand things, that fret and gall those delicate people who, as if their skin was peeled off, feel to the quick everything that touches them. The remedy for this exquisite and painful sensibility is commonly sought from fermented, perhaps from distilled, liquors, which render many lives wretched that would otherwise have been only ridiculous. The tender nerves and low spirits of such poor creatures, would be much relieved by the use of Tar-water, which might prolong and cheer their lives. I do therefore recommend to them the use of a cordial, not only safe and innocent, but giving health and spirit as surely as other cordials destroy them.

I do verily think, there is not any other medicine whatsoever so effectual to restore a crazy constitution, and cheer a dreary mind, or so likely to subvert that gloomy empire of the spleen which tyraniseth over the better sort (as they are called) of these free nations; and maketh them, in spite of their liberty and property, more wretched slaves than even the subjects of absolute power, who breathe clear air in a sunny climate. While men of low degree often enjoy a tranquility and content that no advantage of birth or fortune can equal. Such, indeed, was the case, while the rich alone could afford to be debauched; but when even beggars became debauchees, the case was altered. . . .

To prove the destructive effects of such spirits with regard both to the humane species and individuals, we need not go so far as our colonies, or the savage natives of America. Plain proof may be had nearer home. For, albeit there is in every town or district throughout England, some tough dram-drinker, set up as the Devil's decoy, to draw in proselytes; yet the ruined health and morals, and the beggary of such numbers evidently shew that we need no other enemy to compleat our destruction, than this cheap luxury at the lower end of the state, and that a nation lighted up at both ends must soon be consumed.

It is much to be lamented that our Insulars, who act and think so much for themselves, should yet from grossness of air and diet, grow stupid or doat sooner than other people, who by virtue of elastic air, water-drinking, and light food, preserve their faculties to extreme old age; an advantage which may perhaps be approached, if not equalled, even in these regions, by tar-water, temperance and early hours; the last is a sure addition to life, not only in regard of time, which, being taken from sleep, the image of death, is added to the waking hours, but also in regard of longevity and duration in the vulgar sense. I may say too in regard of spirit and vivacity, which, within the same compass of duration, may truly and properly be affirmed to add to man's life: it being manifest, that one man, by a brisker motion of his spirits and succession of his ideas, shall live more in one hour than another in two: and that the quantity of life is to be estimated, not merely from the duration, but also from the intenseness of living. Which intense living, or, if I may so say, lively life, is not more promoted by early hours as a regimen, than by tar-water as a cordial; which acts, not only as a slow medicine, but hath also an immediate and cheerful effect on the spirits.

George Berkeley

*Siris: a chain of Philosophical
Reflexions and Inquiries* (1743)

GOOD FRIDAY REFLECTIONS: DUELLING

ALL Gallantry and Fashion, one would imagine, should rise out of the Religion and Laws of that Nation wherein they prevail; but, alas! in this Kingdom, gay Characters, and those which lead in the Pleasures and Inclinations of the fashionable World, are such as are readiest to practise Crimes the most abhorrent to Nature, and contradictory to our Faith. A Christian and a Gentleman are made inconsistent Appellations of the same Person; you are not to expect eternal Life, if you do not forgive Injuries, and your mortal Life is uncomfortable, if you are not ready to commit a Murder in Resentment for an Affront: For good Sense as well as Religion is so utterly banished the World, that Men glory in their very Passions, and pursue Trifles with the utmost Vengeance; so little do they know that to Forgive is the most arduous Pitch human Nature can arrive at! A Coward has often Fought, a Coward has often Conquered, but *a Coward never Forgave*. The Power of doing that flows from a Strength of Soul conscious of its own Force, whence it draws a certain Safety, which its Enemy is not of Consideration enough to interrupt; for 'tis peculiar in the Make of a brave Man to have his Friends seem much above him, his Enemies much below him.

Yet though the Neglect of our Enemies may, so intense a Forgiveness as the Love of them is not to be in the least accounted for by the force of Constitution, but is a more spiritual and refined Moral, introduced by him who dy'd for those that persecuted him; yet very justly delivered to us, when we consider ourselves Offenders, and to be forgiven on the reasonable Terms of Forgiving; for who can ask what he will not bestow? Especially when that Gift is attended with a Redemption from the cruellest Slavery to the most acceptable Freedom: For when the Mind is in Contemplation of Revenge, all its Thoughts must surely be tortured with the alternate Pangs of Rancour, Envy, Hatred, and Indignation; and they who profess a Sweet in the Enjoyment of it, certainly never felt the consummate Bliss of Reconciliation. At such an Instant the false Ideas we received unravel, and the Shyness, the Distrust, the secret Scorns, and all the base Satisfactions Men had in each other's Faults and Misfortunes, are dispelled, and their souls appear in their native Whiteness, without the least Streak of that Malice or Distaste which sullied them: And perhaps those very Actions, which (when we looked at them in the oblique Glance with which Hatred doth always see Things) were Horrid and Odious, when observed with honest and open Eyes, are Beauteous and Ornamental.

But if Men are averse to us in the most violent Degree, and

we can never bring them to an amicable Temper, then indeed we are to exert an obstinate Opposition to them; and never let the Malice of our Enemies have so effectual an Advantage over us, as to escape our good Will: For the neglected and despised Tenets of Religion are so Generous, and in so Transcendent and Heroic a manner disposed for publick Good, that it is not in a Man's Power to avoid their Influence; for the Christian is as much inclin'd to your Service when your Enemy, as the moral Man when your Friend.

But the Followers of a Crucified Saviour must root out of their Hearts all Sense that there is any thing great and noble in Pride or Haughtiness of Spirit; yet it will be very difficult to fix that Idea in our Souls, except we can think as worthily of our selves, when we practise the contrary Virtues; we must learn, and be convinced, that there is something Sublime and Heroic in true Meekness and Humility, for they arise from a great, not a groveling Idea of things; for as certainly as Pride proceeds from a mean and narrow View of the little Advantages about a Man's self, so Meekness is founded on the extended Contemplation of the Place we bear in the Universe, and a just Observation how little, how empty, how wavering, are our deepest Resolves and Councils. And as (to a well taught Mind) when you've said an haughty and proud Man, you have spoke a narrow Conception, little Spirit, and despicable Carriage; so when you have said a Man is meek and humble, you have acquainted us that such a Person has arrived at the hardest Task in the World, in an universal Observation round him, to be quick to see his own Faults, and other Men's Virtues, and at the Height of pardoning every Man sooner than himself; you have also given us to understand, that to treat him kindly, sincerely, and respectfully, is but a meer Justice to him that is ready to do us the same Offices. This Temper of Soul keeps us always awake to a just Sense of things, teaches us that we are as well a-kin to Worms as to

Angels; and as nothing is above these, so is nothing below those. It keeps our Understanding tight about us, so that all things appear to us great or little, as they are in Nature, and the sight of Heaven, not as they are gilded or sullied by Accident or Fortune.

It were to be wished that all Men of Sense would think it worth their while to reflect upon the Dignity of Christian Virtues, it would possibly enlarge their Souls into such a Contempt of what Fashion and Prejudice have made honourable, that their Duty, Inclination, and Honour would tend the same way, and make all their Lives an uniform act of Religion and Virtue.

As to the great Catastrophe of this Day, on which the Mediator of the World suffered the greatest Indignities and Death itself for the Salvation of Mankind, it would be worth Gentlemens Consideration, whether from his Example it would not be proper to kill all Inclinations to Revenge; and examine whether it would not be expedient to receive new Notions of what is Great and Honourable.

This is necessary against the Day wherein he who died ignominiously for us *shall descend from Heaven to be our Judge, in Majesty and Glory.* How will the Man who shall die by the Sword of Pride and Wrath, and in Contention with his Brother, appear before him, at *whose Presence Nature shall be in an Agony, and the great and glorious Bodies of Light be obscured; when the Sun shall be darkned, the Moon turned into Blood, and all the Powers of Heaven shaken; when the Heavens themselves shall pass away with a great Noise, and the Elements dissolve with fervent Heat; when the Earth also, and all the Works that are therein, shall be burnt up?*

What may justly damp in our Minds the Diabolical Madness, which prompts us to decide our petty Animosities by the Hazard of Eternity, is, that in that one Act the Criminal does not only highly offend, but forces himself into the

Presence of his Judge; that is certainly his Case who dies in a Duel. I cannot but repeat it, He that dies in a Duel knowingly offends God, and in that very Action rushes into his offended Presence. Is it possible for the Heart of Man to conceive a more terrible Image than that of a departed Spirit in this Condition?

Sir Richard Steele
The Guardian (3 April, 1713)

REFLECTIONS ON ASSASSINATION

THE history of Europe, during the 14th and 15th centuries, abounds with detestable instances of this crime. It prevailed chiefly among the French and Scots, between whom there was a close intercourse at that time, and a surprising resemblance in their national characters. In 1407, the only brother of the king of France was murdered publickly in the streets of Paris; and so far was this horrible action from meeting with proper punishment, that an eminent lawyer was allowed to plead in defence of it before the Peers of France, and avowedly to maintain the lawfulness of assassination. In 1417, it required all the eloquence and authority of the famous Gerson, to prevail on the Council of Constance to condemn this proposition, "That there are some cases in which assassination is a virtue more meritorious in a Knight than in a Squire, and more meritorious in a King than in a Knight." The number of eminent persons who were murdered in France and Scotland, on account either of private, or political, or religious quarrels, during the 15th and 16th centuries, is almost incredible. Even after those causes, which first gave rise to this barbarous practice, were removed; after the jurisdiction of Magistrates, and the authority of laws, were better established, and become more universal; after the progress of learning and philosophy had polished the manners, and humanized the minds of men, this crime continued in some degree. It was towards the close of the 17th century before it disappeared in France. The additional vigour, which the royal authority acquired by the accession of James VI to the throne of England, seems to have put a stop to it in Scotland.

The influence, however, of any national custom, both on the understanding and on the heart, and how far it may go towards perverting or extinguishing moral principles of the greatest importance, is remarkable. The authors of those ages have perfectly imbibed the sentiments of their cotemporaries, with regard to assassination; and they, who had leisure to reflect, and to judge, appear to be no more shocked at this crime, than the persons who committed it during the heat and impetuosity of passion. Buchanan describes the murder of Cardinal Beatoun, and of Rizio, without expressing those feelings which are natural to a man, or that indignation which became an historian. Knox, whose mind was fiercer and more unpolished, relates the death of Beatoun and of the Duke of Guise, not only without censure, but with the utmost exultation. On the other hand, the bishop of Ross mentions the assassination of the earl of Murray, with some degree of applause. Blackwood dwells upon it with the most indecent triumph, and ascribes it directly to the hand of God. Lord Ruthven, the principal actor in the conspiracy against Rizio, wrote an account of it some short time before his own death, and in all his long narrative there is not one expression of regret, or one symptom of compunction, for a crime no less dishonourable than barbarous. Morton, equally guilty of the same crime, entertained the same sentiments concerning it; and in his last moments, neither he himself, nor the Ministers who attended him, seem to have considered it as an action which called for repentance; even then he talks of *David's slaughter* as coolly as if it had been an innocent or commendable deed. The vices of another age astonish and shock us; the vices of our own become familiar, and excite little horror.

William Robertson

*The History of Scotland during the reigns of
Queen Mary and of King James VI* (1759)
Text from fourth edition (1761), Vol. I

POLITICAL LYING

... CONCERNING the Τὸ Φοβερὸν he gives several Rules; one of which is, that terrible Objects should not be too frequently shewn to the People, lest they grow familiar. He says, it is absolutely necessary that the People of *England* should be frighted with the *French* King and the *Pretender* once a Year, but, that the Bears should be chain'd up again till that time Twelve-month. The want of Observing this so necessary a Precept, in bringing out the *Raw-head* and *Bloody-bones* upon every trifling Occasion, has produc'd great Indifference in the Vulgar of late Years. As to the Animating or Encouraging Lyes, he gives the following Rules; That they should not far exceed the common degrees of Probability, and that there should be variety of them, and the same Lye not obstinately insisted upon; that the Promissory or Prognosticating Lyes should not be upon short Days, for fear the Authors should have the Shame and Confusion to see themselves speedily contradicted. He examines by these Rules, that well-meant, but unfortunate Lye of the Conquest of *France*, which continued near twenty Years together; but at last, by being too obstinately insisted upon, it was worn threadbare, and became unsuccessful.

As to the Τὸ Τερατῶδες, or the Prodigious, he has little to advise, but that their Comets, Whales and Dragons, should be sizable; their Storms, Tempests, and Earthquakes, without the reach of a Days Journey of a Man and a Horse.

The Seventh Chapter is wholly taken up in an Enquiry, Which of the two Parties are the greatest Artists in *Political Lying*. He owns the *Tories* have been better believed of late; but, that the *Whigs* have much the greater Genius's amongst them. He attributes the late ill Success of the *Whig-Party* to their glutting the Market, and retailing too much of a bad Commodity at once: When there is too great a Quantity of Worms, it is hard to catch Gudgeons. He proposes a Scheme for the Recovery of the Credit of the *Whig-Party*, which indeed seems to be somewhat Chimerical, and does not savour of that sound Judgment the Author has shown in the rest of the Work. It amounts to this, That the Party should agree to vent nothing but Truth for three Months together, which will give them Credit for six Months Lying afterwards. He owns, that he believes it almost impossible to find fit Persons to execute this Scheme. Towards the end of the Chapter, he inveighs severely against the Folly of Parties, in retaining such Scoundrels and Men of Low Genius's to retail their Lyes; such as most of the present News-Writers are, who besides a strong Bent and Inclination towards the Profession, seem to be wholly ignorant in the Rules of *Pseudology*, and not at all qualified for so weighty a Trust.

John Arbuthnot
*Proposals for printing . . . a Treatise of
the Art of Political Lying . . . (1712)*

A TORY APOLOGIA

IN the summer of the year one thousand seven hundred and ten the queen was prevailed upon to change her parliament and her ministry. The intrigue of the earl of OXFORD might facilitate the means, the violent prosecution of SACHEVEREL, and other unpopular measures, might create the occasion, and encourage her in the resolution: but the true original cause was the personal ill-usage which she received in her private life, and in some trifling instances of the exercise of her power; for indulgence in which she would certainly have left the reins of government in those hands, which had held them ever since her accession to the throne.

I am afraid that we came to court in the same dispositions as all parties have done; that the principal spring of our actions was to have the government of the state in our hands; that our principal views were the conservation of this power, great employments to our selves, and great opportunities of rewarding those who had helped to raise us, and of hurting those who stood in opposition to us. It is however true, that with these considerations of private and party interest, there were others intermingled which had for their object the public good of the nation, at least what we took to be such.

We looked on the political principles, which had generally prevailed in our government from the revolution in one thousand six hundred and eighty eight to be destructive of our true interest, to have mingled us too much in the affairs of the continent, to tend to the impoverishing our people, and to the loosening the bands of our constitution in church and state. We supposed the tory party to be the bulk of the landed interest, and to have no contrary influence blended into its composition. We supposed the whigs to be the remains of a party, formed against the ill designs of the court under king CHARLES the second, nursed up into strength and applied to contrary uses by king WILLIAM the third, and yet still so weak as to lean for support on the presbyterians and the other sectaries, on the bank and the other corporations, on the Dutch and the other allies. From hence we judged it to follow, that they had been forced, and must continue so, to render the national interest subservient to the interest of those who lent them an additional strength, without which they could never be the prevalent party. The view, therefore, of those amongst us, who thought in this manner, was to improve the queen's favor, to break the body of the whigs, to render their supports useless to them, and to fill the employments of the kingdom down to the meanest with tories. We imagined that such measures, joined to the advantages of our numbers and our property, would secure us against all attempts during her reign; and that we should soon become too considerable, not to make our terms in all events which might happen afterwards; concerning which, to speak truly, I believe few or none of us had any very settled resolution.

In order to bring these purposes about, I verily think that the persecution of dissenters entered into no man's head. By the bills for preventing occasional conformity and the growth of schism, it was hoped that their sting would be taken away. These bills were thought necessary for our party interest, and besides were deemed neither unreasonable nor unjust. The good of society may require that no person should be deprived of the protection of the government on account of his opinions on religious matters, but it does not follow from hence that men ought to be trusted in any degree with the preservation of the establishment, who must, to be consistent with their principles, endeavour the subversion of what is established. An indulgence to consciences, which the prejudice of education and long habits have rendered scrupulous, may be agreeable to the rules of good policy and of humanity: yet will it hardly follow from hence, that a government is under any obligation to indulge a tenderness of conscience to come; or to connive at the propagating of these prejudices, and at the forming of these habits. The evil effect is without remedy, and may therefore deserve indulgence; but the evil cause is to be prevented, and can, therefore, be intitled to none. Besides this, the bills I am speaking of, rather than to enact anything new, seemed only to enforce the observation of antient laws; which had been judged necessary for the security of the church and state at a time when the memory of the ruin of both, and of the hands by which the ruin had been wrought, was fresh in the minds of men.

The bank, the east-india company, and in general the moneyed interest, had certainly nothing to apprehend like what they feared, or affected to fear from the tories, an entire subversion of their property. Multitudes of our own party would have been wounded by such a blow. The intention of those, who were the warmest, seemed to me to go no farther then restraining their influence on the legislature, and on matters of state; and finding at a proper season means to make them contribute to the support and ease of a government, under which they enjoyed advantages so much greater than the rest of their fellow subjects. . . The proprietor of the land, and the merchant who brought riches home by the returns of foreign trade, had during two wars bore the whole immense load of the national expences; whilst the lender of money who added nothing to the common stock, throve by the public calamity, and contributed not a mite to the public charge.

Henry St John, Viscount Bolingbroke

*A Letter to Sir William Windham written in the Year
one Thousand seven hundred and seventeen . . .* (1753)

SELF-INTEREST AND THE WAR

BUT if all this be true: If, according to what I have affirmed, we began this War contrary to Reason: If, as the other Party themselves, upon all Occasions, acknowledge, the Success we have had was more than we could reasonably expect: If, after all our Success, we have not made that use of it, which in Reason we ought to have done: If we have made weak and foolish Bargains with our Allies, suffered them tamely to break every Article even in those Bargains to our Disadvantage, and allowed them to treat us with Insolence and Contempt, at the very Instant when we were gaining Towns, Provinces, and Kingdoms for them, at the Price of our Ruin, and without any Prospect of Interest to our selves: If we have consumed all our Strength in attacking the Enemy on the strongest side, where (as the old Duke of *Schomberg* expressed it) *to engage with* France, *was to take a Bull by the Horns*; and left wholly unattempted, that part of the War, which could only enable us to continue or to end it. If all this, I say, be our Case, it is a very obvious Question to ask, by what Motives, or what Management, we are thus become the *Dupes* and *Bubbles* of *Europe*? Sure it cannot be owing to the Stupidity arising from the coldness of our Climate, since those among our Allies, who have given us most Reason to complain, are as far removed from the Sun as our selves.

If in laying open the real Causes of our present Misery, I am forced to speak with some Freedom, I think it will require no Apology; Reputation is the smallest Sacrifice Those can make us, who have been the Instruments of our Ruin; because it is That, for which in all Probability they have the least Value. So that in exposing the Actions of such Persons, I cannot be said, properly speaking, to do them an Injury. But as it will be some Satisfaction to the People, to know by whom they have been so long abused; so it may be of great use to us and our Posterity, not to trust the Safety of their Country in the Hands of those, who act by such Principles, and from such Motives.

I have already observed, that when the Counsels of this War were debated in the late King's Time, my Lord G—n[1] was

1. Godolphin.

then so averse from entring into it, that he rather chose to give up his Employment, and tell the King he could serve him no longer. Upon that Prince's Death, although the Grounds of our Quarrel with *France* had received no manner of Addition, yet this Lord thought fit to alter his Sentiments; for the Scene was quite changed; his Lordship, and the Family with whom he was engaged by so complicated an Alliance, were in the highest Credit possible with the Q—n: The Treasurer's Staff was ready for his Lordship, the Duke was to Command the Army, and the Dutchess by her Employments, and the Favour she was possessed of, to be always nearest Her Majesty's Person; by which the whole Power, at Home and Abroad, would be devolved upon that Family. This was a Prospect so very inviting, that, to confess the Truth, it could not be easily withstood by any who have so keen an Appetite for Wealth or Ambition. By an Agreement subsequent to the Grand Alliance, we were to assist the *Dutch* with Forty thousand Men, all to be Commanded by the D. of *M*.[1] So that whether this War were prudently begun or not, it is plain, that the true Spring or Motive of it, was the aggrandizing a particular Family, and in short, a War of the *General* and the *Ministry*, and not of the *Prince* or *People*; since those very Persons were against it when they knew the Power, and consequently the Profit, would be in other Hands.

With these Measures fell in all that Sett of People, who are called the *Monied Men*; such as had raised vast Sums by Trading with Stocks and Funds, and Lending upon great Interest and Præmiums; whose perpetual Harvest is War, and whose beneficial way of Traffick must very much decline by a Peace.

In that whole Chain of Encroachments made upon us by the *Dutch*, which I have above deduced, and under those several gross Impositions from other *Powers*, if any one should ask, why our G—l continued so easy to the last? I know no

1. Duke of Marlborough.

other way so probable, or indeed so charitable to account for it, as by that unmeasurable Love of Wealth, which his best Friends allow to be his predominant Passion. However, I shall wave any thing that is Personal upon this Subject. I shall say nothing of those great Presents made by several Princes, which the Soldiers used to call Winter-Foraging, and said it was better than that of the Summer; of Two and a half *per Cent.* substracted out of all the Subsidies we pay in those Parts, which amounts to no inconsiderable Sum; and lastly, of the grand Perquisites in a long successful War, which are so amicably adjusted between Him and the *States.*

Jonathan Swift
The Conduct of the Allies . . . (1711)
Text from second edition (1711)

WOOD'S HALFPENCE

BUT it is needless to argue any longer. The Matter is come to an Issue. His Majesty, *Pursuant to the Law,* hath left the *Field* open between *Wood* and the Kingdom of *Ireland. Wood* hath Liberty to *Offer* his Coin, and we have *Law, Reason, Liberty,* and *Necessity* to *Refuse* it: A knavish Jockey may ride an old foundred Jade about the Market, but none are obliged to buy it. I hope the Words *Voluntary* and *Willing to receive it* will be understood, and applied in their true natural Meaning, *as commonly understood by* PROTESTANTS. For if a *Fierce Captain* comes to my Shop to buy Six Yards of Scarlet Cloth, followed by a Porter laden with a Sack of *Wood's* Coin upon his Shoulders; if we are agreed about the Price, and my Scarlet lies ready cut upon the Counter; if he then gives me the *Word of Command* to receive my Money in *Wood's* Coin, and calls me a *Disaffected Jacobite Dog* for refusing it; (although I am as loyal a Subject as himself, and *without Hire*) and thereupon seizes my Cloth, leaving me the Price in this Odious Copper, and bids me take my Remedy: In this Case, I shall hardly be brought to think that I am *left to my own Will.* I shall therefore on such Occasions, first order the Porter aforesaid to go off with his Pack; and then see the Money in *Silver* and *Gold* in my Possession before I Cut or Measure my Cloth. But if a *Common Soldier* drinks his Pot first, and then offers Payment in *Wood*'s Half-pence, the *Landlady* may be under some Difficulty: For if she complains to his *Captain* or *Ensign*, they are likewise OFFICERS, included in this general Order for encouraging these Half-pence to pass as CURRENT MONEY. If she goes to a Justice of Peace, he is also an *Officer*; to whom this general Order is directed. I do therefore advise her to follow my Practice, which I have already begun; and be paid for her Goods before she parts with them. However, I should have been content, for some Reasons, that the *Military Gentlemen* had been excepted by Name; because I have heard it said, that their Discipline is best confined within their own District.

His Majesty, in the Conclusion of his Answer to the Address of the House of Lords, against *Wood*'s Coin, is pleased to say; that *He will do every Thing in his Power to the Satisfaction of His People.* It should seem therefore, that the Recalling the Patent is not to be understood as a Thing *in his Power*: But however, since the Law doth not oblige us to receive this Coin; and consequently the Patent leaves it to our voluntary Choice: There is nothing remaining to preserve us from Ruin, but that the whole Kingdom should continue in a firm determinate Resolution never to receive or utter this FATAL *Coin*: After which, let the *Officers* to whom these Orders are directed, (I would willingly except the *Military*) come with their *Exhortations*, their *Arguments*, and their *Eloquence*, to persuade us to find our Interest in our Undoing. Let *Wood* and his *Accomplices* Travel about the Country with *Cart-Loads* of their *Ware*, and see who will take it off their

Hands: There will be no Fear of his being robbed; for a *Highway-Man* would scorn to touch it.

I am only in Pain how the *Commissioners* of the *Revenue* will proceed in this *Juncture*; because I am told they are obliged by Act of Parliament, to take nothing but *Gold* and *Silver* in Payment for His Majesty's *Customs*: And I think they cannot justly offer this Coinage of Mr. *Wood* to others, unless they will be content to receive it themselves.

The Sum of the whole is this. The *Committee advises the King to send immediate Orders to all His Officers here, that* WOOD's *Coin be suffered and permitted without any Let, Suit, Trouble, &c. to pass and be received as* CURRENT MONEY, *by such as shall be* WILLING *to receive the same.* It is probable, that the first *Willing Receivers* may be those who *Must Receive it whether they will or no*, at least under the Penalty of losing an Office. But the *Landed Undepending Men*, the *Merchants*, the *Shop-keepers* and Bulk of the People, I hope, and am almost confident, will never receive it. What must the Consequence be? The Owners will sell it for as much as they can get. *Wood*'s Half-pence will come to be offered for Six a Penny (yet then he will be a sufficient Gainer) and the *Necessary Receivers* will be Losers of Two Thirds in their *Salaries* or *Pay*.

This puts me in Mind of a Passage I was told many Years ago in *England*. At a Quarter-Sessions in *Leicester*, the Justices had wisely decreed to take off a Half-penny in a Quart from the Price of Ale. One of them who came in after the Thing was determined, being informed of what had passed, said thus, *Gentlemen, You have made an Order, that* Ale *should be sold in our County for three Half-pence a Quart: I desire you will now make another to appoint who must drink it, for By* G— I WILL NOT.

I must beg Leave to caution your *Lordships* and *Worships* in one Particular. *Wood* hath graciously promised to *Load* us at present only with Forty thousand Pounds of his Coin, 'till *the Exigencies of the Kingdom require the Rest.* I intreat you will never suffer Mr. *Wood* to be a Judge of your EXIGENCIES. While there is one Piece of Silver or Gold left in the Kingdom, he will call it an EXIGENCY. He will double his present *Quantum* by Stealth as soon as he can: He will pour his own *Raps* and *Counterfeits* upon us: *France* and *Holland* will do the same; nor will our own Coiners at home be behind them: To confirm which, I have now in my Pocket a *Rap* or Counterfeit Half-penny in Imitation of his, but so ill performed, that in my Conscience, I believe, it is not of his Coining....

I am very sensible, that such a Work as I have undertaken, might have worthily employed a much better Pen. But when a House is attempted to be robbed, it often happens that the weakest in the Family, runs first to stop the Door. All the Assistance I had, were some Informations from an *eminent Person*; whereof I am afraid I have spoiled a few, by endeavouring to make them of a Piece with my own Productions; and the rest I was not able to manage: I was in the Case of *David*, who *could not move in the Armour of* Saul; and therefore I rather chose to attack this *uncircumcised Philistine* (*Wood* I mean) *with a Sling and a Stone.* And I may say for *Wood's* Honour, as well as my own, that he resembles *Goliah* in many Circumstances, very applicable to the present Purpose: For *Goliah had a Helmet of* BRASS *upon his Head, and he was armed with a Coat of Mail, and the Weight of the Coat was five Thousand Shekles of* BRASS, *and he had Greaves of* BRASS *upon his Legs, and a Target of* BRASS *between his Shoulders.* In short, he was like Mr. *Wood*, all over BRASS; and *he defied the Armies of the living God.*

Jonathan Swift

Some Observations Upon a Paper, Call'd, The Report. . . Relating to Wood's Half-pence (1724). Text from *Works . . .* (1735), Vol. IV

The King's Speech

This week has given the public the most abandoned instance of ministerial effrontery ever attempted to be imposed on mankind. The *minister's speech* of last Tuesday, is not to be paralleled in the annals of this country. I am in doubt, whether the imposition is greater on the sovereign, or on the nation. Every friend of his country must lament that a prince of so many great and amiable qualities, whom England truly reveres, can be brought to give the sanction of his sacred name to the most odious measures, and to the most unjustifiable, public declarations, from a throne ever renowned for truth, honour, and unsullied virtue. I am sure, all foreigners, especially the king of Prussia, will hold the minister in contempt and abhorrence. He has made our sovereign declare, *My expectations have been fully answered by the happy effects which the several allies of my crown have derived from this salutary measure* of the Definitive Treaty. *The powers at war with my good brother the king of Prussia, have been induced to agree to such terms of accommodation, as that great prince has approved; and the success which has attended my negociation, has necessarily and immediately diffused the blessings of peace through every part of Europe.* The infamous fallacy of this whole sentence is apparent to all mankind: for it is known, that the king of Prussia did not barely *approve*, but absolutely *dictated*, as conqueror, every article of the terms of peace. No advantage of any kind has accrued to that magnanimous prince from *our negociation*, but he was basely deserted by the *Scottish* prime minister of *England*. He was known by every court in Europe to be scarcely on better terms of friendship *here*, than at *Vienna*; and he was betrayed by us in the *treaty of peace*. What a strain of insolence, therefore, is it in a minister to lay claim to what he is conscious all his efforts tended to prevent, and meanly to arrogate to himself a share in the fame and glory of one of the greatest princes the world has ever seen? The king of *Prussia*, however, has gloriously kept *all* his former *conquests*, and stipulated security for all his allies, even for the *elector of Hanover*. I know in what light this great prince is considered in Europe, and in what manner he has been treated here; among other reasons, perhaps, from some contemptuous expressions he may have used of the *Scot*: expressions which are every day ecchoed by the whole body of *Englishmen* through the southern part of this island.

The *Preliminary Articles of Peace* were such as have drawn the contempt of mankind on our wretched negociators. All our most valuable conquests were agreed to be restored, and *the East-india company* would have been infallibly ruined by a single article of this fallacious and baneful negociation. No hireling of the minister has been hardy enough to dispute this; yet the minister himself has made our sovereign declare, *the satisfaction which he felt at the approaching re-establishment of peace upon conditions so honourable to his crowns and so beneficial to his people*. As to the *entire approbation* of parliament, which is so vainly boasted of, the world knows how that was obtained. The large debt on the *Civil List*, already above half a year in arrear, shews pretty clearly the transactions of the winter. It is, however, remarkable, that the minister's speech dwells on the *entire approbation* given by parliament to the *Preliminary Articles*, which I will venture to say, he must by this time be ashamed of; for he has been brought to confess the total want of that knowledge, accuracy and precision, by which such immense advantages both of trade and territory, were sacrificed to our inveterate enemies. These gross blunders are, indeed, in some measure set right by the *Definitive Treaty*; yet, the most important articles, relative to *cessions, commerce*, and the FISHERY remain as they were, with respect to the *French*. The proud and feeble *Spaniard* too does not RENOUNCE, but only DESISTS *from all pretensions, which he may have formed to the right of Fishing – where?* only *about the island of* NEWFOUNDLAND – till a favourable opportunity arises of *insisting* on it, *there as well as elsewhere.*

John Wilkes
The North Briton, No. 45 (23 April, 1763)

TO THE DUKE OF GRAFTON

MY LORD,

The profound Respect I bear to the gracious Prince, who governs this Country with no less Honour to himself than Satisfaction to his Subjects, and who restores you to your Rank under his Standard, will save you from a Multitude of Reproaches. The Attention I should have paid to your Failings is involuntarily attracted to the Hand that rewards them, and though I am not so partial to the Royal Judgment, as to affirm, that the Favour of a King can remove Mountains of Infamy, it serves to lessen at least, for undoubtedly it divides the Burthen. While I remember how much is due to *his* sacred Character, I cannot, with any decent Appearance of Propriety, call you the meanest and the basest Fellow in the Kingdom. I protest, my Lord, I do not think you so. You will have a dangerous Rival, in that kind of fame to which you have hitherto so happily directed your Ambition, as long as there is one Man living who thinks you worthy of his Confidence, and fit to be trusted with any Share in his Government. I confess you have great intrinsic Merit; but take Care you do not value it too highly. Consider how much of it would be lost to the World, if the King had not graciously affixed his Stamp, and given it Currency among his Subjects. If it be true that a virtuous Man, struggling with Adversity, be a Scene worthy of the Gods, the glorious Contention, between you and the best of Princes, deserves a Audience, equally respectable. I think

I already see other Gods rising from the Earth to behold it. But this Language is too mild for the Occasion. The king is determined, that our Abilities shall not be lost to Society. The Perpetration and Description of new Crimes will find Employment for us both. My Lord, if the Persons, who have been loudest in their Professions of Patriotism, had done their Duty to the Public with the same Zeal and Perseverance that I did, I will not assert that government would have recovered its Dignity, but at least our gracious Sovereign must have spared his Subjects this last Insult, which, if there be any Feeling left among us, they will resent more than even the real Injuries they received from every Measure of your Grace's Administration. In vain would he have looked round him for another Character so consummate as yours. Lord Mansfield shrinks from his Principles; – his Ideas of Government perhaps go farther than your own, but his Heart disgraces the Theory of his Understanding. – Charles Fox is yet in blossom; and as for Mr. Wedderburne, there is something about him, which even Treachery cannot trust. For the present therefore, the best of Princes must have contented himself with Lord Sandwich. – You would long since have received your final Dismission and Reward; and I, my Lord, who do not esteem you the more for the high Office you possess, would willingly have followed you to your Retirement. There is surely something singularly benevolent in the Character of our Sovereign. From the moment he ascended the Throne, there is no Crime, of which human Nature is capable, (and I call upon the Recorder to witness it) that has not appeared venial in his sight. With any other Prince, the shameful Desertion of him in the midst of that Distress, which you alone had created, – in the very Crisis of Danger, when he fancied he saw the Throne already surrounded by Men of Virtue and Abilities, would have outweighed the Memory of all your former Services. But his Majesty is full of Justice, and understands the Doctrine of

Compensations. He remembers with Gratitude how soon you had accommodated your Morals to the Necessities of his Service; – how chearfully you had abandoned the Engagements of private Friendship, and renounced the most solemn Professions to the Public. The Sacrifice of Lord Chatham was not lost upon him. Even the Cowardice and Perfidy of deserting him may have done you no Disservice in his Esteem. The Instance was painful, but the Principle might please.

You did not neglect the Magistrate, while you flattered the *Man*. The Expulsion of Mr. Wilkes predetermined in the Cabinet; – the Power of depriving the Subject of his Birthright, attributed to a Resolution of one Branch of the Legislature; – the Constitution impudently invaded by the House of Commons; – the right of defending it treacherously renounced by the House of Lords: – These are the Strokes, my Lord, which, in the present Reign, recommend to Office, and constitute a Minister.

'Junius'

The Publick Advertiser (22 June, 1771)

'You Cannot Conquer America'

From a speech in the House of Lords, 20 November, 1777

My Lords, this ruinous and ignominious situation, where we cannot act with success, nor suffer with honour, calls upon us to remonstrate in the strongest and loudest language of truth, to rescue the ear of Majesty from the delusions which surround it. The desperate state of our arms abroad is in part known: no man thinks more highly of them than I do: I love and honour the English troops: I know their virtues and their valour: I know they can achieve anything except impossibilities; and I know that the conquest of English America is an impossibility. You cannot, I venture to say it, you cannot conquer America. Your armies last war effected everything that could be effected; and what was it? It cost a numerous army, under the command of a most able general, (Sir Jeffery Amherst) now a noble Lord in this House, a long and laborious campaign, to expel 5000 Frenchmen from French America. My lords, you cannot conquer America. What is your present situation there? We do not know the worst; but we know, that in three campaigns we have done nothing and suffered much. Besides the sufferings, perhaps total loss, of the northern force; the best appointed army that ever took the field, commanded by sir William Howe, has retired from the American lines; he was obliged to relinquish his attempt, and with great delay and danger, to adopt a new and distant plan of operations. We shall soon know, and in any event have reason to lament, what may have happened since. As to conquest, therefore, my lords, I repeat, it is impossible. – You may swell every expence, and every effort, still more extravagantly; pile and accumulate every assistance you can buy or borrow; traffic and barter with every little pitiful German prince, that sells and sends his subjects to the shambles of a foreign prince; your efforts are for ever vain and impotent – doubly so from this mercenary aid on which you rely; for it irritates, to an incurable resentment, the minds of your enemies – to over-run them with the mercenary sons of rapine and plunder; devoting them and their possessions to the rapacity of hireling cruelty! If I were an American, as I am an Englishman, while a foreign troop was landed in my country, I never would lay down my arms – never – never – never.

Your own army is infected with the contagion of these illiberal allies. The spirit of plunder and of rapine is gone forth among them. I know it – and, notwithstanding what the noble Earl, who moved the Address, has given as his opinion of our American army, I know from authentic information and the most experienced officers, that our discipline is deeply wounded. Whilst this is notoriously our sinking situation, America grows and flourishes: whilst our strength and discipline are lowered, theirs are rising and improving.

But, my Lords, who is the man, that in addition to these disgraces and mischiefs of our army, has dared to authorise and associate to our arms the tomahawk and scalping-knife of the savage? To call into civilised alliance, the wild and inhuman savage of the woods; to delegate to the merciless Indian the defence of disputed rights, and to wage the horrors of his barbarous war against our brethren? My Lords, these enormities cry aloud for redress and punishment; unless thoroughly done away, it will be a stain on the national character – it is a violation of the Constitution – I believe it is against law. It is not the least of our national misfortunes, that the strength and character of our army are thus impaired; infected with the mercenary spirit of robbery and rapine—familiarised to the horrid scenes of savage cruelty, it can no longer boast of the noble and generous principles which dignify a soldier; no longer sympathise with the dignity of the royal banner, nor feel the pride, pomp, and circumstance of glorious war, "that makes ambition virtue." What makes ambition virtue? – the sense of honour. But is the sense of honour consistent with a spirit of plunder, or the practice of murder? Can it flow from mercenary motives, or can it prompt to cruel deeds? Besides these murderers and plunderers, let me ask our ministers, what other allies have they acquired? What other powers have they associated to their cause? Have they entered into alliance with the king of the gypsies? Nothing, my Lords, is too low or too ludicrous to be consistent with their counsels.

William Pitt, Earl of Chatham
*The Parliamentary History of England . . .
to the year 1803*, Vol. XIX

III

THE WORLD OF IMAGINATION, FEELING AND COMIC INVENTION: FICTION, HISTORICAL AND OCCASIONAL WRITING

LORD FOPPINGTON'S AGREEABLE LIFE

Characters: Lord Foppington, Loveless, Amanda and Berinthia

Aman. Well, I must own I think Books the best Entertainment in the World.

L. Fop. I am so much of your Ladyship's Mind, Madam; that I have a private Gallery (where I walk sometimes) is furnish'd with nothing but Books and Looking-glasses. Madam, I have guilded 'em, and rang'd 'em, so prettily, before Gad, it is the most entertaining thing in the World to walk and look upon 'em.

Aman. Nay, I love a neat Library too; but 'tis, I think, the Inside of a Book shou'd recommend it most to us.

L. Fop. That, I must confess, I am nat altogether so fand of. Far to mind the inside of a Book, is to entertain ones self with the forc'd Product of another man's Brain. Naw I think a Man of Quality and Breeding may be much diverted with the Natural Sprauts of his own. But to say the truth, Madam, let a Man love reading never so well, when once he comes to know this Tawn, he finds so many better ways of passing away the Four and twenty Hours, that 'twere Ten thousand pities he shou'd consume his time in that. Far example, Madam, my Life; my Life, Madam, is a perpetual Stream of Pleasure, that glides thro' such a Variety of Entertainments, I believe the wisest of our Ancestors never had the least Conception of any of 'em.

I rise, Madam, about Ten a-Clock. I don't rise sooner, because 'tis the worst thing in the World for the Complexion; nat that I pretend to be a Beau; but a Man must endeavour to look wholesome, lest he make so nauseous a Figure in the Side-bax, the Ladies should be compelled to turn their Eyes upon the Play. So at Ten o'clack I say I rise. Naw if I find 'tis a good Day, I resalve to take a turn in the Park, and see the fine Women; So huddle on my Cloaths, and get drest by One. If it be nasty Weather, I take a Turn in the Chocolate-hause; where, as you walk, Madam, you have the prettiest Prospect in the World; you have Looking-glasses all around you — But I'm afraid I tire the Company.

Ber. Not at all. Pray go on.

L. Fop. Why then, Ladies, from thence I go to Dinner at *Lacket's*, and there you are so nicely and delicately serv'd that, stap my Vitals, they shall compose you a Dish, no bigger than a Saucer, shall come to Fifty shillings.

Between eating my Dinner, (and washing my Mauth, Ladies) I spend my time, 'till I go to the Play; where, 'till Nine a-Clack, I entertain my self with looking upon the Company; and usually dispose of one Hour more in leading 'em aut. So there's Twelve of the Four and Twenty pretty well over.

The other Twelve, Madam, are dispos'd of in Two Articles: In the first Four, I toast my self drunk, and in t'other Eight I sleep my self sober again. Thus, Ladies, you see my Life is an eternal raund O of Delights.

Lov. 'Tis a heavenly one, indeed!

Aman. But, my Lord, you *Beaux* spend a great deal of your time in Intrigues: You have given us no Account of them yet.

L. Fop. [*aside.*] Soh, she wou'd enquire into my Amours — That's Jealousie — She begins to be in love with me. Why, Madam [*To Aman.*] — as to time for my Intrigues, I usually make Detachments of it from my other Pleasures, according to the Exigency: Far your Ladyship may please to take notice, that those who intrigue with Women of Quality, have rarely occasion far above half an Hour at a time: People of that Rank being under those Decorums, they can seldom give you a langer View, than will just serve to shoot 'em flying. So that the Course of my other Pleasures is not very much interrupted by my Amours.

Lov. But your Lordship now is become a Pillar of the State; you must attend the weighty Affairs of the Nation.

L. Fop. Sir — as to weighty Affairs — I leave them to weighty Heads. I never intend mine shall be a Burthen to my Body.

Lov. O but you'll find the House will expect your Attendance.

L. Fop. Sir you'll find the House will compound for my Appearance.

Lov. But your Friends will take it ill if you don't attend their particular Causes.

L. Fop. Not, Sir, if I come time enough to give 'em my particular Vote.

Ber. But pray, my Lord, how do you dispose of yourself on *Sundays;* for that, methinks, shou'd hang wretchedly on your hands.

L. Fop. Why, Faith, Madam — *Sunday* — is a vile Day, I must confess. I intend to move for leave to bring in a Bill, That the Players may work upon it, as well as the Hackney Coaches. Tho' this I must say for the Government, it leaves us the Churches to entertain us — But then again, they begin so abominable early, a Man must rise by Candle-light to get dress'd by the Psalm.

Ber. Pray which Church does your Lordship most oblige with your Presence?

L. Fop. Oh, St. *James's*, Madam — There's much the best Company.

Aman. Is there good Preaching too?

L. Fop. Why, Faith, Madam — I can't tell. A man must have very little to do there, that can give an Account of the Sermon.

Sir John Vanbrugh
The Relapse; or Virtue in Danger . . . (1697)

Mrs Sullen's Disagreeable Life

A Gallery in Lady Bountyful's *House*
Mrs. Sullen *and* Dorinda *meeting*

Dor. Morrow, my dear Sister; are you for Church this Morning?

Mrs. Sull. Any where to Pray; for Heaven alone can help me: But, I think, *Dorinda*, there's no Form of Prayer in the Liturgy against bad Husbands.

Dor. But there's a Form of Law in *Doctors-Commons*; and I swear, Sister *Sullen*, rather than see you thus continually discontented, I would advise you to apply to that: For besides the part that I bear in your vexatious Broils, as being Sister to the Husband, and Friend to the Wife; your Example gives me such an Impression of Matrimony, that I shall be apt to condemn my Person to a long Vacation all its Life — But supposing, Madam, that you brought it to a Case of Separation, what can you urge against your Husband? My Brother is, first, the most constant Man alive.

Mrs. Sull. The most constant Husband, I grant'ye.

Dor. He never sleeps from you.

Mrs. Sull. No, he always sleeps with me.

Dor. He allows you a Maintenance suitable to your Quality.

Mrs. Sull. A Maintenance! do you take me, Madam, for an hospital Child, that I must sit down, and bless my Benefactors for Meat, Drink and Clothes? As I take it, Madam, I brought your Brother Ten thousand Pounds, out of which, I might expect some pretty things, call'd Pleasures.

Dor. You share in all the Pleasures that the Country affords.

Mrs. Sull. Country Pleasures! Racks and Torments! dost think, Child, that my Limbs were made for leaping of Ditches, and clambring over Stiles; or that my Parents wisely foreseeing my future Happiness in Country-pleasures, had early instructed me in the rural Accomplishments of drinking fat Ale, playing at Whisk, and smoaking Tobacco with my Husband; or of spreading of Plaisters, brewing of Dietdrinks, and stilling Rosemary-Water with the good old Gentlewoman, my Mother-in-Law.

Dor. I'm sorry, Madam, that it is not more in our power to divert you; I cou'd wish indeed that our Entertainments were a little more polite, or your Taste a little less refin'd: But, pray, Madam, how came the Poets and Philosophers that labour'd so much in hunting after Pleasure, to place it at last in a Country Life?

Mrs. Sull. Because they wanted Money, Child, to find out the Pleasures of the Town: Did you ever see a Poet or Philosopher worth Ten thousand Pound; if you can shew me such a Man, I'll lay you Fifty Pound you'll find him somewhere within the weekly Bills — Not that I disapprove rural Pleasures, as the Poets have painted them; in their Landscape every *Phillis* has her *Coridon*, every murmuring Stream, and every flowry Mead gives fresh Alarms to Love — Besides, you'll find, that their Couples were never marry'd: — But yonder I see my *Coridon*, and a sweet Swain it is, Heaven knows. — Come, *Dorinda*, don't be angry, he's my Husband, and your Brother; and between both is he not a sad Brute?

Dor. I have nothing to say to your part of him, you're the best Judge.

Mrs. Sull. O Sister, Sister! if ever you marry, beware of a sullen, silent Sot, one that's always musing, but never thinks: — There's some Diversion in a talking Blockhead; and since a Woman must wear Chains, I wou'd have the Pleasure of hearing 'em rattle a little. — Now you shall see, but take this by the way; — He came home this Morning at his usual Hour of Four, waken'd me out of a sweet Dream of something else, by tumbling over the Tea-table, which he broke all to pieces. After his Man and he had rowl'd about the Room like sick Passengers in a Storm, he comes flounce into Bed, dead as a Salmon into a Fishmonger's Basket; his Feet cold as Ice, his Breath hot as a Furnace, and his Hands and his Face as greasy as his Flanel Night-cap. — Oh Matrimony! — He tosses up the Clothes with a barbarous swing over his Shoulders, disorders the whole Oeconomy of my Bed, leaves me half naked, and my whole Night's Comfort is the tuneable Serenade of that wakeful Nightingale, his Nose. — O the Pleasure of counting the melancholly Clock by a snoring Husband! . . .

George Farquhar
The Beaux Stratagem (1707)

LOVE IN MARRIAGE

My Brother *Tranquillus* being gone out of Town for some Days, my sister *Jenny* sent me Word she would come and dine with me, and therefore desired me to have no other Company. I took Care accordingly, and was not a little pleased to see her enter the Room with a decent and Matron-like Behaviour, which I thought very much became her. I saw she had a great deal to say to me, and easily discovered in her Eyes, and the Air of her Countenance, that she had abundance of Satisfaction in her Heart, which she longed to communicate. However, I was resolved to let her break into her Discourse her own Way, and reduced her to a thousand little Devices and Intimations to bring me to the Mention of her Husband. But finding I was resolved not to name him, she began of her own Accord; My Husband (said she) gives his humble Service to you: To which I only answered, I hope he is well; and without waiting for a Reply, fell into other Subjects. She at last was out of all Patience, and said, (with a Smile and manner that I thought had more Beauty and Spirit than I had ever observed before in her) I did not think, Brother, you had been so ill-natured. You have seen, ever since I came in, that I had a Mind to talk of my Husband, and you won't be so kind as to give me an Occasion. I did not know, (said I) but it might be a disagreeable Subject to you. You do not take me for so old-fashioned a Fellow as to think of entertaining a young lady with the Discourse of her Husband. I know, nothing is more acceptable than to speak of one who is to be so: but to speak of one who is so! Indeed, *Jenny*, I am a better bred Man than you think me. She shewed a little Dislike at my Raillery; and by her bridling up, I perceived she expected to be treated hereafter not as *Jenny Distaff*, but Mrs. *Tranquillus*. I was very well pleased with this Change in her Humour; and upon talking with her on several Subjects, I could not but fancy, that I saw a great deal of her Husband's Way and Manner, in her Remarks, her Phrases, the Tone of her Voice, and the very Air of her Countenance. This gave me an unspeakable Satisfaction, not only because I had found her an Husband from whom she could learn many Things that were laudable, but also because I looked upon her Imitation of him as an infallible Sign that she entirely loved him. This is an Observation that I never knew fail, though I do not remember that any other has made it. The natural Shyness of her Sex hindered her from telling me the greatness of her own Passion; but I easily collected it, from the Representation she gave me of his. I have every Thing, says she, in *Tranquillus* that I can wish for; and enjoy in him (what indeed you have told me were to be met with in a good husband) the Fondness of a Lover, the Tenderness of a Parent, and the Intimacy of a Friend. It transported me to see her Eyes swimming in Tears of Affection when she spoke: And is there not, Dear Sister, said I, more Pleasure in the Possession of such a Man, than in all the little Impertinences of Balls, Assemblies, and Equipage, which it cost me so much pains to make you contemn? She answered, smiling, *Tranquillus* has made me a sincere Convert in a few Weeks, tho' I am afraid you could not have done it in your whole Life. To tell you truly, I have only one Fear hanging upon me, which is apt to give me Trouble in the midst of all my Satisfactions: I am afraid, you must know, that I shall not always make the same amiable Appearance in his Eye that I do at present. You know, Brother *Bickerstaff*, that you have the Reputation of a Conjuror; and if you have any one Secret in your Art to make your Sister always beautiful, I should be happier than if I were Mistress of all the Worlds you have shown me in a Starry Night — *Jenny* (said I) without having Recourse to Magick, I shall give you one plain Rule, that will not fail of making you always amiable to a Man who has so great a Passion for you, and is of so equal and reasonable a Temper as *Tranquillus*. Endeavour to please, and you must please; be always in the same Disposition as you are when you ask for this Secret, and you may take my Word, you will never want it. An inviolable Fidelity, good Humour, and Complacency of Temper, outlive all the Charms of a fine Face, and make the Decays of it invisible.

We discoursed very long upon this Head, which was equally agreeable to us both; for I must confess, (as I tenderly love her) I take as much Pleasure in giving her Instructions for her Welfare, as she her self does in receiving them....

Sir Richard Steele

The Tatler (8 December, 1709). Text
from collected edition (1710)

NEVER MARRY A FOOL

BEFORE I proceed in the History of the Marry'd Part of my Life, you must allow me to give as impartial an Account of my Husband as I have done of myself: He was a jolly, handsome Fellow, as any Woman need wish for a companion; tall, and well made; rather a little too large, but not so as to be ungentile; he danc'd well, which, *I think*, was the first thing that brought us together: He had an old Father who manag'd the Business carefully, so that he had little of that Part lay on him but now-and-then to appear and show himself; and he took the Advantage of it, for he troubl'd himself very little about it, but went Abroad, kept Company, hunted much, and lov'd it exceedingly.

After I have told you that he was a Handsome Man and a good Sportsman, I have indeed, said all; and unhappy was I – like other young People of our Sex, I chose him for being a handsome, jolly Fellow, as I have said; for he was otherwise a weak, empty-headed, untaught Creature as any Woman could ever desire to be coupled with: And here I must take the Liberty, whatever I have to reproach myself with in my after-Conduct, to turn to my Fellow-Creatures, the Young Ladies of this Country, and speak to them by way of Precaution, If you have any Regard to your future Happiness; any View of living comfortably with a Husband; any Hope of preserving your Fortunes, or restoring them after any Disaster, Never, Ladies, marry a Fool; any Husband rather than a Fool; with some other Husbands you may be unhappy, but with a Fool you will be miserable; with another Husband you *may*, I say, be unhappy, but with a Fool you *must*; nay, if he wou'd, he cannot make you easie; everything he does is so awkward, everything is says is so empty, a Woman of any Sence cannot but be surfeited and sick of him twenty times a-Day: What is more shocking, than for a Woman to bring a handsome, comely Fellow of a Husband, into Company, and then be oblig'd to Blush for him every time she hears him speak; To hear other Gentlemen talk Sence and he able to say nothing? And so look like a Fool; or, which is worse, hear him talk Nonsence, and be laugh'd at for a fool.

In the next Place, there are so many Sorts of Fools, such an infinite Variety of Fools, and so hard it is to know the Worst of the Kind, that I am oblig'd to say, No Fool, Ladies, at all, no kind of Fool; whether a mad Fool, or a sober Fool, a wise Fool, or a silly Fool, take anything but a Fool; *nay*, be anything, be even an Old Maid, the worst of Nature's Curses, rather than take up with a Fool.

Daniel Defoe

The Fortunate Mistress . . . (1724)

POLLY'S UNWISE MARRIAGE

Characters: Peachum, Mrs. Peachum, later Polly

Peach. Dear Wife, be a little pacified. Don't let your Passion run away with your Senses. *Polly*, I grant you, hath done a rash thing.

Mrs. Peach. If she had had only an Intrigue with the Fellow, why the very best Families have excus'd and huddled up a Frailty of that sort. 'Tis Marriage, Husband, that makes it a Blemish.

Peach. But Money, Wife, is the true Fuller's Earth for Reputations, there is not a Spot or a Stain but what it can take out. A rich Rogue now-a-days is fit Company for any Gentleman; and the World, my Dear hath not such a Contempt for Roguery as you imagine. I tell you, Wife, I can make this Match turn to our Advantage.

Mrs. Peach. I am very sensible, Husband, that Captain *Macheath* is worth Money, but I am in doubt whether he hath not two or three Wives already, and then if he should dye in a Session or two, *Polly*'s Dower would come into Dispute.

Peach. That, indeed, is a Point which ought to be consider'd.

AIR XI.　A Soldier and a Sailor.

A Fox may steal your Hens, Sir,
A Whore your Health and Pence, Sir,
Your Daughter rob your Chest Sir,
Your Wife may steal your Rest, Sir,
　A Thief your Goods and Plate.

But this is all but picking,
With Rest, Pence, Chest and Chicken;
It ever was decreed, Sir,
If Lawyer's Hand is fee'd, Sir,
　He steals your whole Estate.

The Lawyers are bitter Enemies to those in our Way.

They don't care that any Body should get a Clandestine Livelihood but themselves.

Mrs. Peachum, Peachum, Polly.

Polly. 'Twas only Nimming *Ned.* He brought in a Damask Window-Curtain, a Hoop-Petticoat, a Pair of Silver Candlesticks, a Perriwig, and one Silk Stocking, from the Fire that happen'd last Night.

Peach. There is not a Fellow that is cleverer in his way, and saves more Goods out of the Fire than *Ned.* But now, *Polly,* to your Affair; for Matters must not be left as they are. You are married then, it seems?

Polly. Yes, Sir.

Peach. And how do you propose to live, Child?

Polly. Like other Women, Sir, upon the Industry of my Husband.

Mrs. Peach. What, is the Wench turn'd Fool? A Highwayman's Wife, like a Soldier's hath as little of his Pay, as of his Company.

Peach. And had not you the common Views of a Gentlewoman in your Marriage, *Polly?*

Polly. I don't know what you mean, Sir.

Peach. Of a Jointure, and of being a Widow.

Polly. But I love him, Sir; how then could I have Thoughts of parting with him?

Peach. Parting with him. Why, that is the whole Scheme and Intention of all Marriage Articles. The comfortable estate of Widowhood, is the only Hope that keeps up a Wife's Spirits. Where is the Woman who would scruple to be a Wife, if she had it in her Power to be a Widow whenever she pleas'd? If you have any Views of this sort, *Polly,* I shall think the Match not so very unreasonable.

Polly. How I dread to hear your Advice! Yet I must beg you to explain yourself.

Peach. Secure what he hath got, have him peach'd the next Sessions, and then at once you are made a rich Widow.

Polly. What, murder the Man I love! The Blood runs cold at my Heart with the very Thought of it.

Peach. Fye, *Polly*! What hath Murder to do in the Affair? Since the thing sooner or later must happen, I dare say, the Captain himself would like that we should get the Reward for his Death sooner than a Stranger. Why, *Polly*, the Captain knows, that as 'tis his Employment to rob, so 'tis ours to take Robbers; every Man in his Business. So that there is no Malice in the Case.

Mrs. Peach. Ay, Husband, now you have nick'd the Matter. To have him peach'd is the only thing could ever make me forgive her.

AIR XII.   Now ponder well, ye Parents dear.

> *Polly. Oh, ponder well! be not severe;*
> *So save a wretched Wife!*
> *For on the Rope that hangs my Dear*
> *Depends poor* Polly's *Life.*

Mrs. Peach. But your Duty to your Parents, Hussy, obliges you to hang him. What would many a Wife give for such an Opportunity!

Polly. What is a Jointure, what is Widow-hood to me? I know my Heart. I cannot survive him.

AIR XIII.   Le printempts rappelle aux armes.

> *The Turtle thus with plaintive crying,*
> *Her Lover dying,*
> *The Turtle thus with plaintive crying,*
> *Laments her Dove.*
> *Down she drops quite spent with sighing,*
> *Pair'd in Death, as pair'd in Love.*

Thus, Sir, it will happen to your poor *Polly.*

Mrs. Peach. What, is the Fool in Love in earnest then? I hate thee for being particular: Why, Wench, thou art a Shame to thy very Sex.

Polly. But hear me, Mother. — If you ever lov'd —

Mrs. Peach. Those cursed Play-books she reads have been her Ruin. One Word more, Hussy, and I shall knock your Brains out, if you have any.

Peach. Keep out of the way, *Polly*, for fear of Mischief, and consider of what is propos'd to you.

Mrs. Peach. Away, Hussy. Hang your Husband, and be dutiful.

John Gay
The Beggar's Opera (1728)

A POLITE VISIT

THE next Morning when our Hero waked, he began to think of paying a Visit to Miss *Tishy Snap*; a Woman of great Merit, and of as great Generosity, yet Mr. *Wild* found a Present was ever most welcome to her, as being a Token of Respect in her Lover. He therefore went directly to a Toy-Shop, and there purchased a genteel Snuff-Box, with which he waited upon his Mistress; whom he found in the most beautiful Undress. Her lovely Hair hung wantonly over her Forehead, being neither white with, nor yet free from Powder; a neat double Clout, which seemed to have been worn a few Weeks only, was pinned under her Chin; some Remains of that Art with which Ladies improve Nature, shone on her Cheeks: her Body was loosely attired, without Stays or Jumps; so that her Breasts had uncontrolled Liberty to display their beauteous Orbs, which they did as low as her Girdle; a thin Covering of

Jumps] under-bodice in place of stays

a rumpled Muslin Handkerchief almost hid them from the Eyes, save in a few Parts, where a good-natured Hole gave Opportunity to the naked Breast to appear. Her Gown was a Sattin of a whitish Colour, with about a dozen little Silver Spots upon it, so artificially interwoven at great distance, that they looked as if they had fallen there by Chance. This flying open, discovered a fine yellow Petticoat, beautifully edged round the Bottom with a narrow Piece of half Gold-Lace, which was now almost become Fringe; beneath this appeared another Petticoat stiffened with Whalebone, vulgarly called a Hoop, which hung six Inches at least below the other; and under this again appeared an under Garment of that colour which Ovid intends when he says,

— *Qui color albus erat nunc est contrarius albo.*

She likewise displayed two pretty Feet covered with Silk, and adorned with Lace; and tied, the right with a handsome Piece of blue Ribband; the left, as more unworthy, with a piece of yellow Stuff, which seemed to have been a Strip of her Upper-Petticoat. Such was the lovely Creature whom Mr. *Wild* attended. She received him at first with some of that Coldness, which women of strict Virtue by a commendable, tho' some-times painful Restraint, enjoin themselves to their Lovers. The Snuff-Box being produced, was at first civilly, and indeed, gently refused: but on a second Application accepted. The Tea-Table was soon called for, at which a Discourse passed between these young Lovers, which, could we set it down with any Accuracy, would be very edifying as well as enter-taining to our Reader; let it suffice then that the Wit, together with the Beauty of this young Creature, so inflamed the Passion of *Wild*, which, tho' an honourable Sort of a Passion, was at the same Time so extremely violent, that it transported him to Freedoms too offensive to the nice Chastity of *Lætitia*; who was, to confess the Truth, more indebted to her own

Strength for the Preservation of her Virtue, than to the awful Respect or Backwardness of her Lover: he was indeed so very urgent in his Addresses, that had he not with many Oaths promised her Marriage, we could scarce have been strictly justified in calling his Passion honourable; but he was so remarkably attached to Decency, that he never offered any Violence to a young Lady without the most earnest Promises of that kind, these being, he said, a Ceremonial due to female Modesty, which cost so little, and were so easily pronounced, that the Omission could arise from nothing but the mere Wantonness of Brutality. The lovely *Lætitia*, either out of Prudence, or perhaps Religion, of which she was a liberal Professor, was deaf to all his Promises, and luckily invincible by his Force; for though she had not yet learnt the Art of well clenching her Fist, Nature had not however left her defenceless: for at the ends of her Fingers she wore Arms, which she used with such admirable Dexterity, that the hot Blood of Mr. *Wild* soon began to appear in several little Spots on his Face, and his *fullblown* Cheeks to resemble that Part which Modesty forbids a Boy to turn up any where but in a public School, after some Pedagogue, strong of Arm, hath exercised his Talents thereon. *Wild* now retreated from the Conflict, and the victorious *Lætitia*, with becoming Triumph and noble Spirit, cried out, "D—n your Eyes, if this be your Way of shewing your Love, I'll warrant I gives you enough on't." She then proceeded to talk of her Virtue, which *Wild* bid her carry to the Devil with her; and thus our Lovers parted.

Henry Fielding
The Life of Mr Jonathan Wild the Great, in
Miscellanies, Vol. III (1743). Text from
second edition of the novel (1754)

THE 'GRISSET'

THE PULSE

PARIS

HAIL ye small sweet courtesies of life, for smooth do ye make the road of it! like grace and beauty which beget inclinations to love at first sight; 'tis Ye who open this door, and let the stranger in.

– Pray, Madame, said I, have the goodness to tell me which way I must turn to go to the Opera comique: – Most willingly, Monsieur, said she, laying aside her work –

I had given a cast with my eye into half a dozen shops as I came along in search of a face not likely to be disordered by such an interruption; till at last, this hitting my fancy, I had walk'd in.

She was working a pair of ruffles as she sat in a low chair on the far side of the shop facing the door –

— *Tres voluntieres;* most willingly, said she, laying her work down upon a chair next her, and rising up from the low chair she was sitting in, with so chearful a movement and so chearful a look, that had I been laying out fifty louis d'ors with her, I should have said – "This woman is grateful."

You must turn, Monsieur, said she, going with me to the door of the shop, and pointing the way down the street I was to take – you must turn first to your left hand – *mais prenez garde* – there are two turns; and be so good as to take the second – then go down a little way and you'll see a church, and when you are pass'd it, give yourself the trouble to turn directly to the right, and that will lead you to the foot of the *pont neuf*, which you must cross – and there, any one will do himself the pleasure to shew you –

She repeated her instructions three times over to me with

the same good natur'd patience the third time as the first – and
if *tones and manners* have a meaning, which certainly they have,
unless to hearts which shut them out – she seem'd really interested, that I should not lose myself.

I will not suppose it was the woman's beauty, notwithstanding she was the handsomest grisset, I think, I ever saw, which
had much to do with the sense I had of her courtesy; only I
remember, when I told her how much I was obliged to her,
that I look'd very full in her eyes, – and that I repeated my
thanks as often as she had done her instructions.

I had not got ten paces from the door, before I found I had
forgot every tittle of what she had said – so looking back and
seeing her still standing in the door of the shop as if to look
whether I went right or not – I returned back to ask her
whether the first turn was to my right or left – for that I had
absolutely forgot — Is it possible! said she, half laughing –
'Tis very possible, replied I, when a man is thinking more of
a woman, than of her good advice.

As this was the real truth – she took it, as every woman
takes a matter of right, with a slight courtesy.

— *Attendez*, said she, laying her hand upon my arm to
detain me, whilst she call'd a lad out of the back-shop, to
get ready a parcel of gloves. I am just going to send him, said
she, with a packet into that quarter, and if you will have the
complaisance to step in, it will be ready in a moment, and
he shall attend you to the place. – So I walk'd in with her to
the far side of the shop, and taking up the ruffle in my hand
which she laid upon the chair, as if I had a mind to sit, she sat
down herself in her low chair and I instantly sat myself down
besides her.

– He will be ready, Monsieur, said she, in a moment –
And in that moment, replied I, most willingly would I say
something very civil to you for all these courtesies. Any one
may do a casual act of good nature, but a continuation of

them shews it is a part of the temperature; and certainly, added I, if it is the same blood which comes from the heart, which descends to the extremes (touching her wrist) I am sure you must have one of the best pulses of any woman in the world – Feel it, said she, holding out her arm. So laying down my hat, I took hold of her fingers in one hand, and applied the two fore-fingers of my other to the artery –

– Would to heaven! my dear Eugenius, thou hadst passed by and beheld me sitting in my black coat, and in my lack-a-day-sical manner, counting the throbs of it, one by one, with as much true devotion as if I had been watching the critical ebb or flow of her fever – How wouldst thou have laugh'd and moralized upon my new profession? – and thou shouldst have laugh'd and moralized on — Trust me, my dear Eugenius, I should have said, "there are worse occupations in this world, *than feeling a woman's pulse.*" – But a Grisset's! thou wouldst have said – and in an open shop! Yorick –

– So much the better: for when my views are direct, Eugenius, I care not if all the world saw me feel it.

THE HUSBAND

PARIS

I had counted twenty pulsations, and was going on fast towards the fortieth, when her husband coming unexpected from a back parlour into the shop, put me a little out in my reckoning. – 'Twas no body but her husband, she said – so I began a fresh score – Monsieur is so good, quoth she, as he pass'd by us, as to give himself the trouble of feeling my pulse – The husband took off his hat, and making me a bow, said, I did him too much honour – and having said that, he put on his hat and walk'd out.

Good God! said I to myself, as he went out – and can this man be the husband of this woman?

Let it not torment the few who know what must have been the grounds of this exclamation, if I explain it to those who do not.

In London a shopkeeper and a shopkeeper's wife seem to be one bone and one flesh: in the several endowments of mind and body, sometimes the one, sometimes the other has it, so as in general to be upon a par, and to tally with each other as nearly as man and wife need to do.

In Paris, there are scarce two orders of beings more different: for the legislative and executive powers of the shop not resting in the husband, he seldom comes there – in some dark and dismal room behind, he sits commerceless in his thrum night-cap, the same rough son of Nature that Nature left him.

The genius of a people where nothing but the monarchy is *salique*, having ceded this department, with sundry others, totally to the women – by a continual higgling with customers of all ranks and sizes from morning to night, like so many rough pebbles shook long together in a bag, by amicable collisions, they have worn down their asperities and sharp angles, and not only become round and smooth, but will receive, some of 'em, a polish like a brilliant — Monsieur *le Mari* is little better than the stone under your feet –

– Surely – surely man! it is not good for thee to sit alone – thou wast made for social intercourse and gentle greetings, and this improvement of our natures from it, I appeal to as my evidence.

– And how does it beat, Monsieur? said she. – With all the benignity, said I, looking quietly in her eyes, that I expected – She was going to say something civil in return – but the lad came into the shop with the gloves – *A propos*, said I, I want a couple of pair myself.

THE GLOVES

PARIS

The beautiful Grisset rose up when I said this, and going behind the counter, reach'd down a parcel and untied it: I advanced to the side over against her: they were all too large. The beautiful Grisset measured them one by one across my hand – It would not alter the dimensions – She begg'd I would try a single pair, which seemed to be the least – She held it open – my hand slipp'd into it at once – It will not do, said I, shaking my head a little – No, said she, doing the same thing.

There are certain combined looks of simple subtlety – where whim, and sense, and seriousness, and nonsense, are so blended, that all the languages of Babel set loose together could not express them – they are communicated and caught so instantaneously, that you can scarce say which party is the infecter. I leave it to your men of words to swell pages about it – it is enough in the present to say again, the gloves would not do; so folding our hands within our arms, we both loll'd upon the counter – it was narrow; and there was just room for the parcel to lay between us. –

The beautiful Grisset look'd sometimes at the gloves, then side-ways to the window, then at the gloves – and then at me: I was not disposed to break silence – I followed her example: so I look'd at the gloves, then to the window, then at the gloves, and then at her – and so on alternately.

I found I lost considerably in every attack – she had a quick black eye, and shot through two such long and silken eyelashes with such penetration, that she look'd into my very heart and reins – it may seem strange, but I could actually feel she did –

– It is no matter, said I, taking up a couple of the pairs next me, and putting them into my pocket.

I was sensible the beautiful Grisset had not ask'd above a single livre above the price – I wish'd she had ask'd a livre more, and was puzzling my brains how to bring the matter about — Do you think, my dear Sir, said she, mistaking my embarrassment, that I could ask a *sous* too much of a stranger – and of a stranger whose politeness, more than his want of gloves, has done me the honour to lay himself at my mercy? – *M'en croyez capable?* – Faith! not I, said I; and if you were, you are welcome — So counting the money into her hand, and with a lower bow than one generally makes to a shop-keeper's wife, I went out, and her lad with his parcel followed me.

Laurence Sterne

A Sentimental Journey through France and Italy (1768), Vol. I

SUPERNATURAL MANIFESTATIONS

As it was now evening, the servant, who conducted *Isabella*, bore a torch before her. When they came to *Manfred*, who was walking impatiently about the gallery, he started and said hastily, take away that light and begone. Then shutting the door impetuously, he flung himself upon a bench against the wall, and bad *Isabella* sit by him. She obeyed trembling. I sent for you, Lady, said he, – and then stopped under great appearance of confusion. My Lord! – Yes, I sent for you on a matter of great moment, resumed he, — dry your tears, young Lady – you have lost your bridegroom. – Yes, cruel fate! and I have lost the hopes of my race! – but *Conrad* was not worthy of your beauty – how! my Lord, said *Isabella*; sure you do not suspect me of not feeling the concern I ought: My duty and affection would have always – think no more of him, interrupted *Manfred*; he was a sickly puny child, and heaven has perhaps taken him away, that I might not trust the honours of my house on so frail a foundation. The line of *Manfred* calls for numerous supports. My foolish fondness for that boy blinded the eyes of my prudence – but it is better as it is. I hope in a few years to have reason to rejoice at the death of *Conrad*.

Words cannot paint the astonishment of *Isabella*. At first she apprehended that grief had disordered *Manfred*'s understanding. Her next thought suggested that this strange discourse was designed to ensnare her: She feared that *Manfred* had perceived her indifference for his son: And in consequence of that idea she replied, Good my Lord, do not doubt my tenderness: My heart would have accompanied my hand. *Conrad* would have engrossed all my care; and wherever fate shall dispose of me, I shall always cherish his memory, and regard your Highness and the virtuous *Hippolita* as my Parents. Curse on *Hippolita*! cried *Manfred*: Forget her from this moment as I do. In short, Lady, you have missed a Husband undeserving of your charms: They shall now be better disposed of. Instead of a sickly boy, you shall have a husband in the prime of his age, who will know how to value your beauties, and who may expect a numerous offspring. Alas! My Lord, said *Isabella*, my mind is too sadly engrossed by the recent catastrophe in your family to think of another marriage. If ever my father returns, and it shall be his pleasure, I shall obey, as I did when I consented to give my hand to your son: But until his return, permit me to remain under your hospitable roof, and employ the melancholy hours in asswaging yours, *Hippolita*'s, and the fair *Matilda*'s affliction.

I desired you once before, said *Manfred* angrily, not to name that woman: From this hour she must be a stranger to you, as she must be to me; – in short, *Isabella*, since I cannot give you my son, I offer you myself. – Heavens! cried *Isabella*, waking from her delusion, what do I hear! You! My

Lord! You! My father-in-law! the father of *Conrad*! The husband of the virtuous and tender *Hippolita*! – I tell you, said *Manfred*, imperiously, *Hippolita* is no longer my wife, I divorce her from this hour. Too long has she cursed me by her unfruitfulness; My fate depends on having sons, – and this night I trust will give a new date to my hopes. At those words he seized the cold hand of *Isabella*, who was half dead with fright and horror. She shrieked and started from him. *Manfred* rose to pursue her, when the moon, which was now up and gleamed in at the opposite casement, presented to his sight the plumes of the fatal helmet, which rose to the height of the windows, waving backwards and forwards in a tempestuous manner, and accompanied with a hollow and rustling sound. *Isabella*, who gathered courage from her situation, and who dreaded nothing so much as *Manfred*'s pursuit of his declaration, cried, Look! My Lord; see, heaven itself declares against your impious intentions! – Heaven nor hell shall impede my designs, said *Manfred*, advancing again to seize the Princess. At that instant the portrait of his grandfather, which hung over the bench where they had been sitting, uttered a deep sigh, and heaved its breast. *Isabella*, whose back was turned to the picture, saw not the motion, nor knew whence the sound came, but started, and said, Hark my Lord! What sound was that? and at the same time made towards the door. *Manfred*, distracted between the flight of *Isabella*, who had now reached the stairs, and yet unable to keep his eyes from the picture which began to move, had however advanced some steps after her, still looking backwards on the portrait, when he saw it quit its pannel, and descend on the floor with a grave and melancholy air. Do I dream? cried *Manfred* returning, or are the devils themselves in league against me? speak, infernal spectre! or, if thou art my grandsire, why dost thou too conspire against thy wretched descendant, who too dearly pays for — e'er he could finish the sentence, the vision sighed again, and made a sign to *Manfred* to follow him. Lead on! cried *Manfred*; I will follow thee to the gulph of perdition.

Horace Walpole, fourth Earl of Orford
The Castle of Otranto, a Gothic Story (1764)

CLARISSA'S ORDEAL BEGINS

Miss Clarissa Harlowe, *To Miss* Howe
[*After her Return from her*]

Harlowe-Place, Feb. 20.

I BEG your excuse for not writing sooner. Alas, my dear, I have sad prospects before me! My Brother and Sister have succeeded in all their views. They have found out another Lover for me; an hideous one! – Yet he is encouraged by every-body. No wonder that I was ordered home so suddenly. At an hour's warning! – No other notice, you know, than what was brought with the chariot that was to carry me back. – It was for fear, as I have been informed [an unworthy fear!] that I should have entered into any concert with Mr. Lovelace had I known their motive for commanding me home; apprehending, 'tis evident, that I should dislike the man they had to propose to me.

And well might they apprehend so: – For who do you think he is? – No other than that *Solmes*! – Could you have believed it? – And they are all determined too; my Mother with the rest! – Dear, dear excellence! how could she be thus brought over, when I am assured, that on his first being proposed she was pleased to say, That had Mr. Solmes the *Indies* in possession, and would endow me with them, she should not think him deserving of her Clarissa?

The reception I met with at my return, so different from

what I used to meet with on every little absence (And now I had been from them three weeks) convinced me that I was to suffer for the happiness I had had in your company and conversation for that most agreeable period. I will give you an account of it.

My Brother met me at the door, and gave me his hand when I stepped out of the chariot. He bowed very low; Pray, Miss, favour me. – I thought it in good humour, but found it afterwards mock-respect: And so he led me in great form, I prattling all the way, inquiring of every-body's health (altho' I was so soon to see them, and there was hardly time for answers) into the Great Parlour; where were my Father, Mother, my two Uncles, and Sister.

I was struck all of a heap as soon as I entered, to see a solemnity, which I had been so little used to on the like occasions in the countenance of every dear relation. They all kept their seats. I ran to my Father, and kneeled: Then to my Mother: And met from both a cold salute: From my Father a blessing but half pronounced: My Mother indeed called me Child; but embraced me not with her usual indulgent ardor.

After I had paid my duty to my Uncles, and my compliments to my Sister, which she received with solemn and stiff form, I was bid to sit down. But my heart was full: And I said it became me to stand, if I *could* stand, upon a reception so awful and unusual. I was forced to turn my face from them, and pull out my handkerchief.

My unbrotherly accuser hereupon stood forth, and charged me with having received no less than *five or six visits* at Miss Howe's from the man they had all so much reason to hate [that was the expression]; notwithstanding the commands I had had to the contrary. And he bid me deny it if I could.

I had never been used, I said, to deny the truth; nor would I now. I owned I had in the three weeks passed seen the person I presumed he meant *oftener* than five or six times [Pray hear

me, Brother, said I; for he was going to flame out]. But he
always asked for Mrs. or Miss Howe when he came.

I proceeded, That I had reason to believe, that both Mrs.
Howe and Miss, as matters stood, would much rather have
excused his visits; but they had more than once apologized,
that having not the same reason my Papa had to forbid him
their house, his rank and fortune intitled him to civility.

You see, my dear, I made not the pleas I might have made.

My Brother seemed ready to give a loose to his passion:
My Father put on the countenance which always portends a
gathering storm: My uncles mutteringly whispered: And
my Sister aggravatingly held up her hands. While I begged
to be heard out; – and my Mother said, Let the *child*, that was
her kind word, be heard.

I hoped, I said, there was no harm done: That it became
not me to prescribe to Mrs. or Miss Howe who should be their
visiters: That Mrs. Howe was always diverted with the raillery
that passed between Miss and him: That I had no reason to
challenge *her* guest for *my* visitor, as I should seem to have
done had I refused to go into their company when he was
with them: That I had never seen him out of the presence of
one or both of those Ladies; and had signified to him once, on
his urging for a few moments private conversation with me,
that unless a Reconciliation were effected between my
family and his, he must not expect that I would countenance
his visits, much less give him an opportunity of that sort.

I told them further, That Miss Howe so well understood
my mind, that she never left me a moment while Mr. Lovelace was there: That when he came, if I was not below in the
Parlour, I would not suffer myself to be called to him: Altho'
I thought it would be an affectation which would give him
advantage rather than the contrary, if I had left company
when he came in; or refused to enter into it when I found he
would stay any time.

My Brother heard me out with such a kind of impatience as shewed he was resolved to be dissatisfied with me, say what I would. The rest, as the event has proved, behaved as if they *would* have been satisfied, had they not further points to carry by intimidating me. All this made it evident, as I mentioned above, that they themselves expected not my voluntary compliance; and was a tacit confession of the disagreeableness of the person they had to propose.

I was no sooner silent than my *Brother* swore, altho' in my Father's presence (swore, unchecked either by eye or countenance) That for his part, he would *never* be reconciled to that Libertine. And that he would renounce me for a Sister, if I encouraged the addresses of a man so obnoxious to them all. –

A man who had like to have been my Brother's murderer, my *Sister* said, with a face even bursting with restraint of passion.

The poor Bella has, you know, a plump high-fed face, if I may be allowed the expression. You, I know, will forgive me for this liberty of speech sooner than I can forgive myself: Yet how can one be such a reptile as not to turn when trampled upon!

My Father, with vehemence both of action and voice [my Father has, you know, a terrible voice when he is angry!] told me that I had met with too much indulgence in being allowed to refuse *this* gentleman, and the *other* gentleman; and it was now *his* turn to be obeyed.

Very true, my *Mother* said: – And hoped his will would not now be disputed by a child so favoured.

To shew they were all of a sentiment, my Uncle *Harlowe* said, He hoped his beloved Niece only wanted to know her Father's will, to obey it.

And my Uncle *Antony*, in his rougher manner, added, That surely I would not give them reason to apprehend, that I thought my Grandfather's favour to me had made me independent of them all. – If I did, he would tell me, the Will *could* be set aside, and *should*.

I was astonished, you must needs think. – Whose addresses now, thought I, is this treatment preparative to? – Mr. Wyerley's again? – or whose? And then, as high comparisons, where *self* is concerned, sooner than low, come into young peoples heads: Be it for whom it will, this is wooing as the English did for the heiress of Scotland in the time of Edward the Sixth. But that it could be for Solmes, how should it enter into my head?

I did not know, I said, that I had given occasion for this harshness. I hoped I should always have a just sense of every one's favour to me, superadded to the duty I owed as a Daughter and a Niece: But that I was so much surprised at a reception so unusual and unexpected, that I hoped my Papa and Mamma would give me leave to retire, in order to recollect myself.

No one gainsaying, I made my silent compliments, and withdrew; – leaving my Brother and Sister, as I thought, pleased; and as if they wanted to congratulate each other on having occasioned so severe a beginning to be made with me.

I went up to my chamber, and there with my faithful Hannah deplored the determined face which the new proposal it was plain they had to make me wore.

I had not recovered myself when I was sent for down to Tea. I begged by my maid to be excused attending; but on the repeated command, went down with as much chearfulness as I could assume; and had a new fault to clear myself of: For my Brother, so pregnant a thing is determined ill-will, by intimations equally rude and intelligible, charged my desire of being excused coming down, to Sullens, because a certain person had been spoken against, upon whom, as he supposed, my fancy ran.

I could easily answer you, Sir, said I, as such a reflection deserves: But I forbear. If I do not find a Brother in *you*, you shall have a Sister in *me*.

Pretty meekness! Bella whisperingly said; looking at my Brother, and lifting up her lip in contempt.

He, with an imperious air, bid me *deserve* his Love, and I should be sure to *have* it.

As we sat, my Mother, in her admirable manner, expatiated upon brotherly and sisterly love, indulgently blamed my Brother and Sister for having taken up displeasure too lightly against me; and politically, if I may so say, answered for my obedience to my Father's will. – *Then it would be all well*, my Father was pleased to say: *Then they should doat upon me*, was my Brother's expression; *Love me as well as ever*, was my Sister's: And my Uncles, *That I then should be the pride of their hearts.* – But, alas! what a forfeiture of all these must I make!

This was the reception I had on my return from you.

Mr. Solmes came in before we had done Tea. My Uncle Antony presented him to me, as a gentleman he had a particular friendship for. My Uncle Harlowe in terms equally favourable for him. My Father said, Mr. Solmes is my friend, Clarissa Harlowe. My Mother looked at him, and looked at me, now-and-then, as he sat near me, I thought with concern. – I at *her*, with eyes appealing for pity. At *him*, when I could glance at him, with disgust little short of affrightment. While my Brother and Sister Mr. *Solmes*'d him, and *Sirr*'d him up, at every word. So caressed in short, by all; – yet such a wretch! – But I will at present only add, My humble thanks and duty to your honoured Mother (to whom I will particularly write, to express the grateful Sense I have of her goodness to me); and that I am

> *Your ever obliged,*
> CL. HARLOWE.

> Samuel Richardson
> *Clarissa, or The History of a Young Lady . . . (1747–8)*
> Text from the third edition (1751), Vol. I

A Misunderstanding

Sophia was in her Chamber reading, when her Aunt came in. The Moment she saw Mrs. *Western*, she shut the Book with so much Eagerness, that the good Lady could not forbear asking her, What Book that was which she seemed so much afraid of shewing? 'Upon my Word, Madam,' answered *Sophia*, 'it is a Book which I am neither ashamed nor afraid to own I have read. It is the Production of a young Lady of Fashion, whose good Understanding, I think, doth Honour to her Sex, and whose good Heart is an Honour to Human Nature.' Mrs. *Western* then took up the Book, and immediately after threw it down, saying, — 'Yes, the Author is of a very good Family; but she is not much among People one knows. I have never read it; for the best Judges say, there is not much in it.' 'I dare not, Madam, set up my own Opinion,' says *Sophia*, 'against the best Judges, but there appears to me a great deal of human Nature in it; and in many Parts, so much true Tenderness and Delicacy, that it hath cost me many a Tear.' 'Ay, and do you love to cry then?' says the Aunt. 'I love a tender Sensation,' answered the Niece, 'and would pay the Price of a Tear for it at any time.' 'Well, but shew me,' said the Aunt, 'what you was reading when I came in; there was something very tender in that, I believe, and very loving too. You blush, my dear *Sophia*. Ah! Child, you should read Books, which would teach you a little Hypocrisy, which would instruct you how to hide your Thoughts a little better.' 'I hope, Madam,' answered *Sophia*, 'I have no Thoughts which I ought to be ashamed of discovering.' 'Ashamed! no,' cries the Aunt, 'I don't think you have any Thoughts which you ought to be ashamed of; and yet, Child, you blushed just now when I mentioned the Word *Loving*. Dear *Sophy*, be assured you have not one Thought which I am not well acquainted with; as well, Child, as the *French* are with our Motions, long before we put them in Execution. Did you think, Child, because you have been able to impose upon your Father, that you could impose upon me? Do you imagine I did not know the Reason of your over-acting all that Friendship for Mr. *Blifil* yesterday? I have seen a little too much of the World, to be so deceived. Nay, nay, do not blush again. I tell you it is a Passion you need not be ashamed of. – It is a Passion I myself approve, and have already brought your Father into the Approbation of. Indeed, I solely consider your Inclination; for I would always have that gratified, if possible, though one may sacrifice higher Prospects. Come, I have News which will delight your very Soul. Make me your Confident, and I will undertake you shall be happy to the very Extent of your Wishes.' 'La, Madam,' says *Sophia*, looking more foolishly than ever she did in her Life, 'I know not what to say. – Why, Madam, should you suspect?' – 'Nay, no Dishonesty,' returned Mrs. *Western*. 'Consider, you are speaking to one of your own Sex, to an Aunt, and I hope you are convinced you speak to a Friend. Consider, you are only revealing to me what I know already, and what I plainly saw yesterday through that most artful of all Disguises, which you had put on, and which must have deceived any one who had not perfectly known the World. Lastly, consider it is a Passion which I highly approve.' 'La, Madam,' says *Sophia*, 'you come upon one so unawares, and on a sudden. To be sure, Madam, I am not blind, – and certainly, if it be a Fault to see all human Perfections assembled together. – But is it possible my Father and you, Madam, can see with my Eyes?' 'I tell you,' answered the Aunt, 'we do entirely approve; and this very Afternoon your Father hath appointed for you to receive your Lover.' 'My Father, this Afternoon!' cries *Sophia*, with the Blood starting from her Face. – 'Yes, Child,' said the Aunt, 'this Afternoon. You know the Impetuosity of my Brother's Temper. I acquainted him with the Passion which

I first Discovered in you that Evening when you fainted away in the Field. I saw it in your Fainting. I saw it immediately upon your Recovery. I saw it that Evening at Supper, and the next Morning at Breakfast; (you know, Child, I have seen the World.) Well, I no sooner acquainted my Brother, but he immediately wanted to propose it to *Allworthy*. I proposed it Yesterday, *Allworthy* consented, (as to be sure he must with Joy) and this Afternoon, I tell you, you are to put on all your best Airs.' 'This Afternoon!' cries *Sophia*. 'Dear Aunt, you frighten me out of my Senses.' 'O, my Dear,' said the Aunt, 'you will soon come to yourself again; for he is a charming young Fellow, that's the Truth on't.' 'Nay, I will own,' says *Sophia*, 'I know none with such Perfections. So brave, and yet so gentle; so witty, yet so inoffensive; so humane, so civil, so genteel, so handsome! What signifies his being base born, when compared with such Qualifications as these?' 'Base born! what do you mean?' said the Aunt, 'Mr. *Blifil* base born!' *Sophia* turned instantly pale at this Name, and faintly repeated it. Upon which the Aunt cried, 'Mr. *Blifil*, ay, Mr. *Blifil*, of whom else have we been talking?' 'Good heavens,' answered *Sophia*, ready to sink, 'of Mr. *Jones*, I thought; I am sure I know no other who deserves –' 'I protest,' cries the Aunt, 'you frighten me in your Turn. Is it Mr. *Jones*, and not Mr. *Blifil* who is the Object of your Affection?' 'Mr. *Blifil*,' repeated *Sophia*. 'Sure it is impossible you can be in Earnest; if you are, I am the most miserable Woman alive.' Mrs. *Western* now stood a few Moments silent, while Sparks of fiery Rage flashed from her Eyes. At length, collecting all her Force of Voice, she thundered forth in the following articulate Sounds:

'And is it possible you can think of disgracing your Family by allying yourself to a Bastard? Can the Blood of the *Westerns* submit to such Contamination! If you have not Sense sufficient to restrain such monstrous Inclinations, I

thought the Pride of our Family would have prevented you
from giving the least Encouragement to so base an Affection;
much less did I imagine you would ever have had the Assurance to own it to my Face.'

'Madam,' answered *Sophia*, trembling, 'what I have said
you have extorted from me. I do not remember to have ever
mentioned the Name of Mr. *Jones*, with Approbation, to any
one before; nor should I now, had I not conceived he had had
your Approbation. Whatever were my Thoughts of that
poor unhappy young Man, I intended to have carried them
with me to my Grave. – To that Grave where only now, I
find, I am to seek Repose.' — Here she sunk down in her
Chair, drowned in her Tears, and, in all the moving Silence
of unutterable Grief, presented a Spectacle which must have
affected almost the hardest Heart.

Henry Fielding

The History of Tom Jones, a Foundling (1749)
Text from fourth edition (1750), Vol. II

COMMODORE TRUNNION IS PERSUADED TO MARRY

THE lieutenant, fraught with this piece of intelligence,
watched for an opportunity, and as soon as he perceived the
commodore's features a little unbended from that ferocious
contraction they had retained so long, ventured to inform
him that Pickle's sister lay at the point of death, and that she
had left him a thousand pounds in her will. This piece of news
overwhelmed him with confusion, and Mr. Hatchway im-
puting his silence to remorse, resolved to take advantage of
that favourable moment, and counselled him to go and visit
the poor young woman, who was dying for love of him. But
his admonition happened to be somewhat unseasonable; for

Trunnion no sooner heard him mention the cause of her disorder than his morosity recurring, he burst out into a violent fit of cursing, and forthwith betook himself again to his hammock, where he lay uttering in a low growling tone of voice, a repetition of oaths and imprecations, for the space of four-and-twenty hours, without ceasing. This was a delicious meal to the lieutenant, who eager to inhance the pleasure of the entertainment, and at the same time conduce to the success of the cause he had espoused, invented a stratagem, the execution of which had all the effect he could desire. He prevailed upon Pipes, who was devoted to his service, to get upon the top of the chimney belonging to the commodore's chamber, at midnight, and to lower down by a rope a bunch of stinking whitings, which being performed, he put a speaking-trumpet to his mouth, and hollowed down the vent, in a voice like thunder, "Trunnion! Trunnion! turn out and be spliced, or lie still and be damned." This dreadful note, the terror of which was increased by the silence and darkness of the night, as well as the eccho of the passage through which it was conveyed, no sooner reached the ears of the astonished commodore, than turning his eye towards the place from whence this solemn address seemed to proceed, he beheld a glittering object that vanished in an instant. Just as his superstitious fear had improved the apparation into some supernatural messenger cloathed in shining array, his opinion was confirmed by a sudden explosion, which he took for thunder, though it was no other than the noise of a pistol fired down the chimney by the boatswain's mate, according to the instructions he had received; and he had time enough to descend before he was in any danger of being detected by his commander, who could not for a whole hour recollect himself from the amazement and consternation which had overpowered his faculties.

At length, however, he got up, and rang his bell with great

agitation. He repeated the summons more than once, but no regard being paid to this alarm, his dread returned with double terror, a cold sweat bedewed his limbs, his knees knocked together, his hair bristled up, and the remains of his teeth were shattered to pieces in the convulsive vibrations of his jaws.

In the midst of this agony he made one desperate effort, and bursting open the door of his apartment, bolted into Hatchway's chamber, which happened to be on the same floor. There he found the lieutenant in a counterfeit swoon, who pretended to wake from his trance in an ejaculation of "Lord have mercy upon us!" And being questioned by the terrified commodore with regard to what had happened, assured him he had heard the same voice and clap of thunder by which Trunnion himself had been discomposed.

Pipes, whose turn it was to watch, concurred in giving evidence to the same purpose; and the commodore not only owned that he had heard the voice, but likewise communicated his vision, with all the aggravation which his disturbed fancy suggested.

A consultation immediately ensued, in which Mr. Hatchway very gravely observed, that the finger of God was plainly perceivable in those signals; and that it would be both sinful and foolish to disregard his commands, especially as the match proposed was, in all respects, more advantageous than any that one of his years and infirmities could reasonably expect; declaring that for his own part he would not endanger his soul and body by living one day longer under the same roof with a man who despised the holy will of heaven; and Tom Pipes adhered to the same pious resolution.

Trunnion's perseverance could not resist the number and diversity of considerations that assaulted it; he revolved in silence all the opposite motives that occurred to his reflection; and after having been, to all appearance, bewildered in the labyrinth of his own thoughts, he wiped the sweat from his forehead, and heaving a piteous groan, yielded to their remonstrances in these words: "Well, since it must be so, I think we must e'en grapple. But damn my eyes! 'tis a damned hard case that a fellow of my years should be compell'd, d'ye see, to beat up to windward all the rest of his life, against the current of his own inclination."

This important article being discussed, Mr. Hatchway set out in the morning to visit the despairing shepherdess, and was handsomely rewarded for the enlivening tidings with which he blessed her ears. Sick as she was, she could not help laughing heartily at the contrivance, in consequence of which her swain's assent had been obtained, and gave the lieutenant ten guineas for Tom Pipes in consideration of the part he acted in the farce.

In the afternoon the commodore suffered himself to be conveyed to her apartment, like a felon to execution, and was received by her in a languishing manner and genteel dishabille, accompanied by her sister-in-law; who was, for very obvious reasons, extremely solicitous about her success. Though the lieutenant had tutored him touching his behaviour at this interview, he made a thousand wry faces before he could pronounce the simple salutation of *How 'dye?* to his mistress; and after his counsellor had urged him with twenty or thirty whispers, to each of which he had replied aloud, "Damn your eyes, I won't," he got up, and halting towards the couch on which Mrs. Grizzle reclined, in a state of strange expectation, he seized her hand and pressed it to his lips; but this piece of gallantry he performed in such a reluctant, uncouth, indignant manner, that the nymph had need of all her resolution to endure the compliment without shrinking; and he himself was so disconcerted at what he had done, that he instantly retired to the other end of the room, where he sat silent, and broiled with shame and vexation. Mrs. Pickle, like a sensible matron, quitted the place, on pretence of going to the nursery; and Mr. Hatchway taking the hint, recollected that he had left his tobacco-pouch in the parlour, whither he immediately descended, leaving the two lovers to their mutual endearments. Never had the commodore found himself in such a disagreeable dilemma before. He sat in an agony of suspense, as if he every moment dreaded the dissolution of nature; and the imploring sighs of his future bride added, if possible, to the pangs of his distress. Impatient of his situation, he rolled his eye around in quest of some relief, and unable to contain himself, exclaimed, "Damnation seize the fellow and his pouch too! I believe he has sheered off and left me here in the stays." Mrs. Grizzle, who could not help taking some notice of this manifestation of chagrin, lamented her unhappy fate in being so disagreeable to him, that he could not put up with her company for a few moments without repining; and began in very tender terms to reproach him with his inhumanity and indifference. To this expostulation he replied, "Zounds! what would the woman have? let the parson do his office when he wool, here I am ready to be reeved in the matrimonial block, d'ye see, and damn all nonsensical palaver." So saying, he retreated, leaving his mistress not at all disobliged at his plain dealing.

Tobias Smollett

The Adventures of Peregrine Pickle (1751)
Text from third edition (1765)

HINGES AND HOBBY-HORSES

EVERY day for at least ten years together did my father resolve to have it mended, — 'tis not mended yet; — no family but ours would have borne with it an hour – and what is most astonishing, there was not a subject in the world upon which

my father was so eloquent, as upon that of door-hinges. —
And yet at the same time, he was certainly one of the greatest
bubbles to them, I think, that history can produce: his
rhetoric and conduct were at perpetual handy-cuffs. — Never
did the parlour-door open – but his philosophy or his principles fell a victim to it; — three drops of oyl with a feather,
and a smart stroke of a hammer, had saved his honour for ever.

— Inconsistent soul that man is! – languishing under
wounds, which he has the power to heal! – his whole life
a contradiction to his knowledge! – his reason, that precious
gift of God to him – (instead of pouring in oyl) serving but to
sharpen his sensibilities, — to multiply his pains and render
him more melancholy and uneasy under them! – Poor unhappy creature, that he should do so! — are not the necessary
causes of misery in this life enow, but he must add voluntary
ones to his stock of sorrow; — struggle against evils which
cannot be avoided, and submit to others, which a tenth part
of the trouble they create him, would remove from his heart
for ever?

By all that is good and virtuous, if there are three drops of
oyl to be got, and a hammer to be found within ten miles of
Shandy-Hall – the parlour-door hinge shall be mended this
reign.

*

When corporal *Trim* had brought his two mortars to bear, he
was delighted with his handy-work above measure; and
knowing what a pleasure it would be to his master to see
them, he was not able to resist the desire he had of carrying
them directly into his parlour.

Now next to the moral lesson I had in view in mentioning
the affair of *hinges*, I had a speculative consideration arising
out of it, and it is this.

bubbles] dupes

Had the parlour door open'd and turn'd upon its hinges, as a door should do —

— Or for example, as cleverly as our government has been turning upon its hinges — (that is, in case things have all along gone well with your worship, – otherwise I give up my simile) – in this case, I say, there had been no danger either to master or man, in Corporal *Trim*'s peeping in: the moment he had beheld my father and my uncle *Toby* fast asleep — the respectfulness of his carriage was such, he would have retired as silent as death, and left them both in their arm-chairs, dreaming as happy as he had found them: but the thing was morally speaking so very impracticable, that for the many years in which this hinge was suffered to be out of order, and amongst the hourly grievances my father submitted to upon its account – this was one; that he never folded his arms to take his nap after dinner, but the thoughts of being unavoidably awakened by the first person who should open the door, was always uppermost in his imagination, and so incessantly step'd in betwixt him and the first balmy presage of his repose, as to rob him, as he often declared, of the whole sweets of it.

"*When things move upon bad hinges*, an' please your lordships, *how can it be otherwise?*"

Pray what's the matter? Who is there? cried my father, waking, the moment the door began to creak. — I wish the smith would give a peep at that confounded hinge. — 'Tis nothing, an' please your honour, said *Trim*, but two mortars I am bringing in. — They shan't make a clatter with them here, cried my father hastily. — If Dr. *Slop* has any drugs to pound, let him do it in the kitchen. – May it please your honour, cried *Trim*, they are two mortar-pieces for a siege next summer, which I have been making out of a pair of jack-boots, which *Obadiah* told me your honour had left off wearing. — By Heaven! cried my father, springing out of his chair, as he swore – I have not one appointment belonging to me, which I set so much store by, as I do by these jack-boots — they were our great-grandfather's, brother *Toby* — they were *hereditary*. Then I fear, quoth my uncle *Toby*, *Trim* has cut off the entail. — I have only cut off the tops, an' please your honour, cried *Trim* — I hate *perpetuities* as much as any man alive, cried my father — but these jack-boots, continued he (smiling, though very angry at the same time), have been in the family, brother, ever since the civil wars; — Sir *Roger Shandy* wore them at the battle of *Marston Moor*. — I declare I would not have taken ten pounds for them. — I'll pay you the money, brother *Shandy*, quoth my uncle *Toby*, looking at the two mortars with infinite pleasure, and putting his hand into his breeches pocket as he viewed them — I'll pay you the ten pounds this moment with all my heart and soul. –

Brother *Toby*, replied my father, altering his tone, you care not what money you dissipate and throw away, provided, continued he, 'tis but upon a SIEGE. – Have I not one hundred and twenty pounds a year, besides my half pay? cried my uncle *Toby*. – What is that, replied my father, hastily, – to ten pounds for a pair of jack-boots? – twelve guineas for your *pontoons*? – half as much for your *Dutch* draw-bridge? – to say nothing of the train of little brass-artillery you bespoke last week, with twenty other preparations for the siege of *Messina*: believe me, dear brother *Toby*, continued my father, taking him kindly by the hand – these military operations of yours are above your strength; – you mean well, brother, – but they carry you into greater expences than you were first aware of; – and take my word, — dear *Toby*, they will in the end quite ruin your fortune, and make a beggar of you. — What signifies it if they do, brother, replied my uncle *Toby*, so long as we know 'tis for the good of the nation? –

My father could not help smiling for his soul; – his anger

at the worst was never more than a spark; – and the zeal an[d]
simplicity of *Trim* — and the generous (tho' hobby-horsica[l])
gallantry of my uncle *Toby*, brought him into perfect goo[d]
humour with them in an instant.

Generous souls! – God prosper you both, and your mortar
pieces too, quoth my father to himself!

Laurence Sterne

The Life and Opinions of Tristram Shandy,
Gentleman, Vol. III (1761)

A HOME-COMING

JUST then a woman passed them on the road, and discovere[d]
some signs of wonder at the attitude of Harley, who stood
with his hands folded together, looking with a moistened ey[e]
on the fallen pillars of the hut. He was too much entranced i[n]
thought to observe her at all; but Edwards civilly accosting
her, desired to know, if that had not been the school-house[,]
and how it came into the condition in which they now saw
it? "Alack a day!" said she, "it was the school-house indeed[,]
but to be sure, Sir, the squire has pulled it down, because i[t]
stood in the way of his prospects." — "What! how! prospects! pulled down!" cried Harley. "Yes, to be sure, Sir; an[d]
the green, where the children used to play he has ploughed up[,]
because, he said, they hurt his fence on the other side of it.['']
— "Curses on his narrow heart," cried Harley, "that coul[d]
violate a right so sacred! Heaven blast the wretch!

> "And from his derogate body never spring
>   A babe to honour him!" —

But I need not, Edwards, I need not (recovering himself a[
little), he is cursed enough already: to him the noblest sourc[e]

of happiness is denied; and the cares of his sordid soul shall gnaw it, while thou sittest over a brown crust, smiling on those mangled limbs that have saved thy son and his children!" "If you want any thing with the school-mistress, Sir," said the woman, "I can shew you the way to her house." He followed her without knowing whither he went.

They stopped at the door of a snug habitation, where sat an elderly woman with a boy and a girl before her, each of whom held a supper of bread and milk in their hands. "There, Sir, is the school-mistress." – "Madam," said Harley, "was not an old venerable man school-master here some time ago?" – "Yes, Sir, he was; poor man! the loss of his former school-house, I believe, broke his heart, for he died soon after it was taken down; and as another has not yet been found, I have that charge in the mean time." "And this boy and girl, I presume, are your pupils?" – "Ay, Sir, they are poor orphans, put under my care by the parish; and more promising children I never saw." "Orphans!" said Harley. "Yes, Sir, of honest creditable parents as any in the parish; and it is a shame for some folks to forget their relations, at a time when they have most need to remember them." — "Madam," said Harley, "let us never forget that we are all relations." He kissed the children.

"Their father, Sir," continued she, "was a farmer here in the neighbourhood, and a sober industrious man he was; but nobody can help misfortunes: what with bad crops, and bad debts, which are worse, his affairs went to wreck, and both he and his wife died of broken hearts. And a sweet couple they were, Sir; there was not a properer man to look on in the county than John Edwards, and so indeed were all the Edwardses." "What Edwardses?" cried the old soldier hastily. "The Edwardses of South-hill; and a worthy family they were." – "South-hill!" said he, in languid voice, and fell back into the arms of the astonished Harley. The school-mistress ran for some water, and a smelling-bottle, with the assistance of which they soon recovered the unfortunate Edwards. He stared wildly for some time, then folding his orphan grand-children in his arms, "Oh! my children, my children!" he cried, "have I found you thus? My poor Jack! art thou gone? I thought thou shouldst have carried thy father's grey hairs to the grave! and these little ones" – his tears choaked his utter-ance, and he fell again on the necks of the children.

"My dear old man!" said Harley, "Providence has sent you to relieve them; it will bless me, if I can be the means of assisting you." – "Yes, indeed, Sir," answered the boy; "father, when he was a-dying, bade God bless us; and prayed, that if grandfather lived, he might send him to support us." – "Where did they lay my boy?" said Edwards. – "In the Old Church-yard," replied the woman, "hard by his mother." – "I will show it you," answered the boy; "for I have wept over it many a time, when first I came amongst strange folks." He took the old man's hand, Harley laid hold of his sister's, and they walked in silence to the churchyard.

There was an old stone, with the corner broken off, and some letters, half covered with moss, to denote the names of the dead: there was a cyphered R. E. plainer than the rest: it was the tomb they sought. "Here it is, grandfather," said the boy. Edwards gazed upon it without uttering a word: the girl, who had only sighed before, now wept outright: her brother sobbed, but he stifled his sobbing. "I have told sister," said he, "that she should not take it so to heart; she can knit already, and I shall soon be able to dig: we shall not starve, sister, indeed we shall not, nor shall grandfather neither."— The girl cried afresh; Harley kissed off her tears as they flowed, and wept between every kiss.

Henry Mackenzie
The Man of Feeling (1771)

An Idyllic Community

THE place of our retreat was in a little neighbourhood, consisting of farmers, who tilled their own grounds, and were equal strangers to opulence and poverty. As they had almost all the conveniences of life within themselves, they seldom visited towns or cities in search of superfluity. Remote from the polite, they still retained the primæval simplicity of manners; and frugal by habit, they scarce knew that temperance was a virtue. They wrought with chearfulness on days of labour; but observed festivals as intervals of idleness and pleasure. They kept up the Christmas carol, sent true love-knots on Valentine morning, eat pancakes on Shrove-tide, shewed their wit on the first of April, and religiously cracked nuts on Michaelmas eve. Being apprized of our approach, the whole neighbourhood came out to meet their minister, dressed in their finest cloaths, and preceded by a pipe and tabor: A feast also was provided for our reception, at which we sate cheerfully down; and what the conversation wanted in wit, was made up in laughter.

Our little habitation was situated at the foot of a sloping hill, sheltered with a beautiful underwood behind, and a prattling river before; on one side a meadow, on the other a green. My farm consisted of about twenty acres of excellent land, having given an hundred pound for my predecessor's good-will. Nothing could exceed the neatness of my little enclosures: the elms and hedge-rows appearing with inexpressible beauty. My house consisted of but one story, and was covered with thatch, which gave it an air of great snugness; the walls on the inside were nicely whitewashed, and my daughters undertook to adorn them with pictures of their own designing. Though the same room served us for parlour and kitchen, that only made it the warmer. Besides, as it was kept with the utmost neatness, the dishes, plates, and coppers, being well scoured, and all disposed in bright rows on the shelves, the eye was agreeably relieved, and did not want richer furniture. There were three other apartments, one for my wife and me, another for our two daughters, within our own, and the third, with two beds, for the rest of the children.

The little republic to which I gave laws was regulated in the following manner: by sunrise we all assembled in our common apartment; the fire being previously kindled by the servant. After we had saluted each other with proper ceremony, for I always thought fit to keep up some mechanical forms of good breeding, without which freedom ever destroys friendship, we all bent in gratitude to that Being who gave us another day. This duty being performed, my son and I went to pursue our usual industry abroad, while my wife and daughters employed themselves in providing breakfast, which was always ready at a certain time. I allowed half an hour for this meal, and an hour for dinner; which time was taken up in innocent mirth between my wife and daughters, and in philosophical arguments between my son and me.

As we rose with the sun, so we never pursued our labours after it was gone down, but returned home to the expecting family; where smiling looks, a neat hearth, and pleasant fire, were prepared for our reception. Nor were we without guests: sometimes farmer Flamborough, our talkative neighbour, and often the blind piper, would pay us a visit, and taste our gooseberry wine; for the making of which we had lost neither the receipt nor the reputation. These harmless people had several ways of being good company; while one played, the other would sing some soothing ballad, Johnny Armstrong's last good night, or the cruelty of Barbara Allen. The night was concluded in the manner we began the morning, my youngest boys being appointed to read the lessons of the day, and he that read loudest, distinctest, and best, was to have an halfpenny to put into the poor's box.

Oliver Goldsmith
The Vicar of Wakefield (1766). Text
from second edition (1766)

A Good Priest

Ouranius is a holy Priest, full of the spirit of the Gospel, watching, labouring, and praying for a poor *country village*. Every soul in it is as dear to him as himself; and he loves them all, as he loves himself; because he *prays* for them all, as often as he prays for himself.

If his whole life is one continual exercise of great zeal and labour, hardly ever satisfy'd with any degrees of care and watchfulness, 'tis because he has learn'd the great value of souls, by so often appearing before God, as an *intercessor* for them.

He never thinks he can love, or do enough for his flock; because he never considers them in any other view, than as so many persons, that by receiving the gifts and graces of God, are to become his *hope*, his *joy*, and his *crown of rejoicing*.

He goes about his Parish, and visits every body in it; but visits in the same spirit of piety that he preaches to them; he visits them to encourage their virtues, to assist them with his advice and counsel, to discover their manner of life, and to know the state of their souls, that he may *intercede* with God for them, according to their *particular necessities*.

When *Ouranius* first entered into holy orders, he had a *haughtiness* in his temper, a great *contempt* and *disregard* for all foolish and unreasonable people; but he has *pray'd away* this spirit, and has now the greatest tenderness for the most obstinate sinners; because he is always hoping, that God will sooner or later hear those *prayers* that he makes for their repentance.

The *rudeness*, *ill-nature*, or *perverse* behaviour of any of his flock, used at first to betray him into impatience; but it now raises no other passion in him, than a desire of being upon his knees in prayer to God for them. Thus have his *prayers* for others, *alter'd* and *amended* the state of his own heart.

It would strangely delight you to see with what *spirit* he converses, with what *tenderness* he reproves, with what *affection* he exhorts, and with what *vigor* he preaches; and 'tis all owing to this, because he reproves, exhorts, and preaches to those, for whom he first *prays* to God.

This devotion softens his heart, enlightens his mind, sweetens his temper, and makes every thing that comes from him, instructive, amiable and affecting.

At his first coming to his little *Village*, it was as disagreeable to him as a *prison*, and every day seem'd too tedious to be endured in so retir'd a place. He thought his Parish was too full of *poor* and *mean* people, that were none of them fit for the conversation of a *Gentleman*.

This put him upon a close application to his studies. He kept much at home, writ *notes* upon *Homer* and *Plautus*, and sometimes thought it hard to be called to pray by any poor body, when he was just in the midst of one of *Homer's* battels.

This was his *polite*, or I may rather say, *poor*, *ignorant* turn of mind, before devotion had got the government of his heart.

But now his days are so far from being tedious, or his parish too great a retirement, that he now only wants more time to do that variety of good which his soul thirsts after. The solitude of his little Parish is become matter of great comfort to him, because he hopes that God has plac'd him and his flock there, to make it their way to heaven.

He can now not only converse with, but gladly attend and

wait upon the poorest kind of people. He is now daily watching over the *weak* and *infirm*, humbling himself to perverse, rude, ignorant people, wherever he can find them; and is so far from desiring to be considered as a *Gentleman*, that he desires to be used as the *servant* of all; and in the spirit of his Lord and Master *girds himself*, and is glad to *kneel down* and *wash* any of their *feet*.

He now thinks the poorest creature in his Parish good enough, and great enough, to deserve the humblest attendances, the kindest friendships, the tenderest offices, he can possibly shew them.

He is so far now from wanting agreeable company, that he thinks there is no better conversation in the world, than to be talking with *poor* and *mean* people about the kingdom of Heaven.

William Law
A Serious Call to a Devout and Holy Life (1729)

Mr Barnabas Visits Joseph

Mr. *Barnabas* (for that was the Clergyman's Name) came as soon as sent for; and having first drank a Dish of Tea with the Landlady, and afterwards a Bowl of Punch with the Landlord, he walked up to the Room where *Joseph* lay: but, finding him asleep, returned to take the other Sneaker, which when he had finished, he again crept softly up to the Chamber-Door, and, having opened it, heard the Sick Man talking to himself in the following manner:

"O most adorable *Pamela*, most virtuous Sister! whose Example could alone enable me to withstand all the Temptations of Riches and Beauty, and to preserve my Virtue pure and chaste, for the Arms of my dear *Fanny*, if it had pleased

Heaven that I should ever have come unto them. What Riches, or Honours, or Pleasures can make us amends for the Loss of Innocence? Doth not that alone afford us more Consolation, than all worldly Acquisitions? What but Innocence and Virtue could give any Comfort to such a miserable Wretch as I am? Yet these can make me prefer this sick and painful Bed to all the Pleasures I should have found in my Lady's. These can make me face Death without Fear; and though I love my *Fanny* more than ever Man loved a Woman; these can teach me to resign myself to the Divine Will without repining. O thou delightful charming Creature! if Heaven had indulged thee to my Arms, the poorest, humblest State would have been a Paradise; I could have liv'd with thee in the lowest Cottage, without envying the Palaces, the Dainties, or the Riches of any Man breathing. But I must leave thee, leave thee for ever, my dearest Angel, I must think of another World, and I heartily pray thou may'st meet Comfort in this." – *Barnabas* thought he had heard enough; so down stairs he went, and told *Tow-wouse* he could do his Guest no Service: for that he was very light-headed, and had uttered nothing but a Rhapsody of Nonsense all the time he stayed in the Room.

The Surgeon returned in the Afternoon, and found his Patient in a higher Fever, as he said, than when he left him, though not delirious; for notwithstanding Mr. *Barnabas's* Opinion, he had not been once out of his Senses since his Arrival at the Inn.

Mr. *Barnabas* was again sent for, and with much difficulty prevailed on to make another Visit. As soon as he entered the Room, he told *Joseph*, "He was come to pray by him, and to prepare him for another World: In the first place therefore, he hoped he had repented of all his Sins." *Joseph* answered, "He hoped he had: but there was one thing which he knew not whether he should call a Sin; if it was, he feared he should

die in the Commission of it; and that was, the Regret of parting with a young Woman, whom he loved as tenderly as he
did his Heartstrings." *Barnabas* bad him be assured, that "any
Repining at the Divine Will was one of the greatest Sins he
could commit; that he ought to forget all carnal Affections,
and think of better things." *Joseph* said, "That neither in this
World nor the next, he could forget his *Fanny*, and that the
Thought, however grievous, of parting from her for ever,
was not half so tormenting, as the Fear of what she would
suffer, when she knew his Misfortune." *Barnabas* said, "That
such Fears argued a Diffidence and Despondence very criminal; that he must divest himself of all human Passions, and fix
his Heart above." *Joseph* answered, "That was what he desired
to do, and should be obliged to him, if he would enable him
to accomplish it." *Barnabas* replied, "That must be done by
Grace." *Joseph* besought him to discover how he might attain
it. *Barnabas* answered, "By Prayer and Faith." He then questioned him concerning his Forgiveness of the Thieves. *Joseph*
answered, "He feared, that was more than he could do: for
nothing would give him more Pleasure than to hear they
were taken." "That," cries *Barnabas*, "is for the sake of
Justice." "Yes," said *Joseph*, "but if I was to meet them again,
I am afraid I should attack them, and kill them too, if I could."
"Doubtless," answered *Barnabas*, "it is lawful to kill a Thief:
but can you say, you forgive them as a Christian ought?"
Joseph desired to know what that Forgiveness was. "That is,"
answered *Barnabas*, "to forgive them as – as – it is to forgive
them as – in short, it is to forgive them as a Christian." *Joseph*
replied, "He forgave them as much as he could." "Well,
well," said *Barnabas*, "that will do." He then demanded of
him, "If he remembered any more Sins unrepented of; and if
he did, he desired him to make haste and repent of them as
fast as he could: that they might repeat over a few Prayers
together." *Joseph* answered, "He could not recollect any great

Crimes he had been guilty of, and that those he had committed, he was sincerely sorry for." *Barnabas* said that was enough, and then proceeded to Prayer with all the Expedition he was master of; Some Company then waiting for him below in the Parlour, where the Ingredients for Punch were all in Readiness; but no one would squeeze the Oranges till he came.

Henry Fielding

The History of the Adventures of Joseph Andrews . . . (1742)
Text from fourth edition (1749), Vol. I

A TEST OF FAITH

THE time was now come when they were to attend Mr. Whitfield to Kingswood; where, when they arrived after a sultry walk, they found about ten thousand people assembled; the trees and hedges being lined with spectators. There had been a violent storm of thunder and lightning: but this was dispelled by a single ejaculation; and Providence was pleased so visibly to interpose, in causing the weather to clear up just as he began, that Mr. Whitfield could not avoid taking notice of it in his discourse to the people, and to hint, "that the course of nature had been altered in favour of his harangue." The sun now shone, and all was hushed; and notwithstanding the distance of some part of the audience, they all heard distinctly; for, indeed, the wind was extremely favourable.

Whilst all was thus in a profound calm for near an hour, every one being attentive to the voice of the preacher, on a sudden the skies again grew black, and the assembly was alarmed a second time, by a most tremendous volley of thunder and lightning, and a storm of rain.

A remarkable difference now appeared between the Saints

and the Sinners. Those whom curiosity, or perhaps some less justifiable motive, had brought thither, scampered away with the utmost precipitation, to trees or hedges, or some occasional sheds which had been erected amongst the coal-works, to avoid the impending storm; whilst those who either were, or fancied they were, possessed of true faith, scorned to flinch, or to discover the least regard to their bodies, whilst they were thus refreshing their souls with the heavenly dew of Mr. Whitfield's eloquence.

Mr. Whitfield now very dextrously shifted his discourse to the present occasion, and observed, "that although Providence had, at their first meeting, so miraculously put a stop to the rain; yet he had now, with the same gracious intention, permitted it to rain again, to try the zeal of his audience, and to distinguish his sincere votaries from pretenders and hypocrites; and he did not doubt, but, together with the rain, God would shower down upon them 'the gracious dew of his blessing,' and refresh them with his spirit." And this compliment many of them thought a sufficient consolation for their being wet to the skin.

Richard Graves
The Spiritual Quixote . . . (1773), Vol. II

IN THE TAVERN OF THE ELECT

BEING now well tired with the days Fatigue, our thirsty Veins and drooping Spirits call'd for the assistance of a Cordial Flask. In order to gratifie our craving Appetites with this Refreshment, we stood a while debating what Tavern we should choose to enrich our Minds with unadulterated Juice. My friend recollected a little Sanctified *Aminadab* in *Finch Lane*, whose Purple *Nectar* had acquir'd a Singular Reputation among the Staggering Zealots of the Sober Fraternity, who are allow'd, of late, to be as good Judges of the comfortable Creature, as a *Protestant Priest*, or a *Latitudinarian* Fuddle-Cap, who (as Rooks play) drink Wine on *Sundays*.

To this Salutiferous Fountain of Natures choicest *Juleps*, our inclination led us, tho' we knew the little Ruler of the Mansion intended it chiefly for Watering the Lambs of Grace and not to Succour the Evil Off-spring of a Reprobate Generation.

When we had entred our Land of Promise, which over-flow'd with more Healthful Riches than either Milk or Honey, we found all things were as silent as the Mourning Attendance at a Rich Mans Funeral; no Ringing of *Bar-bell*, Bawling of *Drawers*, or Ratling of *Pot-lidds*: But a general Hush order'd to be kept thro' the whole Family, as a warning to all Tiplers, at their Entrance, how they make a Noise to awake the Spirit, least it move the Masters and Drawers to stand still when you call 'em; and refuse to draw you any more Wine, for fear the Inward Man should break out into open Disorder.

In the Entry we met two or three blushing Saints, who had been holding forth so long over the Glass, that had it not been for their flapping *Umbrella's*, puritanical Coats, and diminutive Cravats, shap'd like the Rose of a Parsons Hatband, I should have taken them by their Scarlet Faces, to be good Christians. They pass'd by us as upright and as stiff, as so many Figures in a *Raree-show*, as if a touch of the Hat, had been committing of Sacrilege, or a Ceremonious Nod, a rank Idolatry.

A Drunken-look'd Drawer, disguis'd in a Sober garb, like a Wolf in Sheeps Clothing, or the Devil in a Fryars Habit, show'd us into the Kitchin, where we told him we were desirous of being, as Crickets covet Ovens for the sake of warmth: Several of Father *Ramseys* slouching Disciples sat hovering over their Half-pints, like so many Coy Gossips over their Quarterns of Brandy, as if they were afraid any body should see 'em; and cast as many froward looks upon us Swords-men, as so many Misers would do upon a couple of spunging Acquaintance; as if they took us for some of the wild *Irish*, that should have Cut their Throats in the beginning of the late Revolution.

However we bid our selves Welcome into their Company; and were forc'd for want of Room, the Kitchen being well fill'd, to mix higgle-de-piggle-de, as the Rooks amongst the Crowes upon the Battlements of a Church-Steeple: They leering at us under their Bongraces, with as much contempt, as so many *Primitive Christians* at a couple of *Pagans*.

We, like true Protestant Topers, who scorn the Hippocrisie of tipling by half pints, as if we Drank rather to wash away our *Sins* than our *Sorows*, appear'd bare-fac'd, call'd for a Quart at once, and soon discover'd our Religion by our Drinking; whilst they, like true Puritans, gifted with abundance of holy cheats, will never be Catch'd over more than half a Pint, tho' they'll drink Twenty at a Sitting.

The Wine prov'd extraordinary, which indeed was no more than we expected, when we found our selves surrounded with so many Spiritual Mumchances, whose Religious looks shew them to be true Lovers of what the Righteous are too apt to esteem as the chiefest Blessing of Providence.

We had not sat long, observing the Humours of the drowthy Saints about us, but several amongst them began to look as chearful, as if they had drown'd the terrible apprehensions of Futurity, and thought no more of Damnation, than a Whore of a Twelve-months standing.

The Drawer now was constantly imploy'd in replenishing their Scanty Measures; for once warm'd, they began to drink so fast, 'twas the Business of one Servant to keep them doing. Notwithstanding their great aversion to external ceremony, one pluck'd off his hat, and ask'd his next Neighbour *What do'st thou think, Friend, this cost me? But before thou tellest me, let me Drink; and I hope thou understand'st my meaning.* This I suppose, was their canting method of paying more than ordinary Veneration to some peculiar Thoughts; which by this stratagem were render'd Intelligible to each other: For I took Notice this Allegorical method of drinking some obliging Health, was observ'd thro' the whole Society, with the reverence of uncover'd Heads, under a crafty pretence of examining into the price of each other's Hat; and when they were desirous to Elevate their Lethargick Spirits with the circulation of a Bumper, one fills it, and offers the prevailing Temptation to his left Hand Companion, in these words, saying, *Friend, does the Spirit move thee to receive the good Creature thus plentifully?* The other replys, *Yea, do thou take and enjoy the fruits of thy own Labour, and by the help of Grace I will drink another as full.* Thus did the liquorish Saints quaff it round as merrily, after their precise and Canting manner, as so many Country Parsons over a Tub of Ale, when freed from the remarks of their censorious Parishoners, till, like reprobate Sinners, who have not the fear of Providence before their Eyes, they were deluded by Satan into a wicked state of Drunkenness.

Edward Ward
The London Spy, IV (February, 1699)

COFFEE HOUSE RUMOURS

WHEN I consider this great City in its several Quarters and Divisions, I look upon it as an Aggregate of various Nations distinguished from each other by their respective Customs, Manners and Interests. The Courts of two Countries do not so much differ from one another, as the Court and City in their peculiar ways of Life and Conversation. In short, the

Inhabitants of St *James*'s, notwithstanding they live under the same Laws, and speak the same Language, are a distinct People from those of *Cheapside*, who are likewise removed from those of the *Temple* on the one side, and those of *Smithfield* on the other, by several Climates and Degrees in their way of Thinking and Conversing together.

For this Reason, when any publick Affair is upon the Anvil, I love to hear the Reflections that arise upon it in the several Districts and Parishes of *London* and *Westminster*, and to ramble up and down a whole Day together, in order to make my self acquainted with the Opinions of my ingenious Countrymen. By this means I know the Faces of all the principal Politicians within the Bills of Mortality; and as every Coffee-house has some particular Statesman belonging to it, who is the Mouth of the Street where he lives, I always take care to place my self near him, in order to know his Judgment on the present Posture of Affairs. The last Progress that I made with this Intention, was about three Months ago, when we had a Current Report of the King of *France*'s Death. As I foresaw this would produce a new Face of things in *Europe*, and many curious Speculations in our *British* Coffee-houses, I was very desirous to learn the Thoughts of our most eminent Politicians on that Occasion.

That I might begin as near the Fountain-head as possible, I first of all called in at St. *James*'s, where I found the whole outward Room in a Buzz of Politics. The Speculations were but very indifferent towards the Door, but grew finer as you advanced to the upper end of the Room, and were so very much improved by a Knot of Theorists, who sate in the inner Room, within the Steams of the Coffee-Pot, that I there heard the whole *Spanish* Monarchy disposed of, and all the Line of *Bourbon* provided for in less than a Quarter of an Hour.

I afterwards called in at *Giles*'s where I saw a Board of *French* Gentlemen sitting upon the Life and Death of their

Grand Monarque. Those among them who had espoused the Wigg Interest, very positively affirmed, that he departed this Life about a Week since, and therefore proceeded without any further Delay to the Release of their Friends on the Gallies, and to their own Re-establishment; but finding they could not agree among themselves, I proceeded on my intended Progress.

Upon my Arrival at *Jenny Man's*, I saw an *alerte* young Fellow that cocked his Hat upon a Friend of his who entered just at the same time with my self, and accosted him after the following manner. Well *Jack*, the old Prig is dead at last. Sharp's the Word. Now or never Boy. Up to the Walls of *Paris* directly. With several other deep Reflections of the same Nature.

I met with very little variation in the Politics between *Charing-Cross* and *Covent-Garden*. And upon my going into *Will's* I found their Discourse was gone off from the Death of the *French* King to that of Monsieur *Boileau, Racine, Corneille*, and several other Poets, whom they regretted on this Occasion, as Persons who would have obliged the World with very noble Elegies on the Death of so great a Prince, and so eminent a Patron of Learning.

At a Coffee-house near the *Temple*, I found a couple of young Gentlemen engaged very smartly in a Dispute on the Succession to the *Spanish* Monarchy. One of them seemed to have been retained as Advocate for the Duke of *Anjou*, the other for his Imperial Majesty. They were both for regulating the Title to that Kingdom by the Statute Laws of *England*; but finding them going out of my Depth I passed forward to *Paul's* Church-yard, where I listned with great Attention to a learned Man, who gave the Company an Account of the deplorable State of *France* during the Minority of the *deceased* King.

I then turned on my right Hand into *Fish-street*, where the chief Politician of that Quarter, upon hearing the News, (after having taken a Pipe of Tobacco, and ruminated for some time) If, says he, the King of *France* is certainly dead, we shall have plenty of Mackerel this Season; our Fishery will not be disturbed by Privateers, as it has been for these ten Years past. He afterwards considered how the Death of this great Man would affect our Pilchards, and by several other Remarks infused a general Joy into his whole Audience.

I afterwards entered a By-Coffee-house that stood at the upper End of a narrow Lane, where I met with a Nonjuror, engaged very warmly with a Laceman who was the great Support of a neighbouring Conventicle. The Matter in Debate was, whether the *late French* King was most like *Augustus Cæsar*, or *Nero*. The Controversie was carried on with great Heat on both sides, and as each of them looked upon me very frequently during the Course of their Debate, I was under some Apprehension that they would appeal to me, and therefore laid down my Penny at the Barr, and made the best of my way to *Cheapside*.

I here gazed upon the Signs for some time before I found one to my Purpose. The first Object I met in the Coffee-room was a Person who expressed a great Grief for the Death of the *French* King; but upon his explaining himself, I found his Sorrow did not arise from the Loss of the Monarch, but for his having sold out of the Bank about three Days before he heard the News of it: Upon which a Haberdasher, who was the Oracle of the Coffee-house, and had his Circle of Admirers about him, called several to witness that he had declared his Opinion above a Week before, that the *French* King was certainly dead; to which he added, that considering the late Advices we had received from *France*, it was impossible that it could be otherwise. As he was laying these together, and dictating to his Hearers with great Authority, there came in a Gentleman from *Garraway's*, who told us that there were several Letters from *France* just come in, with Advice that the King was in good Health, and was gone out a Hunting the very Morning the Post came away: Upon which the Haberdasher stole off his Hat that hung upon a Wooden Pegg by him, and retired to his Shop with great Confusion. This Intelligence put a Stop to my Travels, which I had prosecuted with much Satisfaction; not being a little pleased to hear so many different Opinions upon so great an Event, and to observe how naturally upon such a Piece of News every one is apt to consider it with a regard to his particular Interest and Advantage.

Joseph Addison
The Spectator (12 June, 1712)

THE CITIZEN CONNOISSEUR

Characters: Lord Ogleby, Mr. Sterling, Canton, Mrs. Heidelberg,
Miss Sterling, Fanny

Lord Ogle. Great improvements indeed, Mr. Sterling! wonderful improvements! The four seasons in lead, the flying Mercury, and the basin with Neptune in the middle, are all in the very extreme of fine taste. You have as many rich figures as the man at Hyde Park Corner.

Sterl. The chief pleasure of a country house is to make improvements, you know, my Lord. I spare no expense, not I. – This is quite another-guess sort of a place than it was when I first took it, my Lord. We were surrounded with trees. I cut down above fifty to make the lawn before the house, and let in the wind and the sun – smack-smooth, as you see. – Then I made a green house out of the old laundry, and turned the brew-house into a pinery. – The high octagon summer-house, you see yonder, is raised on the mast of a ship, given me by an East India captain who has turned many a thousand of my money. It commands the whole road. All the coaches and chariots, and chaises, pass and repass under your eye. I'll mount you up there in the afternoon, my Lord. 'Tis the pleasantest place in the world to take a pipe and a bottle – and so you shall say, my Lord.

Lord Ogle. Ay – or a bowl of punch, or a can of flip, Mr. Sterling; for it looks like a cabin in the air. – If flying chairs were in use, the captain might make a voyage to the Indies in it still, if he had but a fair wind.

Canton. Ha! ha! ha! ha!

Mrs. Heidel. My brother's a little comacal in his ideas, my Lord! – But you'll excuse him. – I have a little gothick dairy, fitted up entirely in my own taste. – In the evening I shall hope for the honour of your lordship's company to take a dish of tea there, or a sullabub warm from the cow.

Lord Ogle. I have every moment a fresh opportunity of admiring the elegance of Mrs. Heidelberg – the very flower of delicacy and cream of politeness.

Mrs. Heidel. O my Lord! ⎱
Lord Ogle. O Madam! ⎰ *Leering at each other.*

Sterl. How d'ye like these close walks, my Lord?

Lord Ogle. A most excellent serpentine! It forms a perfect maze, and winds like a true-lover's knot.

Sterl. Ay – here's none of your strait lines here – but all taste – zig zag – crinkum-crankum – in and out – right and left – to and again – twisting and turning like a worm, my Lord!

Lord Ogle. Admirably laid out indeed, Mr. Sterling! one can hardly see an inch beyond one's nose anywhere in these walks. – You are a most excellent economist of your land, and make a little go a great way. – It lies together in as small parcels as if it was placed in pots out at your window in Gracechurch Street.

Canton. Ha! ha! ha! ha!

Lord Ogle. What d'ye laugh at, Canton?

Canton. Ah! que cette similitude est drole! So clever what you say, mi Lor.

Lord Ogle. (to Fanny). You seem mightily engaged, madam. What are those pretty hands so busily employed about?

Fanny. Only making up a nosegay, my Lord! – Will your lordship do me the honour of accepting it?

(*presenting it.*

Lord Ogle. I'll wear it next my heart, madam! – I see the young creature doats on me. (*apart.*

Miss Sterl. Lord, sister! you've loaded his Lordship with a bunch of flowers as big as the cook or the nurse carry to town on Monday morning for a beaupot. – Will your Lordship give me leave to present you with this rose and a sprig of sweet briar?

Lord Ogle. The truest emblems of yourself, Madam! all sweetness and poignancy. – A little jealous, poor soul! (*apart.*

Sterl. Now, my lord, if you please, I'll carry you to see my Ruins.

Mrs. Heidel. You'll absolutely fatigue his lordship with over walking, brother!

Lord Ogle. Not at all, Madam! We're in the Garden of Eden, you know; in the region of perpetual spring, youth, and beauty. (*leering at the women.*

Mrs. Heidel. Quite the man of qualaty, I pertest. (*apart.*

Canton. Take a my arm, mi Lor!

(*Lord Ogleby leans on him.*

Sterl. I'll only show his Lordship my ruins, and the cascade, and the Chinese bridge, and then we'll go in to breakfast.

Lord Ogle. Ruins, did you say, Mr. Sterling?

Sterl. Ay, ruins, my Lord! and they are reckoned very fine ones too. You would think them ready to tumble on your head. It has just cost me a hundred and fifty pounds to put

beaupot] large ornamental vase

my ruins in thorough repair. – This way, if your Lordship pleases.

Lord Ogle. (*going, stops*). What steeple's that we see yonder? the parish church, I suppose.

Sterl. Ha! ha! ha! that's admirable. It is no church at all, my Lord! it is a spire that I have built against a tree, a field or two off, to terminate the prospect. One must always have a church, or an obelisk, or a something, to terminate the prospect, you know. That's a rule in taste, my Lord!

Lord Ogle. Very ingenious, indeed! For my part, I desire no finer prospect, than this I see before me (*leering at the women.*) – Simple, yet varied; bounded, yet extensive. – Get away, Canton! (*pushing away* Canton.) I want no assistance – I'll walk with the ladies.

Sterl. This way, my Lord!

Lord Ogle. Lead on, sir! – We young folks here will follow you. – Madam! – Miss Sterling! – Miss Fanny! I attend you.

      (*Exit after* Sterling, *gallanting the ladies.*

       George Colman and David Garrick
          The Clandestine Marriage (1766)

IN MR CARMINE'S STUDIO

Characters: Mr. Carmine, Mr. Puff, later a Boy and Lady Pentweazel.

Puff. Why, thou Post-painter, thou Dauber, thou execrable White-washer, thou — Sirrah, have you so soon forgot the wretched State, from whence I drag'd you. The first Time I set Eyes on you, Rascal! what was your Occupation then? Scribbling, in scarce legible Letters, Coffee, Tea and Chocolate on a Bawdy-house Window in *Goodman's-fields*.

Carm. The Meanness of my Original demonstrates the Greatness of my Genius.

Puff. Genius! Here's a Dog. Pray, how high did your Genius
soar? To the daubing diabolical Angels for Alehouses,
Dogs with Chains for Tanners Yards, Rounds of Beef and
roasted Pigs for Porridge Island.

Carm. Hannibal *Scratchi* did the same.

Puff. From that contemptible State did not I raise you to the
Cat and *Fiddle* in *Petticoat-lane;* the *Goose* and *Gridiron* in
Paul's Church-yard; the first live Things you ever drew,
Dog....

Enter Boy.

Boy. Sir, my Lady *Pen* —

Carm. Send her to the — Show her up Stairs. Dear *Puff* —

Puff. Oh! Sir, I can be calm; I only wanted to let you see I had
not forgot, tho' perhaps you may.

Carm. Sir, you are very obliging. Well, but now as all is over,
if you will retreat a small Time — Lady *Pentweazel* sits for
her Picture, and she's —

Puff. I have some Business at next Door; I suppose in half an
Hour's Time —

Carm. I shall be at Leisure. Dear *Puff* —

Puff. Dear *Carmine* —   (*Exit Puff.*

Carm. Son of a Whore — Boy, shew the Lady up Stairs.

Enter Lady Pentweazel.

Lady. Fine Pieces! – very likely Pieces! and, indeed, all alike;
Hum! Lady *Fussock* – and, ha! ha! ha! Lady *Glumstead*, by
all that's ugly – Pray now, Mr. *Carmine*, how do you Lim-
ners contrive to overlook the Ugliness, and yet preserve
the Likeness.

Carm. The Art, Madam, may be convey'd in two Words;
where Nature has been severe, we soften; where she has
been kind, we aggravate.

Lady. Very ingenus, and very kind, truly. Well, good Sir, I bring you a Subject that will demand the Whole of the first Part of your Skill; and, if you are at Leisure, you may begin directly.

Carm. Your Ladyship is here a little ungrateful to Nature, and cruel to yourself; even Lady *Pentweazel*'s Enemies (if such there be) must allow she is a fine Woman.

Lady. Oh! your Servant, good Sir. Why I have had my Day, Mr. *Carmine*; I have had my Day.

Carm. And have still, Madam. The only Difference I shall make between what you were, and what you are, will be no more than what *Rubens* has distinguished between *Mary de Medicis* a Virgin and a Regent.

Lady. Mr. *Carmine*, I vow you are a very judicious Person. I was always said to be like that Family. When my Piece was first done, the Limner did me after *Venus de Medicis*, which I suppose might be one of *Mary*'s Sisters; but Things must change; to be sitting for my Picture at this Time of Day; ha! ha! – but my Daughter *Sukey*, you must know, is just married to Mr. Deputy *Dripping*, of *Candlewick-Ward*, and would not be said nay; so it is not so much for the Beauty, as the Similitude. Ha! ha!

Carm. True, Madam; ha! ha! but if I hit the Likeness, I must preserve the Beauty. – Will your Ladyship be seated.

(She sits.

Lady. I have heard, good Sir, that every Body has a more betterer and more worserer Side of the Face than the other – now which will you chuse?

Carm. The right Side, Madam – the left – now, if you please, the full – Your Ladyship's Countenance is so exactly proportion'd, that I must have it all; no Feature can be spar'd.

Lady. When you come to the Eyes, Mr. *Carmine*, let me know, that I may call up a Look.

Carm. Mighty well, Madam – Your Face a little nearer to the

Left, nearer me – your Head more up – Shoulders back – and Chest forward.

Lady. Bless me, Mr. *Carmine*, don't mind my Shape this Bout; for I'm only in Jumps. – Shall I send for my Tabbys?

Carm. No, Madam, we'll supply that for the present – Your Ladyship was just now mentioning a Daughter – is she – your Face a little more towards me – Is she the sole Inheritor of her Mother's Beauty? Or – have you –

Lady. That? ha! ha! ha! – why that's my youngest of all, except *Caleb.* I have had, Mr. *Carmine*, live born, and christen'd – stay – don't let me lye now – One – Two – Three – Four – Five — Then I lay fallow — but the Year after I had Twins — they came in Mr. *Pentweazel's* Sheriffralty; then *Roger*, then *Robin*, then *Reuben* — in short, I have had twenty as fine Babes, as ever trod in Shoe of Leather.

Carm. Upon my Word, Madam, your Ladyship is an admirable Member of the Commonwealth; 'tis a thousand Pities that, like the *Romans*, we have not some Honours to reward such distinguish'd Merit.

Samuel Foote
Taste (1752)

SECOND THOUGHTS

I HAD been now thirteen Days on Shore, and had been eleven Times on Board the Ship; in which Time I had brought away all that one Pair of Hands could well be suppos'd capable to bring, tho' I believe verily, had the calm Weather held, I should have brought away the whole Ship Piece by Piece: But preparing the 12th Time to go on Board, I found the Wind begin to rise; however at low Water I went on Board, and tho' I thought I had rumag'd the Cabbin so effectually,

Jumps] See footnote on p. 160   *Tabbys*] striped or watered silks

as that nothing more could be found, yet I discover'd a Locker with Drawers in it, in one of which I found two or three Razors, and one Pair of large Sizzers, with some ten or a Dozen of good Knives and Forks; in another I found about Thirty six Pounds value in Money, some *European* Coin, some *Brasil*, some Pieces of Eight, some Gold, some Silver.

I smil'd to my self at the Sight of this Money, O Drug! Said I aloud, what art thou good for, Thou art not worth to me, no not the taking off of the Ground, one of those Knives is worth all this Heap, I have no Manner of use for thee, e'en remain where thou art, and go to the Bottom as a Creature whose Life is not worth saving. However, upon Second Thoughts, I took it away, and wrapping all this in a Piece of Canvas, I began to think of making another Raft....

Daniel Defoe

The Life and Strange Surprizing Adventures
of Robinson Crusoe . . . (1719)

MOLL BECOMES A THIEF

FOR a little Relief I had put off my House and took Lodgings, and as I was reducing my Living so, I sold off most of my Goods, which put a little Money in my Pocket, and I liv'd near a Year upon that, spending very sparingly, and eeking things out to the utmost; but still when I look'd before me, my Heart would sink within me at the inevitable approach of Misery and Want: O let none read this part without seriously reflecting on the Circumstances of a desolate State, and how they would grapple with want of Friends and want of Bread; it will certainly make them think not of sparing what they have only, but of looking up to Heaven for support, and of the wise Man's Prayer, *Give me not Poverty least I steal.*

Let 'em remember that a time of Distress, is a time of dreadful Temptation, and all the Strength to resist is taken away; Poverty presses, the Soul is made Desparate by Distress, and what can be done? It was one Evening, when being brought, as I may say, to the last Gasp, I think I may truly say I was Distracted and Raving, when prompted by I know not what Spirit, and as it were, doing I did not know what, or why; I dress'd me, for I had still pretty good Cloaths, and went out: I am very sure I had no manner of Design in my Head, when I went out, I neither knew or consider'd where to go, or on what Business; but as the Devil carried me out, and laid his Bait for me, so he brought me to be sure to the place, for I knew not whether I was going or what I did.

Wandring thus about I knew not whether, I pass'd by an Apothecary's Shop in *Leadenhall-street*, where I saw lye on a Stool just before the Compter a little Bundle wrapt in a white Cloth, beyond it stood a Maid Servant with her Back to it, looking up towards the top of the Shop, where the Apothecary's Apprentice, as I suppose, was standing up on the Compter, with his Back also to the Door, and a Candle in his Hand, looking and reaching up to the upper Shelf, for something he wanted, so that both were engag'd, and no Body else in the Shop.

This was the Bait; and the Devil who laid the Snare, prompted me, as if he had spoke, for I remember, and shall never forget it, 'twas like a Voice spoken over my Shoulder, take the Bundle; be quick; do it this Moment; it was no sooner said but I step'd into the Shop, and with my Back to the Wench, as if I had stood up for a Cart that was going by, I put my Hand behind me and took the Bundle, and went off with it, the Maid or Fellow not perceiving me, or any one else.

It is impossible to express the Horror of my Soul all the while I did it. When I went away I had no Heart to run, or scarce to mend my pace; I cross'd the Street indeed, and went down the first turning I came to, and I think it was a Street that went thro' into *Fenchurch-street*, from thence I crossed and turn'd thro' so many ways and turnings, that I could never tell which way it was, nor where I went. I felt not the Ground I stept on, and the farther I was out of Danger, the faster I went, till tyr'd and out of Breath, I was forc'd to sit down on a little Bench at a Door, and then found I was got into *Thames-street*, near *Billingsgate*: I rested me a little and went on, my Blood was all in a Fire, my Heart beat as if I was in a sudden Fright: In short, I was under such a Surprize that I knew not whether I was a going, or what to do.

After I had tyr'd my self thus with walking a long way about, and so eagerly, I began to consider and make home to my Lodging, where I came about Nine a Clock at Night.

What the Bundle was made up for, or on what Occasion laid where I found it, I knew not, but when I came to open it, I found there was a Suit of Child-bed Linnen in it, very good and almost new, the Lace very fine; there was a Silver Porringer of a Pint, a small Silver Mug and Six Spoons, with some other Linnen, a good Smock, and Three Silk Hand-kerchiefs, and in the Mug in a Paper, Eighteen Shillings and Six-pence in Money.

All the while I was opening these things I was under such dreadful Impressions of Fear, and in such Terror of Mind, tho' I was perfectly safe, that I cannot express the manner of it; I sat me down and cried most vehemently: Lord, *said I*, what am I now? a Thief! why I shall be taken next time and be carried to *Newgate* and be Try'd for my Life! and with that I cry'd again a long time, and I am sure, as poor as I was, if I had durst for fear, I would certainly have carried the Things back again; but that went off after a while: Well, I went to Bed for that Night, but slept little, the Horror of the Fact was upon my Mind, and I knew not what I said or did all

Night, and all the next Day: Then I was impatient to hear some News of the Loss; and would fain know how it was, whether they were a Poor Bodies Goods, or a Rich; perhaps, *said I*, it may be some poor Widow like me, that had pack'd up these Goods to go and sell them for a little Bread for herself and a poor Child, and are now starving and breaking their Hearts, for want of that little they would have fetch'd, and this Thought tormented me worse than all the rest, for three or four Days.

But my own Distresses silenc'd all these Reflections, and the prospect of my own Starving, which grew every Day more frightful to me, harden'd my Heart by degrees; it was then particularly heavy upon my Mind, that I had been reform'd and had, as I hop'd, repented of all my pass'd wickednesses; that I had liv'd a sober, grave, retir'd Life for several Years, but now I should be driven by the dreadful Necessity of my Circumstances to the Gates of Destruction, Soul and Body; and two or three times I fell upon my Knees, praying to God, as well as I could, for Deliverance; but I cannot but say, my Prayers had no hope in them; I knew not what to do, it was all Fear without, and Dark within; and I reflected on my pass'd Life as not repented of, that Heaven was now beginning to punish me, and would make me as miserable as I had been wicked.

Had I gone on here I had perhaps been a true Penitent; but I had an evil Counsellor within, and he was continually prompting me to relieve my self by the worst means; so one Evening he tempted me again by the same wicked Impulse that had said, *take that Bundle*, to go out again and seek for what might happen.

I went out now by Day-light, and wandred about I knew not whether, and in search of I knew not what, when the Devil put a Snare in my way of a dreadful Nature indeed, and such a one as I have never had before or since; going thro'

Aldersgate-street, there was a pretty little Child had been at a Dancing-School, and was a going home all alone, and my Prompter, like a true Devil, set me upon this innocent Creature; I talk'd to it, and it prattl'd to me again, and I took it by the Hand and led it a long till I came to a pav'd Alley that goes into *Bartholomew-Close*, and I led it in there; the Child said that was not its way home; I said, yes, my Dear, it is, I'll show you the way home; the Child had a little Necklace on of Gold Beads, and I had my Eye upon that, and in the dark of the Alley I stoop'd, pretending to mend the Child's Clog that was loose, and took off her Necklace, and the Child never felt it, and so led the Child on again: Here, I say, the Devil put me upon killing the Child in the dark Alley, that it might not Cry, but the very thought frighted me so that I was ready to drop down, but I turn'd the Child about and bad it go back again, for that was not its way home; the Child said so she would, and I went thro' into *Bartholomew-Close*, and then turn'd round to another Passage that goes into *Long-lane*, so away into *Charterhouse-Yard*, and out into *St. John's-street*; then crossing into *Smithfield*, went down *Chick-lane*, and into *Field-lane*, to *Holbourn-bridge*, when mixing with the Crowd of People usually passing there, it was not possible to have been found out; and thus I made my second Sally into the World.

The thoughts of this Booty put out all the thoughts of the first, and the Reflections I had made wore quickly off; Poverty harden'd my Heart, and my own Necessities made me regardless of any thing: The last Affair left no great Concern upon me, for as I did the poor Child no harm, I only thought, I had given the Parents a just Reproof for their Negligence, in leaving the poor Lamb to come home by it self, and it would teach them to take more Care another time.

This String of Beads was worth about Twelve or Fourteen Pounds; I suppose it might have been formerly the

Mother's, for it was too big for the Child's wear, but that, perhaps, the Vanity of the Mother to have her Child look Fine at the Dancing School, had made her let the Child wear it, and no doubt the Child had a Maid sent to take care of it, but she, like a careless Jade, was taken up perhaps with some Fellow that had met her, and so the poor Baby wandred till it fell into my Hands.

However, I did the Child no harm, I did not so much as fright it, for I had a great many tender Thoughts about me yet, and did nothing but what, as I may say, meer Necessity drove me to.

Daniel Defoe

The Fortunes and Misfortunes of the Famous Moll Flanders
. . . (1722). Text from the third edition (1722)

CAPTAIN OAKUM ORDERS A SICK PARADE

THIS inhuman order shocked us extremely, as we knew it would be impossible to carry some of them on the deck, without imminent danger of their lives; but as we likewise knew it would be to no purpose for us to remonstrate against it, we repaired to the quarter-deck in a body, to see this extraordinary muster; Morgan observing by the way, that the captain was going to send to the other world, a great many evidences to testify against himself. – When we appeared upon deck, the captain bade the doctor, who stood bowing at his right hand, look at these lazy lubberly sons of bitches, who were good for nothing on board but to eat the king's provision, and encourage idleness in the skulkers. – The surgeon grinned approbation, and taking the list, began to examine the complaints of each as they could crawl to the place appointed. – The first who came under his cognizance was a poor fellow just freed of a fever, which had weakened him so much, that he could hardly stand. – Mr Mackshane (for that was the doctor's name) having felt his pulse, protested he was as well as any man in the world; and the captain delivered him over to the boatswain's mate, with orders that he should receive a round dozen at the gangway immediately, for counterfeiting himself sick: – but, before the discipline could be executed, the man dropt down on the deck, and had well nigh perished under the hands of the executioner. – The next patient, to be considered, laboured under a quartan ague, and being then in his interval of health, discovered no other symptoms of distemper, than a pale meagre countenance, and emaciated body; upon which, he was declared fit for duty, and turned over to the boatswain; – but being resolved to disgrace the doctor, died upon the forecastle next day, during his cold fit. – The third complained of a pleuritic stitch, and spitting of blood, for which doctor Mackshane prescribed exercise at the pump to promote expectoration; but whether this was improper for one in his situation, or that it was used to excess, I know not, but in less than half an hour he was suffocated with a deluge of blood that issued from his lungs. – A fourth, with much difficulty, climbed to the quarter-deck, being loaded with a monstrous ascites, or dropsy, that invaded his chest so much, he could scarce fetch his breath; but this disease being interpreted into fat, occasioned by idleness and excess of eating, he was ordered, with a view to promote perspiration and enlarge his chest, to go aloft immediately: It was in vain for this unwieldy wretch to alledge his utter incapacity, the boatswain's driver was commanded to whip him up with the cat and nine tails: The smart of this application made him exert himself so much, that he actually arrived at the foot-hook-shrouds; but when the enormous weight of his body had nothing else to support it than his weakened arms, either out of spite or necessity he quitted his hold, and plumped into the sea, where he must have been drowned, had not a sailor, who was in a boat along-side, saved his life, by keeping him afloat, till he was hoisted on board by a tackle. – It would be tedious and disagreeable to describe the fate of every miserable object that suffered by the inhumanity and ignorance of the captain and surgeon, who so wantonly sacrificed the lives of their fellow-creatures. Many were brought up in the height of fevers, and rendered delirious by the injuries they received in the way. – Some gave up the ghost in the presence of their inspectors; and others, who were ordered to their duty, languished a few days at work among their fellows, and then departed without any ceremony.

Tobias Smollett
The Adventures of Roderick Random (1748)

MRS SINCLAIR'S DEATHBED

THERE were no less than Eight of her cursed daughters surrounding her bed when I entered; one of her partners, Polly Horton, at their head; and now Sally, her other partner, and *Madam* Carter, as they called her (for they are all *Madams* with one another) made the number Ten: All in shocking dishabille, and without stays, except Sally, Carter, and Polly; who, not daring to leave her, had not been in bed all night.

The other Seven seemed to have been but just up, risen perhaps from their customers in the fore-house, and their nocturnal Orgies, with faces, three or four of them, that had run, the paint lying in streaky seams not half blowz'd off, discovering coarse wrinkled skins: The hair of some of them of divers colours, obliged to the black-lead comb where black was affected; the artificial jet, however, yielding apace to the natural brindle: That of others plaistered with oil and powder; the oil predominating: But every one's hanging about her ears and neck in broken curls, or ragged ends; and each at my entrance taken with one motion, stroaking their matted locks with both hands under their coifs, mobs, or pinners, every one of which was awry. They were all slip-shoed; stockenless some; only under-petticoated all; their gowns, made to cover straddling hoops, hanging trollopy, and tangling about their heels; but hastily wrapt round them, as soon as I came upstairs. And half of them (unpadded, shoul-der-bent, pallid-lipt, limber-jointed wretches) appearing, from a blooming Nineteen or Twenty perhaps over-night, haggard well-worn strumpets of Thirty-eight or Forty.

I am the more particular in describing to thee the appear-ance these creatures made in my eyes when I came into the room, because I believe thou never sawest any of them, much less a group of them, thus unprepared for being seen. I, for my part, never did before; nor had I now, but upon this occasion, been thus *favoured*. If thou *hadst*, I believe thou wouldst hate a profligate woman, as one of Swift's Yahoos, or Virgil's obscene Harpyes, squirting their ordure upon the Trojan trenchers; since the persons of such in their retirements are as filthy as their minds – Hate them as much as I do; and as much as I admire, and next to adore a truly-virtuous and elegant woman: For to me it is evident, that as a neat and clean woman must be an angel of a creature, so a sluttish one is the impurest animal in nature.

But these were the veterans, the chosen band; for now-and-then flitted in, to the number of half a dozen or more, by turns, subordinate sinners, under-graduates, younger than some of the chosen phalanx, but not less obscene in their appearance, tho' indeed not so much beholden to the plaster-ing fucus; yet unprop by stays, squalid, loose in attire, slug-gish-haired, under-petticoated only as the former, eyes half-opened, winking and pinking, mispatched, yawning, stretch-ing, as if from the unworn-off effects of the midnight revel;

all armed in succession with supplies of cordials (of which every one present was either taster or partaker) under the direction of the busier Dorcas, who frequently popp'd in, to see her slops duly given and taken.

But when I approached the *old wretch*, what a spectacle presented itself to my eyes!

Her misfortune had not at all sunk, but rather, as I thought, increased her flesh; rage and violence perhaps swelling her muscular features. Behold her then, spreading the whole tumbled bed with her huge quaggy carcase: Her mill-post arms held up; her broad hands clenched with violence; her big eyes, goggling and flaming-red as we may suppose those of a salamander; her matted griesly hair, made irreverend by her wickedness (her clouted head-dress being half off) spread about her fat ears and brawny neck; her livid lips parched, and working violently; her broad chin in convulsive motion; her wide mouth, by reason of the contraction of her forehead (which seemed to be half-lost in its own frightful furrows) splitting her face, as it were, into two parts; and her huge tongue hideously rolling in it; heaving, puffing, as if for breath; her bellows-shaped and various-coloured breasts ascending by turns to her chin, and descending out of sight, with the violence of her gaspings.

This was the spectacle, as recollection has enabled me to describe it, that this wretch made to my eye, when I approached her bed-side, surrounded, as I said, by her suffragans and daughters, who surveyed her with scouling frighted attention, which one might easily see had more in it of horror and self-concern (and *self condemnation* too) than of love or pity; as who should say, See! what we ourselves must one day be!

Samuel Richardson

Clarissa, or The History of a Young Lady . . . (1747–8)
Text from third edition (1751), Vol. VIII

On the Brink of Eternity

*The Place of Execution. The Gallows and Ladders at the
farther End of the Stage. A Crowd of Spectators*
Blunt *and* Lucy

Lucy. Heavens! What a Throng!

Blunt. How terrible is Death when thus prepar'd!

Lucy. Support them, Heaven; thou only can support them; all other Help is vain.

Officer within. Make Way there; make Way, and give the Prisoners Room!

Lucy. They are here. Observe them well. How humble and composed young *Barnwell* seems! But *Millwood* looks wild, ruffled with Passion, confounded and amazed.

Enter Barnwell, Millwood, *Officers and Executioner*

Barn. See, *Millwood*, see our Journey's at an End: Life, like a Tale that's told, is past away; that short but dark and unknown Passage, Death, is all the Space 'tween us and endless Joys, or Woes eternal.

Mill. Is this the End of all my flattering Hopes? Were Youth and Beauty given me for a Curse, and Wisdom only to insure my Ruin? They were, they were, Heaven thou hast done thy worst. Or if thou hast in Store some untried Plague, somewhat that's worse than Shame, Despair and Death, unpitied Death, confirm'd Despair and Soul confounding Shame; something that Men and Angels can't describe, and only Fiends, who bear it, can conceive; now, pour it now on this devoted Head, that I may feel the worst thou canst inflict, and bid Defiance to thy utmost Power!

Barn. Yet ere we pass the dreadful Gulph of Death, yet ere you're plunged in everlasting Woe, O bend your stubborn Knees, and harder Heart, humbly to deprecate the Wrath divine. Who knows but Heaven, in your dying Moments, may bestow that Grace and Mercy which your Life despised.

Mill. Why name you Mercy to a Wretch like me? Mercy's beyond my Hope; almost beyond my Wish. I can't repent, nor ask to be forgiven.

Barn. O think what 'tis to be for ever, ever miserable; nor with vain Pride oppose a Power, that's able to destroy you.

Mill. That will destroy me: I feel it will. A Deluge of Wrath is pouring on my Soul. Chains, Darkness, Wheels, Racks, sharp stinging Scorpions, molten Lead, and Seas of Sulphur, are light to what I feel.

Barn. O! add not to your vast Account Despair; a Sin more injurious to Heaven, than all you've yet committed.

Mill. O! I have sinn'd beyond the Reach of Mercy.

Barn. O say not so: 'tis Blasphemy to think it. As yon bright Roof is higher than the Earth, so and much more, does Heaven's Goodness pass our Apprehension. O what created Being shall presume to circumscribe Mercy, that knows no Bounds?

Mill. This yields no Hope. Tho' Mercy may be boundless, yet 'tis free: and I was doom'd, before the World began, to endless pains, and thou to Joys eternal.

Barn. O gracious Heaven! extend thy Pity to her: Let thy rich Mercy flow in plenteous Streams, to chase her Fears, and heal her wounded Soul!

Mill. It will not be: Your prayers are lost in Air, or else returned perhaps with double Blessing, to your Bosom: They help not me.

Barn. Yet hear me, *Millwood.*

Mill. Away, I will not hear thee: I tell thee, Youth, I am by Heaven devoted a dreadful Instance of its Power to punish. (Barnwell *seems to pray.*) If thou wilt pray, pray for thyself, not me. How doth his fervent Soul mount with his Words, and both ascend to Heaven! that Heaven, whose Gates are shut with adamantine Bars against my Prayers, had I the Will to pray. I cannot bear it. Sure 'tis the worst of Torments to behold others enjoy that Bliss which we must never taste!

Officer. The utmost Limit of your Time's expired.

Mill. Incompassed with Horror, whither must I go? I wou'd not live — nor die — That I cou'd cease to be — or ne'er had been!

Barn. Since Peace and Comfort are denied her here, may she find Mercy where she least expects it, and this be all her Hell. – From our Example may all be taught to fly the first approach of Vice; but, if o'ertaken

> *By strong Temptation, Weakness, or Surprize,*
> *Lament their Guilt and by Repentance rise.*
> *Th' Impenitent alone die unforgiv'n:*
> *To sin's like Man, and to forgive like Heav'n.*

George Lillo

The London Merchant; or the History of George Barnwell (1731). Text from the seventh edition (1740)

JUDGE JEFFREYS

His Friendship and Conversation lay much among the good Fellows and Humourists; and his Delights were, accordingly, Drinking, Laughing, Singing, Kissing, and all the Extravagances of the Bottle. He had a Set of Banterers, for the most Part, near him; as, in old Time, great Men kept Fools to make them merry. And these Fellows, abusing one another and their Betters, were a Regale to him. And no Friendship or Dearness could be so great, in private, which he would not use ill, and to an extravagant Degree, in Publick. No one, that had any Expectations from him, was safe from his publick Contempt and Derision, which some of his Minions, at the

Bar, bitterly felt. Those above, or that could hurt, or benefit, him, and none else, might depend on fair Quarter at his Hands. When he was in Temper, and Matters indifferent came before him, he became his Seat of Justice better than any other I ever saw in his Place. He took a Pleasure in mortifying fraudulent Attornies, and would deal forth his Severities with a Sort of Majesty. He had extraordinary natural Abilities, but little acquired, beyond what Practice in Affairs had supplied. He talk'd fluently, and with Spirit; and his Weakness was that he could not reprehend without scolding; and in such *Billingsgate* Language, as should not come out of the Mouth of any Man. He call'd it *giving a Lick with the rough Side of his Tongue*. It was ordinary to hear him say *Go, you are a filthy, lousy, knitty Rascal;* with much more of like Elegance. Scarce a Day past that he did not chide some one, or other, of the Bar, when he sat in the Chancery: And it was commonly a Lecture of a Quarter of an Hour long. And they used to say, *This is yours; my Turn will be to Morrow*. He seemed to lay nothing of his Business to Heart nor care what he did, or left undone; and spent, in the Chancery Court, what Time he thought fit to spare. Many Times, on Days of Causes at his House, the Company have waited five hours in a Morning, and, after Eleven, he hath come out inflamed, and staring like one distracted. And that Visage he put on when he animadverted on such as he took Offence at, which made him a Terror to real Offenders; whom also he terrified, with his Face and Voice, as if the Thunder of the Day of Judgment broke over their Heads: And nothing ever made Men tremble like his vocal Inflictions. He loved to insult, and was bold without Check; but that only when his Place was uppermost. To give an Instance. A City Attorney was petition'd against for some Abuse; and Affidavit was made that, when he was told of my Lord Chancellor, *My Lord Chancellor*, said he, *I made him;* meaning his being a Means to bring him early into

City Business. When this Affidavit was read, *Well*, said the Lord Chancellor, *then I will lay my Maker by the Heels*. And, with that Conceit, one of his best old Friends went to Jail. One of these Intemperances was fatal to him. There was a Scrivener of *Wapping* brought to hearing for Relief against a Bummery Bond; the Contingency of losing all being shewed, the Bill was going to be dismissed. But one of the Plaintiff's Counsel said that he was a strange Fellow, and sometimes went to Church, sometimes to Conventicles; and none could tell what to make of him; and *it was thought he was a Trimmer*. At that the Chancellor fired; and *A Trimmer*, said he! *I have heard much of that Monster, but never saw one. Come forth, Mr.* Trimmer, *turn you round, and let us see your Shape*: And, at that Rate, talk'd so long that the poor Fellow was ready to drop under him; but, at last, the Bill was dismissed with Costs, and he went his Way. In the Hall, one of his Friends asked him how he came off? *Came off*, said he, *I am escaped from the Terrors of that Man's Face, which I would scarce undergo again to save my Life; and I shall certainly have the frightful Impression of it as long as I live*. Afterwards, when the Prince of *Orange* came, and all was in Confusion, this Lord Chancellor, being very obnoxious, disguised himself in order to go beyond Sea. He was in a Seaman's Garb and drinking a Pot in a Cellar. This Scrivener came into the Cellar after some of his Clients; and his Eye caught that Face which made him start; and the Chancellor, seeing himself eyed, feign'd a Cough, and turn'd to the Wall with his Pot in his Hand. But Mr. *Trimmer* went out, and gave Notice that he was there; whereupon the Mob flow'd in, and he was in extreme Hazard of his Life; but the Lord Mayor saved him and lost himself. For the Chancellor being hurried with such Croud and Noise before him, and appearing so dismally, not only disguised but disorder'd; and there having been an Amity betwixt them, as also a Veneration on the Lord Mayor's Part, he had not Spirits to sustain the Shock, but fell down in a Swoon; and, in not many hours after, died. But this Lord *Jeffries* came to the Seal without any Concern at the Weight of Duty incumbent upon him; for, at the first, being merry over a Bottle with some of his old Friends, one of them told him that he would find the Business heavy. *No*, he said, *I'll make it light*. But, to conclude with a strange Inconsistency, he would drink, and be merry, kiss and slaver, with these bon Companions over Night, as the way of such is, and, the next Day, fall upon them, ranting and scolding with a virulence insufferable.

Roger North

The Life of the Right Honourable Francis
North, Baron of Guilford ... (1742)

PLOTS AND PARTIES IN THE REIGN OF CHARLES II

IT was the favor and countenance of the Parliament, which had chiefly encouraged the rumor of plots; but the nation had got so much into that vein of credulity, and every necessitous villain was so much incited by the success of Oates and Bedloe, that even during the vacation the people were not allowed to remain in tranquillity. There was one Dangerfield, a fellow who had been burned in the hand for crimes, transported, whipped, pilloried four times, fined for cheats, outlawed for felony, convicted of false coining, and exposed to all the public infamy which the laws could inflict on the basest and most shameful enormities. The credulity of the people, and the humor of the times enabled even this man to become a person of consequence. He was the author of a new incident, called the *meal-tub plot*, from the place where some papers, regarding it, were found. The bottom of this affair it is difficult, and not very material, to discover. It only appears, that Dangerfield, under pretence of betraying the conspiracies of the Presby-

terians, had been countenanced by some Catholics of condition, and had even been admitted to the Duke's presence
and the King's. And that under pretence of revealing new
popish plots, he had obtained access to Shaftesbury and some
of the popular leaders. Which side he intended to cheat, is
uncertain; or whether he did not rather mean to cheat both:
But he soon found, that the belief of the nation was more
open to a popish than a presbyterian plot; and he resolved to
strike in with the prevailing humor. Though no weight could
be laid on his testimony, great clamor was raised; as if the
Court, by way of retaliation, had intended to load the Presbyterians with the guilt of a false conspiracy. It must be
confessed that the present period, by the prevalence and
suspicion of such mean and ignoble arts on all sides, throws
a great stain on the British annals.

One of the most innocent artifices, practised by party-men
at this time, was the additional ceremony, pomp, and expence,
with which a pope-burning was celebrated in London: The
spectacle served to entertain, and amuse, and enflame, the
populace. The Duke of Monmouth likewise came over without leave, and made a triumphant procession thro' many parts
of the kingdom, extremely caressed and admired by the
people. All these arts seemed requisite to support the general
prejudices, during the long interval of Parliament. Great
endeavors were also used to obtain the King's consent for
the meeting of that assembly. Seventeen peers presented a
petition to this purpose. Many of the corporations imitated
the example. Notwithstanding several marks of displeasure,
and even a menacing proclamation from the King, petitions
came from all parts, earnestly insisting on a session of Parliament. The danger of popery, and the terrors of the plot,
were never forgotten in any of these addresses.

Tumultuous petitioning was one of the chief artifices, by
which the malcontents in the last reign had attacked the

crown: And tho' the manner of subscribing and delivering petitions was now somewhat limited by act of Parliament, the thing itself still remained; and was an admirable expedient for infesting the Court, for spreading discontent, and for uniting the nation in any popular clamor. As the King found no law, by which he could punish those importunate, and, as he deemed them, undutiful sollicitations, he was obliged to encounter them by popular applications of a contrary tendency. Wherever the church and court party prevailed, addresses were framed, containing expressions of the highest regard to his majesty, the most entire acquiescence in his wisdom, the most dutiful submission to his prerogative, and the deepest *abhorrence* of those who endeavored to encroach upon it, by prescribing to him any time for assembling the Parliament. Thus the nation came to be distinguished into *Petitioners* and *Abhorrers*. Factions indeed were at this time extremely animated against each other. The very means by which each party denominated its antagonist, discover the virulence and rancor which prevailed. For besides Petitioner and Abhorrer, appellations which were soon forgot, this year[1] is remarkable for being the epoch of the well-known epithets of WHIG and TORY, by which, and sometimes without any material difference, this island has been so long divided. The court party reproached their antagonists with their affinity to the fanatical conventiclers in Scotland, who were known by the name of Whigs: The country party found a resemblance between the courtiers and the popish banditti in Ireland, to whom the appellation of Tory was affixed. And after this manner, these foolish terms of reproach came into public and general use; and even at present seem not nearer their end than when they were first invented.

David Hume

The History of Great Britain. . . ., Vol. II (1757)
1. 1680.

MAHOMET

THE communication of ideas requires a similitude of thought and language: the discourse of a philosopher would vibrate without effect on the ear of a peasant; yet how minute is the distance of *their* understandings, if it be compared with the contact of an infinite and a finite mind, with the word of God expressed by the tongue or the pen of a mortal? The inspiration of the Hebrew prophets, of the apostles and evangelists of Christ, might not be incompatible with the exercise of their reason and memory; and the diversity of their genius is strongly marked in the style and composition of the books of the Old and New Testament. But Mahomet was content with a character, more humble, yet more sublime, of a simple editor: the substance of the Koran, according to himself or his disciples, is uncreated and eternal; subsisting in the essence of the Deity, and inscribed with a pen of light on the table of his everlasting decrees. A paper copy in a volume of silk and gems, was brought down to the lowest heaven by the angel Gabriel, who, under the Jewish œconomy, had indeed been dispatched on the most important errands; and this trusty messenger successively revealed the chapters and verses to the Arabian prophet. Instead of a perpetual and perfect measure of the divine will, the fragments of the Koran were produced at the discretion of Mahomet; each revelation is suited to the emergencies of his policy or passion; and all contradiction is removed by the saving maxim, that any text of scripture is abrogated or modified by any subsequent passage. The word of God, and of the apostle, was diligently recorded by his disciples on palm-leaves and the shoulder-bones of mutton; and the pages, without order or connection, were cast into a domestic chest in the custody of one of his wives. Two years after the death of Mahomet, the sacred volume was collected and published by his friend and successor

Abubeker: the work was revised by the caliph Othman, in the thirtieth year of the Hegira; and the various editions of the Koran assert the same miraculous privilege of an uniform and incorruptible text. In the spirit of enthusiasm or vanity, the prophet rests the truth of his mission on the merit of his book, audaciously challenges both men and angels to imitate the beauties of a single page, and presumes to assert that God alone could dictate this incomparable performance. This argument is most powerfully addressed to a devout Arabian, whose mind is attuned to faith and rapture, whose ear is delighted by the music of sounds, and whose ignorance is incapable of comparing the productions of human genius. The harmony and copiousness of style will not reach, in a version, the European infidel: he will peruse with impatience the endless incoherent rhapsody of fable, and precept, and declamation, which seldom excites a sentiment or an idea, which sometimes crawls in the dust, and is sometimes lost in the clouds. The divine attributes exalt the fancy of the Arabian missionary; but his loftiest strains must yield to the sublime simplicity of the book of Job, composed in a remote age, in the same country and in the same language. If the composition of the Koran exceed the faculties of a man, to what superior intelligence should we ascribe the Iliad of Homer or the Philippics of Demosthenes? In all religions, the life of the founder supplies the silence of his written revelation: the sayings of Mahomet were so many lessons of truth; his actions so many examples of virtue; and the public and private memorials were preserved by his wives and companions. At the end of two hundred years, the *Sonna* or oral law was fixed and consecrated by the labours of Al Bochari, who discriminated seven thousand two hundred and seventy-five genuine traditions, from a mass of three hundred thousand reports, of a more doubtful or spurious character. Each day the pious author prayed in the temple of Mecca, and performed his ablutions with the water of Zemzem: the pages were successively deposited on the pulpit, and the sepulchre of the apostle; and the work has been approved by the four orthodox sects of the Sonnites.

The mission of the ancient prophets, of Moses and of Jesus, had been confirmed by many splendid prodigies; and Mahomet was repeatedly urged, by the inhabitants of Mecca and Medina, to produce a similar evidence of his divine legation; to call down from heaven the angel or the volume of his revelation, to create a garden in the desert, or to kindle a conflagration in the unbelieving city. As often as he is pressed by the demands of the Koreish, he involves himself in the obscure boast of vision and prophecy, appeals to the internal proofs of his doctrine, and shields himself behind the providence of God, who refuses those signs and wonders that would depreciate the merit of faith and aggravate the guilt of infidelity. But the modest or angry tone of his apologies betrays his weakness and vexation; and these passages of scandal establish, beyond suspicion, the integrity of the Koran. The votaries of Mahomet are more assured than himself of his miraculous gifts, and their confidence and credulity encrease as they are farther removed from the time and place of his spiritual exploits. They believe or affirm that trees went forth to meet him; that he was saluted by stones; that water gushed from his fingers; that he fed the hungry, cured the sick, and raised the dead; that a beam groaned to him; that a camel complained to him; that a shoulder of mutton informed him of its being poisoned; and that both animate and inanimate nature were equally subject to the apostle of God. His dream of a nocturnal journey is seriously described as a real and corporeal transaction. A mysterious animal, the Borak, conveyed him from the temple of Mecca to that of Jerusalem: with his companion Gabriel, he successively ascended the seven heavens, and received and repaid the salutations of the patriarchs, the prophets, and the angels, in their respective mansions. Beyond the seventh heaven, Mahomet alone was permitted to proceed; he passed the veil of unity, approached within two bow-shots of the throne, and felt a cold that pierced him to the heart, when his shoulder was touched by the hand of God. After this familiar though important conversation, he again descended to Jerusalem, remounted the Borak, returned to Mecca, and performed in the tenth part of a night the journey of many thousand years. According to another legend, the apostle confounded in a national assembly the malicious challenge of the Koreish. His resistless word split asunder the orb of the moon; the obedient planet stooped from her station in the sky, accomplished the seven revolutions round the Caaba, saluted Mahomet in the Arabian tongue, and suddenly contracting her dimensions, entered at the collar, and issued forth through the sleeve, of his shirt. The vulgar are amused with these marvellous tales; but the gravest of the Musulman doctors imitate the modesty of their master, and indulge a latitude of faith or interpretation. They might speciously allege, that in preaching the religion, it was needless to violate the harmony, of nature; that a creed unclouded with mystery may be excused from miracles; and that the sword of Mahomet was not less potent than the rod of Moses.

Edward Gibbon
The History of the Decline and Fall of the
Roman Empire, Vol. V (1788)

THE DARKER SIDE OF ROMAN RULE

IF a man were called to fix the period in the history of the world, during which the condition of the human race was most happy and prosperous, he would, without hesitation, name that which elapsed from the death of Domitian to the accession of Commodus. The vast extent of the Roman empire was governed by absolute power, under the guidance of virtue and wisdom. The armies were restrained by the firm but gentle hand of four successive emperors, whose characters and authority commanded involuntary respect. The forms of the civil administration were carefully preserved by Nerva, Trajan, Hadrian, and the Antonines, who delighted in the image of liberty, and were pleased with considering themselves as the accountable ministers of the laws. Such princes deserved the honour of restoring the republic, had the Romans of their days been capable of enjoying a rational freedom.

The labours of these monarchs were over-paid by the immense reward that inseparably waited on their success; by the honest pride of virtue, and by the exquisite delight of beholding the general happiness of which they were the authors. A just, but melancholy reflection, embittered, however, the noblest of human enjoyments. They must often have recollected the instability of a happiness which depended on the character of a single man. The fatal moment was perhaps approaching, when some licentious youth, or some jealous tyrant, would abuse, to the destruction, that absolute power, which they had exerted for the benefit of their people. The ideal restraints of the senate and the laws might serve to display the virtues, but could never correct the vices, of the emperor. The military force was a blind and irresistible instrument of oppression; and the corruption of Roman manners would always supply flatterers eager to applaud, and ministers prepared to serve, the fear or the avarice, the lust or the cruelty, of their masters.

These gloomy apprehensions had been already justified by the experience of the Romans. The annals of the emperors exhibit a strong and various picture of human nature, which we should vainly seek among the mixed and doubtful characters of modern history. In the conduct of those monarchs we may trace the utmost lines of vice and virtue; the most exalted perfection, and the meanest degeneracy of our own species. The golden age of Trajan and the Antonines had been preceded by an age of iron. It is almost superfluous to enumerate the unworthy successors of Augustus. Their unparalleled vices, and the splendid theatre on which they were acted, have saved them from oblivion. The dark unrelenting Tiberius, the furious Caligula, the feeble Claudius, the profligate and cruel Nero, the beastly Vitellius, and the timid inhuman Domitian, are condemned to everlasting infamy. During fourscore years (excepting only the short and doubtful respite of Vespasian's reign) Rome groaned beneath an unremitting tyranny, which exterminated the ancient families of the republic, and was fatal to almost every virtue, and every talent, that arose in that unhappy period.

Under the reign of these monsters, the slavery of the Romans was accompanied with two peculiar circumstances, the one occasioned by their former liberty, the other by their extensive conquests, which rendered their condition more completely wretched than that of the victims of tyranny in any other age or country. From these causes were derived 1. The exquisite sensibility of the sufferers; and, 2. the impossibility of escaping from the hand of the oppressor.

I. When Persia was governed by the descendants of Sefi, a race of princes, whose wanton cruelty often stained their divan, their table, and their bed, with the blood of their favourites, there is a saying recorded of a young nobleman, that he never departed from the sultan's presence, without satisfying himself whether his head was still on his shoulders. The experience of every day might almost justify the scepticism of Rustan. Yet the fatal sword suspended above him by a single thread, seems not to have disturbed the slumbers, or interrupted the tranquillity of the Persian. The monarch's frown, he well knew, could level him with the dust; but the stroke of lightning or apoplexy might be equally fatal; and it was the part of a wise man, to forget the inevitable calamities of human life in the enjoyment of the fleeting hour. He was dignified with the appellation of the king's slave; had, perhaps, been purchased from obscure parents, in a country which he had never known, and was trained up from his infancy in the severe discipline of the seraglio. His name, his wealth, his honours, were the gift of a master, who might, without injustice, resume what he had bestowed. Rustan's knowledge, if he possessed any, could only serve to confirm his habits by prejudices. His language afforded not words for any form of government, except absolute monarchy. The history of the East informed him, that such had ever been the condition of mankind. The Koran, and the interpreters of that divine book, inculcated to him, that the sultan was the descendant of the prophet, and the vicegerent of heaven; that patience was the first virtue of a Mussulman, and unlimited obedience the great duty of a subject.

The minds of the Romans were very differently prepared for slavery. Oppressed beneath the weight of their own corruption and of military violence, they for a long while preserved the sentiments, or at least the ideas, of their freeborn ancestors. The education of Helvidius and Thrasea, of Tacitus and Pliny, was the same as that of Cato and Cicero. From Grecian philosophy, they had imbibed the justest and most liberal notions of the dignity of human nature, and the origin of civil society. The history of their own country had taught them to revere a free, a virtuous, and a victorious commonwealth; to abhor the successful crimes of Cæsar and Augustus; and inwardly to despise those tyrants whom they adored with the most abject flattery. As magistrates and senators, they were admitted into the great council, which had once dictated laws to the earth, whose name still gave a sanction to the acts of the monarch, and whose authority was so often prostituted to the vilest purposes of tyranny. Tiberius, and those emperors who adopted his maxims, attempted to disguise their murders by the formalities of justice, and perhaps enjoyed a secret pleasure in rendering the senate their accomplice as well as their victim. By this assembly, the last of the Romans were condemned for imaginary crimes and real virtues. Their infamous accusers assumed the language of independent patriots, who arraigned a dangerous citizen before the tribunal of his country; and the public service was rewarded by riches and honours. The servile judges professed to assert the majesty of the commonwealth, violated in the person of its first magistrate, whose clemency they most applauded when they trembled the most at his inexorable and impending cruelty. The tyrant beheld their baseness with just contempt, and encountered their secret sentiments of detestation with sincere and avowed hatred for the whole body of the senate.

II. The division of Europe into a number of independent states, connected, however, with each other, by the general resemblance of religion, language, and manners, is productive of the most beneficial consequences to the liberty of mankind. A modern tyrant, who should find no resistance either in his own breast, or in his people, would soon experience a gentle restraint from the example of his equals, the dread of present censure, the advice of his allies, and the apprehension of his enemies. The object of his displeasure, escaping from the narrow limits of his dominions, would easily obtain, in a happier climate, a secure refuge, a new fortune adequate to his merit, the freedom of complaint, and perhaps the means of revenge. But the empire of the Romans filled the world, and when that empire fell into the hands of a single person, the world became a safe and dreary prison for his enemies. The slave of Imperial despotism, whether he was condemned to drag his gilded chain in Rome and the senate, or to wear out a life of exile on the barren rock of Seriphus, or the frozen banks of the Danube, expected his fate in silent despair. To resist was fatal, and it was impossible to fly. On every side he was encompassed with a vast extent of sea and land, which he could never hope to traverse without being discovered, seized, and restored to his irritated master. Beyond the frontiers, his anxious view could discover nothing, except the ocean, inhospitable deserts, hostile tribes of barbarians, of fierce manners and unknown language, or dependent kings, who would gladly purchase the emperor's protection by the sacrifice of an obnoxious fugitive. "Wherever you are," said Cicero to the exiled Marcellus, "remember that you are equally within the power of the conqueror."

Edward Gibbon

The History of the Decline and Fall of the Roman Empire,
Vol. I (1776). Text from second edition (1782)

IV

THE CRITICISM OF THE ARTS

POETRY AND THE PASSIONS

Now the proper Means for Poetry, to attain both its subordinate and final End, is by exciting Passion. First, The subordinate End of Poetry, which is to please, is attained by exciting Passion, because every one who is pleased is moved, and either desires, or rejoices, or admires, or hopes, or the like. As we are moved by Pleasure which is Happiness, to do every thing we do, we may find upon a little Reflection, That every Man is incited by some Passion or other, either to Action, or to Contemplation; and Passion is the Result either of Action or of Contemplation, as long as either of them please, and the more either of them pleases, the more they are attended with Passion. The Satisfaction that we receive from Geometry it self comes from the joy of having found out Truth, and the Desire of finding more. And the satiety that seizes us upon too long a Lecture, proceeds from nothing but from the weariness of our Spirits, and consequently from the cessation or the decay of those two pleasing Passions. But,

Secondly, Poetry attains its final End, which is the reforming the Minds of Men, by exciting of Passion. And here I dare be bold to affirm, that all Instruction whatever depends upon Passion. The Moral Philosophers themselves, even the dryest of them, can never instruct and reform, unless they move; for either they make Vice odious and Virtue lovely, or they deter you from one by the Apprehension of Misery, or they incite you to the other by the Happiness they make you expect from it; or they work upon your Shame, or upon your Pride, or upon your Indignation. And therefore Poetry instructs and reforms more powerfully than Philosophy can do, because it moves more powerfully: And therefore it instructs more easily too. For whereas all Men have Passions, and great Passions of one sort or another, and whereas those Passions will be employed, and whatever way they move, they that way draw the Man, it follows, that Philosophy can instruct but hardly, because it moves but gently: for the violent Passions not finding their account in those faint emotions, begin to rebel and fly to their old Objects, whereas Poetry, at the same time that it instructs us powerfully, must reform us easily; because it makes the very Violence of the Passions contribute to our Reformation.

John Dennis

The Grounds of Criticism in Poetry . . . (1704)

THE NECESSITY FOR BAD POETRY

FARTHERMORE, it were great Cruelty and Injustice, if all such Authors as cannot write in the other Way, were prohibited from writing at all. Against this, I draw an Argument from what seems to me an undoubted Physical Maxim, That Poetry is a *natural* or *morbid Secretion from the Brain*. As I would not suddenly stop a Cold in the Head, or dry up my Neighbour's Issue, I would as little hinder him from necessary Writing. It may be affirm'd with great truth, that there is hardly any human Creature past Childhood, but at one time or other has had some Poetical Evacuation, and no question was much the better for it in his Health; so true is the Saying, *Nascimur Poetæ*: Therefore is the Desire of Writing properly term'd *Pruritus*, the *Titillation of the Generative Faculty of the Brain;* and the Person is said to *conceive*; Now such as conceive must *bring forth*. I have known a Man thoughtful, melancholy, and raving for divers days, but forthwith grow wonderfully easy, lightsome and cheerful, upon a Discharge of the peccant Humour, in exceeding purulent Metre. Nor can I question, but abundance of untimely Deaths are occasion'd by want of this laudable Vent of unruly Passions; yea, perhaps, in poor Wretches, (which is very lamentable) for meer Want of Pen, Ink, and Paper! From hence it follows, that a Suppression of the very worst Poetry is of dangerous consequence to the State: We find by Experience, that the same Humours which vent themselves in Summer in *Ballads* and *Sonnets*, are condens'd by the Winter's Cold into *Pamphlets* and *Speeches* for and against the *Ministry*: Nay I know not, but many times a Piece of Poetry may be the most innocent Composition of a *Minister himself*.

Alexander Pope (or others of the 'Scriblerus' circle)
'The Art of Sinking in Poetry' in *Miscellanies in Prose and Verse* Vol. III (1727)

GENIUS

NOR are we only ignorant of the dimensions of the human mind in general, but even of our own. That a man may be scarce less ignorant of his own powers, than an oyster of its pearl, or a rock of its diamond; that he may possess dormant, unsuspected abilities, till awakened by loud calls, or stung up by striking emergencies, is evident from the sudden eruption of some men, out of perfect obscurity, into publick admiration, on the strong impulse of some animating occasion; not more to the world's great surprize, than their own. Few authors of distinction but have experienced something of this nature, at the first beamings of their yet unsuspected genius on their hitherto dark Composition: The writer starts at it, as at a lucid meteor in the night; is much surprized; can scarce believe it true. During his happy confusion it may be said to him, as to Eve at the lake,

> What there thou seest, fair creature, is thyself.
>   Milt[on]

Genius, in this view, is like a dear friend in our company under disguise; who, while we are lamenting his absence, drops his mask, striking us, at once, with equal surprize and joy. This sensation, which I speak of in a writer, might favour, and so promote, the fable of poetic inspiration: A poet of a strong imagination, and stronger vanity, on feeling it, might naturally enough realize the world's mere compliment, and think himself truly inspired. Which is not improbable; for enthusiasts of all kinds do no less.

Since it is plain that men may be strangers to their own abilities; and by thinking meanly of them without just cause, may possibly lose a name, perhaps a name immortal; I would find some means to prevent these evils. Whatever promotes virtue, promotes something more, and carries its good influence beyond the *moral* man: To prevent these evils, I borrow two golden rules from *ethics*, which are no less golden in *Composition* than in life. 1st. *Know thyself;* 2ndly, *Reverence thyself*: I design to repay ethics in a future letter, by two rules from rhetoric for its service.

1st. *Know thyself*. Of ourselves it may be said, as Martial says of a bad neighbour,

> Nil tam prope, proculque nobis.

Therefore dive deep into thy bosom; learn the depth, extent bias, and full fort of thy mind; contract full intimacy with the stranger within thee; excite and cherish every spark of intellectual light and heat, however smothered under former negligence, or scattered through the dull, dark mass of common thoughts; and collecting them into a body, let thy genius rise (if a genius thou hast) as the sun from chaos; and if I should then say, like an *Indian*, *Worship it*, (though too bold) yet should I say little more than my second rule enjoins, (*viz.*) *Reverence thyself*.

That is, let not great examples, or authorities, browbeat thy reason into too great a diffidence of thyself: Thyself so reverence, as to prefer the native growth of thy own mind to the richest import from abroad; such borrowed riches make us poor. The man who thus reverences himself, will soon find the world's reverence to follow his own. His works will stand distinguished; his the sole property of them; which property alone can confer the noble title of an *author*; that is, of one who (to speak accurately) *thinks* and *composes*; while other invaders of the press, how voluminous and learned soever, (with due respect be it spoken) only *read*, and *write*.

This is the difference between those two luminaries in literature, the well-accomplished scholar, and the divinely-inspired enthusiast; the *first* is, as the bright morning star; the *second*, as the rising sun. The writer who neglects those two rules above will never stand alone; he makes one of a group, and thinks in wretched unanimity with the throng: Incumbered with the notions of others, and impoverished by their abundance, he conceives not the least embryo of new thought; opens not the least vista thro' the gloom of ordinary writers, into the bright walks of rare imagination, and singular design; while the true genius is crossing all publick roads into fresh untrodden ground; he, up to the knees in antiquity, is treading the sacred footsteps of great examples, with the blind veneration of a bigot saluting the papal toe; comfortably hoping full absolution for the sins of his own understanding, from the powerful charm of touching his idol's infallibility.

Edward Young
Conjectures on Original Composition . . . (1759)

HOMER

OUR Author's Work is a wild Paradise, where if we cannot see all the Beauties so distinctly as in an order'd Garden, it is only because the Number of them is infinitely greater. 'Tis like a copious Nursery which contains the Seeds and first Productions of every kind, out of which those who follow'd him have but selected some particular Plants, each according to his Fancy, to cultivate and beautify. If some things are too luxuriant, it is owing to the Richness of the Soil; and if others are not arriv'd to Perfection or Maturity, it is only because they are over-run and opprest by those of a stronger Nature.

It is to the Strength of this amazing Invention we are to attribute that unequal'd Fire and Rapture, which is so forcible in *Homer*, that no Man of a true Poetical Spirit is Master of himself while he reads him. What he writes is of the most animated Nature imaginable; every thing moves, every thing lives, and is put in Action. If a Council be call'd, or a Battel fought, you are not coldly inform'd of what was said or done as from a third Person; the Reader is hurry'd out of himself by the Force of the Poet's Imagination, and turns in one place to a Hearer, in another to a Spectator. The Course of his Verses resembles that of the Army he describes.

Οἱ δ'ἄρ ἴσαν, ὡσεί τε πυρὶ χθὼν πᾶσα νέμοιτο.

They pour along like a Fire that sweeps the whole Earth before it.
'Tis however remarkable that his Fancy, which is every where

vigorous, is not discover'd immediately at the beginning of his Poem in its fullest Splendor: It grows in the Progress both upon himself and others, and becomes on Fire like a Chariot-Wheel, by its own Rapidity. Exact Disposition, just Thought, correct Elocution, polish'd Numbers, may have been found in a thousand; but this Poetical *Fire*, this *Vivida vis animi*, in a very few. Even in Works where all those are imperfect or neglected, this can over-power Criticism, and make us admire even while we dis-approve. Nay, where this appears, tho' attended with Absurdities, it brightens all the Rubbish about it, 'till we see nothing but its own Splendor. This *Fire* is discern'd in *Virgil*, but discern'd as through a Glass, reflected, and more shining than warm, but every-where equal and constant: In *Lucan* and *Statius*, it bursts out in sudden, short, and interrupted Flashes: In *Milton*, it glows like a Furnace kept up to an uncommon Fierceness by the Force of Art: In *Shakespear*, it strikes before we are aware, like an accidental Fire from Heaven: But in *Homer*, and in him only, it burns every where clearly, and every where irresistibly.

Alexander Pope
Preface to *The Iliad of Homer* . . . (1715)

IN DEFENCE OF MEDIAEVAL PROLIXITY

"These oakès greatè be not down yhewe
First at a stroke, but by a *long processe*,
Nor long stories a word may not expresse."

THESE "*long processes*" indeed suited wonderfully with the attention and simple curiosity of the age in which Lydgate lived. Many *a stroke* have he and the best of his contemporaries spent upon a *sturdy old story*, till they blunted their own edge and that of their readers; at least a modern reader will find it so: but it is a folly to judge of the understanding and of the patience of those times by our own. They loved, I will not say tediousness, but length and a train of circumstances in a narration. The vulgar do so still: it gives an air of reality to facts, it fixes the attention, raises and keeps in suspense their expectation, and supplies the defects of their little and lifeless imagination; and it keeps pace with the slow motion of their own thoughts. Tell them a story, as you would tell it to a man of wit, it will appear to them as an object seen in the night by a flash of lightning; but, when you have placed it in various lights and in various positions, they will come at last to see and feel it as well as others. But we need not confine ourselves to the vulgar, and to understandings beneath our own. *Circumstance* ever was, and ever will be, the life and the essence both of oratory and of poetry. It has in some sort the same effect upon every mind that it has upon that of the populace; and I fear the quickness and delicate impatience of these polished times, in which we live, are but the fore-runners of the decline of all those beautiful arts which depend upon the imagination.

Thomas Gray
'Some Remarks on the Poems of John Lydgate,'
in *Works . . .* ed. T. J. Matthias (1814), Vol. II

CLASSICAL AND GOTHIC UNITY

WHEN an architect examines a Gothic structure by Grecian rules, he finds nothing but deformity. But the Gothic architecture has it's own rules, by which when it comes to be examined, it is seen to have it's merit, as well as the Grecian. The question is not, which of the two is conducted in the simplest or truest taste: but, whether there be not sense and design in both, when scrutinized by the laws on which each is projected.

The same observation holds of the two sorts of poetry. Judge of the *Faery Queen* by the classic models, and you are shocked with it's disorder: consider it with an eye to it's Gothic original, and you find it regular. The unity and simplicity of the former are more complete: but the latter has that sort of unity and simplicity, which results from it's nature.

The Faery Queen then, as a Gothic poem, derives it's METHOD as well as the other characters of it's composition, from the established modes and ideas of chivalry.

It was usual, in the days of knight-errantry, at the holding of any great feast, for Knights to appear before the Prince, who presided at it, and claim the privilege of being sent on any adventure, to which the solemnity might give occasion. For it was supposed that, when such a *throng of knights and barons bold*, as Milton speaks of, were got together, the distressed would flock in from all quarters, as to a place where they knew they might find and claim redress for all their grievances.

This was the real practice, in the days of pure and ancient chivalry. And an image of this practice was afterwards kept up in the castles of the great, on any extraordinary festival or solemnity: of which, if you want an instance, I refer you to the description of a feast made at Lisle in 1453, in the court of Philip the Good, Duke of Burgundy, for a crusade against the Turks: As you may find it given at large in the memoirs of *Matthieu de Conci*, *Olivier de la Marche*, and *Monstrelet*.

That feast was held for *twelve* days: and each day was distinguished by the claim and allowance of some adventure.

Now laying down this practice, as a foundation for the poet's design, you will see how properly the *Faery Queen* is conducted.

— "I devise, says the poet himself in his Letter to Sir W.

Raleigh, that the Faery Queen kept her annual feaste xii days: upon which xii several days, the occasions of the xii several adventures hapened; which being undertaken by xii several knights, are in these xii books severally handled."

Here you have the poet delivering his own method, and the reason of it. It arose out of the order of his subject. And would you desire a better reason for his choice? . . .

If you ask then, what is this *Unity* of Spenser's Poem? I say, It consists in the relation of it's several adventures to one common *original*, the appointment of the Faery Queen; and to one common *end*, the completion of the Faery Queen's injunctions. The knights issued forth on their adventures on the breaking up of this annual feast; and the next annual feast, we are to suppose, is to bring them together again from the atchievement of their several charges.

This, it is true, is not the classic unity, which consists in the representation of one entire action: but it is an Unity of another sort, an unity resulting from the respect which a number of related actions have to one common purpose. In other words, It is an unity of *design*, and not of action.

This Gothic method of design in poetry may be, in some sort, illustrated by what is called the Gothic method of design in Gardening. A wood or grove cut out into many separate avenues or glades was amongst the most favourite of the works of art, which our fathers attempted in this species of cultivation. These walks were distinct from each other, had, each, their several destination, and terminated on their own proper objects. Yet the whole was brought together and considered under one view by the relation which these various openings had, not to each other, but to their common and concurrent center. You and I are, perhaps, agreed that this sort of gardening is not of so true a taste as that which *Kent*[1] *and Nature* have brought us acquainted with; where the

1. William Kent (1684–1748), landscape-gardener. See pp. 271–4.

supreme art of the Designer consists in disposing his ground and objects into an *entire landskip*; and grouping them, if I may use the term, in so easy a manner, that the careless observer, tho' he be taken with the symmetry of the whole, discovers no art in the combination . . .

This, I say, may be the truest taste in gardening, because the simplest: Yet there is a manifest regard to unity in the other method; which has had it's admirers, as it may have again, and is certainly not without it's *design* and beauty.

But to return to our poet. Thus far he drew from Gothic ideas, and these ideas, I think, would lead him no farther. But, as Spenser knew what belonged to classic composition, he was tempted to tie his subject still closer together by *one* expedient of his own, and by *another* taken from his classic models.

His *own* was to interrupt the proper story of each book, by dispersing it into several; involving by this means, and as it were intertwisting the several actions together, in order to give something like the appearance of one action to his twelve adventures. And for this conduct, as absurd as it seems, he had some great examples in the Italian poets, tho' I believe, they were led into it by different motives.

The *other* expedient which he borrowed from the classics, was by adopting one superior character, which should be seen throughout. Prince Arthur, who had a separate adventure of his own, was to have his part in each of the other; and thus several actions were to be embodied by the interest which one principal Hero had in them all. It is even observable, that Spenser gives this adventure of Prince Arthur, in quest of Gloriana, as the proper subject of his poem. And upon this idea the late learned editor of the Faery Queen has attempted, but I think without success, to defend the Unity and simplicity of its fable. The truth was, the violence of classic prejudices forced the poet to affect this appearance of unity, tho' in contradiction to his Gothic system. And, as far as we can judge of the tenour of the whole work from the finished half of it, the adventure of Prince Arthur, whatever the author pretended, and his critic too easily believed, was but an after thought; and at least with regard to the *historical fable*, which we are now considering, was only one of the expedients by which he would conceal the disorder of his Gothic plan.

And if this was his design, I will venture to say that both his expedients were injudicious. Their purpose was to ally two things, in nature incompatible, the Gothic, and the classic unity; the effect of which misalliance was to discover and expose the nakedness of the Gothic.

I am of opinion then, considering the Faery Queen as an epic or *narrative* poem constructed on Gothic ideas, that the Poet had done well to affect no other unity than that of *design*, by which his subject was connected.

Richard Hurd
Letters on Chivalry and Romance (1762)

THE FAIRY WAY OF WRITING

THERE is a kind of Writing, wherein the Poet quite loses sight of Nature, and entertains his Reader's Imagination with the Characters and Actions of such Persons as have many of them no Existence, but what he bestows on them. Such are Fairies, Witches, Magicians, Demons, and departed Spirits. This Mr. *Dryden* calls *the Fairy way of Writing*, which is, indeed, more difficult than any other that depends on the Poet's Fancy, because he has no Pattern to follow in it, and must work altogether out of his own Invention.

There is a very odd turn of Thought required for this sort of Writing, and it is impossible for a Poet to succeed in it, who has not a particular Cast of Fancy, and an Imagination naturally fruitful and superstitious. Besides this, he ought to be very well versed in Legends and Fables, antiquated Romances, and the Traditions of Nurses and old Women, that he may fall in with our natural Prejudices, and humour those Notions which we have imbibed in our Infancy. For, otherwise, he will be apt to make his Fairies talk like People of his own Species, and not like other Setts of Beings, who converse with different Objects, and think in a different manner from that of Mankind:

> *Sylvis deducti caveant, me judice, Fauni*
> *Ne velut innati triviis, ac pene forenses,*
> *Aut nimium teneris juvenentur versibus* – Hor[ace]

I do not say with Mr. *Bays* in the *Rehearsal*, that Spirits must not be confined to speak Sense, but it is certain their Sense ought to be a little discoloured, that it may seem particular, and proper to the Person and the Condition of the Speaker.

These Descriptions raise a pleasing kind of Horrour in the Mind of the Reader, and amuse his Imagination with the Strangeness and Novelty of the Persons who are represented in them. They bring up into our Memory the Stories we have heard in our Childhood, and favour those secret Terrours and Apprehensions to which the Mind of Man is naturally subject. We are pleased with surveying the different Habits and Behaviours of Foreign Countries; how much more must we be delighted and surprised when we are led, as it were, into a new Creation, and see the Persons and Manners of another Species? Men of cold Fancies, and Philosophical Dispositions, object to this kind of Poetry, that it has not Probability enough to affect the Imagination. But to this it may be answered, that we are sure, in general, there are many intellectual Beings in the World besides our selves, and several Species of Spirits, who are subject to different Laws and Oeconomies from those of Mankind; when we see, therefore, any of these represented naturally, we cannot look upon the Representation as altogether impossible; nay, many are prepossest with such false Opinions, as dispose them to believe these particular Delusions; at least, we have all heard so many pleasing Relations in favour of them, that we do not care for seeing through the Falshood, and willingly give our selves up to so agreeable an Imposture.

The Ancients have not much of this Poetry among them, for, indeed, almost the whole Substance of it owes its Original to the Darkness and Superstition of later Ages, when pious Frauds were made use of to amuse Mankind, and frighten them into a Sense of their Duty. Our Forefathers looked upon Nature with more Reverence and Horrour, before the World was enlightned by Learning and Philosophy, and loved to astonish themselves with the Apprehensions of Witchcraft, Prodigies, Charms and Enchantments. There was not a Village in *England* that had not a Ghost in it, the Churchyards were all haunted, every large Common had a Circle of Fairies belonging to it, and there was scarce a Shepherd to be met with who had not seen a Spirit.

Among all the Poets of this Kind our *English* are much the best, by what I have yet seen, whether it be that we abound with more Stories of this Nature, or that the Genius of our Country is fitter for this sort of Poetry. For the *English* are naturally Fanciful, and very often disposed by that Gloominess and Melancholly of Temper, which is so frequent in our Nation, to many wild Notions and Visions, to which others are not so liable.

Among the *English*, *Shakespear* has incomparably excelled all others. That noble Extravagance of Fancy, which he had in so great Perfection, thoroughly qualified him to touch this weak superstitious Part of his Reader's Imagination; and made him capable of succeeding, where he had nothing to support him besides the Strength of his own Genius. There is something so wild and yet so solemn in the Speeches of his Ghosts, Fairies, Witches and the like Imaginary Persons, that we cannot forbear thinking them natural, tho' we have no Rule by which to judge of them, and must confess, if there are such Beings in the World, it looks highly probable they should talk and act as he has represented them.

Joseph Addison
The Spectator (1 July, 1712). Text from
collected edition, Vol. VI (1713)

SHAKESPEARE THE MAGICIAN

WHEN the hand of time shall have brushed off his present Editors and Commentators, and when the very name of *Voltaire*, and even the memory of the language in which he has written, shall be no more, the *Apalachian* mountains, the banks of the *Ohio*, and the plains of *Scotia* shall resound with the accents of this Barbarian: In his native tongue he shall roll the genuine passions of nature; nor shall the griefs of *Lear* be alleviated, or the charms and wit of *Rosalind* be abated by time. There is indeed nothing perishable about him, except that very learning which he is said so much to want. He had not, it is true, enough for the demands of the age in which he lived, but he had perhaps too much for the reach of his genius, and the interest of his fame. *Milton* and he will carry the decayed remnants and fripperies of antient mythology into more distant ages than they are by their own force intitled to extend; and the metamorphoses of *Ovid*, upheld by them, lay in a new claim to unmerited immortality.

Shakespeare is a name so interesting, that it is excusable to stop a moment, nay it would be indecent to pass him without the tribute of some admiration. He differs essentially from all other writers: Him we may profess rather to feel than to understand; and it is safer to say, on many occasions, that we are possessed by him, than that we possess him. And no wonder; – He scatters the seeds of things, the principles of character and action, with so cunning a hand yet with so careless an air, and, master of our feelings, submits himself so little to our judgment, that every thing seems superior. We discern not his course, we see no connection of cause and effect, we are rapt in ignorant admiration, and claim no kindred with his abilities. All the incidents, all the parts, look like chance, whilst we feel and are sensible that the whole is design. His Characters not only act and speak in strict conformity to nature, but in strict relation to us; just so much is shewn as is requisite, just so much is impressed; he commands every passage to our heads and to our hearts, and moulds us as he pleases, and that with so much ease, that he never betrays his own exertions. We see these Characters act from the mingled motives of passion, reason, interest, habit and complection, in all their proportions, when they are supposed to know it not themselves; and we are made to acknowledge that their actions and sentiments are, from those motives, the necessary result. He at once blends and distinguishes every thing; – every thing is complicated, every thing is plain. I restrain the further expressions of my admiration lest they should not seem applicable to man; but it is really astonishing that a mere human being, a part of humanity only, should so perfectly comprehend the whole; and that he should possess such exquisite art, that whilst every woman and every child shall feel the whole effect, his learned Editors and Commentators should yet so very frequently mistake or seem ignorant of the cause. A sceptre or a straw are in his hands of equal efficacy; he needs no selection; he converts every thing into excellence; nothing is too great, nothing is too base. Is a character efficient like *Richard*, it is every thing we can wish: Is it otherwise, like *Hamlet*, it is productive of equal admiration: Action produces one mode of excellence and inaction another: The Chronicle, the Novel, or the Ballad; the king, or the beggar, the hero, the madman, the sot or the fool; it is all one; – nothing is worse, nothing is better: The same genius pervades and is equally admirable in all. Or, is a character to be shewn in progressive change, and the events of years comprized within the hour; – with what a Magic hand does he prepare and scatter his spells! The Understanding must, in the first place, be subdued; and lo! how the rooted prejudices of the child spring up to confound the man! The Weird sisters rise, and order is extinguished. The laws of nature give way, and leave nothing in our minds but wildness and horror. No pause is allowed us for reflection: Horrid sentiment, furious guilt and compunction, air-drawn daggers, murders, ghosts, and inchantment, shake and *possess us wholly*. In the mean time the *process* is completed. *Macbeth* changes under our eye, *the milk of human kindness is converted to gall; he has supped full of horrors*, and his *May of life is fallen into the sear, the yellow leaf;* whilst we, the fools of amazement, are insensible to the shifting of place and the lapse of time, and till the curtain drops, never once wake to the truth of things, or recognize the laws of existence. – On such an occasion, a fellow, like *Rymer*, waking from his trance, shall lift up his Constable's staff, and charge this great Magician, this daring *practicer of arts inhibited*, in the name of *Aristotle*, to surrender; whilst *Aristotle* himself, disowning his wretched Officer, would fall prostrate at his feet and acknowledge his supremacy. – O supreme of Dramatic excellence! (*might he say*,) not to me be imputed the insolence of fools. The bards of *Greece* were confined within the narrow circle of the Chorus, and hence they found themselves constrained to practice, for the most part, the precision, and copy the details of nature. I followed them, and knew not that a larger circle might be drawn, and the Drama extended to the whole reach of human genius. Convinced, I see that a more compendious *nature* may be obtained; a nature of *effects* only, to which neither the relations of place, or continuity of time, are always essential. Nature, condescending to the faculties and apprehensions of man, has drawn through human life a regular chain of visible causes and effects: But Poetry delights in surprize, conceals her steps, seizes at once upon the heart, and obtains the Sublime of things without betraying the rounds of her ascent: True Poesy is *magic*, not *nature*; an effect from causes hidden or unknown. To the Magician I prescribed no laws; his law and his power are one; his power is his law.

Maurice Morgann
*Essay on the Dramatic Character
of Sir John Falstaff* (1777)

SHAKESPEARE AND THE UNITIES

To the unities of time and place he has shewn no regard, and perhaps a nearer view of the principles on which they stand will diminish their value, and withdraw from them the veneration which, from the time of *Corneille*, they have very generally received, by discovering that they have given more trouble to the poet, than pleasure to the auditor.

The necessity of observing the unities of time and place arises from the supposed necessity of making the drama credible. The criticks hold it impossible, that an action of months or years can be possibly believed to pass in three hours; or that the spectator can suppose himself to sit in the theatre, while ambassadors go and return between distant kings, while armies are levied and towns besieged, while an exile wanders and returns, or till he whom they saw courting his mistress, shall lament the untimely fall of his son. The mind revolts from evident falsehood, and fiction loses its force when it departs from the resemblance of reality.

From the narrow limitation of time necessarily arises the contraction of place. The spectator, who knows that he saw the first act at *Alexandria*, cannot suppose that he sees the next at *Rome*, at a distance to which not the dragons of *Medea* could, in so short a time, have transported him; he knows with certainty that he has not changed his place, and he knows that place cannot change itself; that what was a house cannot become a plain; that what was *Thebes* can never be *Persepolis*.

Such is the triumphant language with which a critick exults over the misery of an irregular poet, and exults commonly without resistance or reply. It is time therefore to tell him by the authority of *Shakespeare*, that he assumes, as an unquestionable principle, a position, which, while his breath is forming it into words, his understanding pronounces to be false. It is false, that any representation is mistaken for reality; that any dramatick fable in its materiality was ever credible, or, for a single moment, was ever credited.

The objection arising from the impossibility of passing the first hour at *Alexandria*, and the next at *Rome*, supposes, that when the play opens, the spectator really imagines himself at *Alexandria*, and believes that his walk to the theatre has been a voyage to *Egypt*, and that he lives in the days of *Antony* and *Cleopatra*. Surely he that imagines this may imagine more. He that can take the stage at one time for the palace of the *Ptolemies*, may take it in half an hour for the promontory of *Actium*. Delusion, if delusion be admitted, has no certain limitation; if the spectator can be once persuaded, that his old acquaintance are *Alexander* and *Cæsar*, that a room illuminated with candles is the plain of *Pharsalia*, or the bank of *Granicus*, he is in a state of elevation above the reach of reason, or of truth, and from the heights of empyrean poetry, may despise the circumscriptions of terrestrial nature. There is no reason why a mind thus wandering in extasy should count the clock, or why an hour should not be a century in that calenture of the brains that can make the stage a field.

The truth is, that the spectators are always in their senses, and know, from the first act to the last, that the stage is only a stage, and that the players are only players. They came to hear a certain number of lines recited with just gesture and elegant modulation. The lines relate to some action, and an action must be in some place; but the different actions that compleat a story may be in places very remote from each other; and where is the absurdity of allowing that space to represent first *Athens*, and then *Sicily*, which was always known to be neither *Sicily* nor *Athens*, but a modern theatre?

Samuel Johnson
Preface to *The Plays of Shakespeare* ... (1765)

THOMSON AS A NATURE POET

THOMSON was blessed with a strong and copious fancy; he hath enriched poetry with a variety of new and original images, which he painted from nature itself, and from his own actual observations: his descriptions have therefore a distinctness and truth, which are utterly wanting to those of poets who have only copied from each other, and have never looked abroad on the objects themselves. Thomson was accustomed to wander away into the country for days and for weeks, attentive to, "each rural sight, each rural sound;" while many a poet who has dwelt for years in the Strand, has attempted to describe fields and rivers, and generally succeeded accordingly.

Hence that nauseous repetition of the same circumstances; hence that disgusting impropriety of introducing what may be called a set of hereditary images, without proper regard to the age, or climate, or occasion in which they were formerly used. Though the diction of the Seasons is sometimes harsh and inharmonious, and sometimes turgid and obscure, and though in many instances, the numbers are not sufficiently diversified by different pauses, yet is this poem on the whole, from the numberless strokes of nature in which it abounds, one of the most captivating and amusing in our language, and which, as its beauties are not of a transitory kind, as depending on particular customs and manners, will ever be perused with delight. The scenes of Thomson are frequently as wild and romantic as those of Salvator Rosa, varied with precipices and torrents, and "castled cliffs," and deep vallies, with piny mountains, and the gloomiest caverns. Innumerable are the little circumstances in his descriptions, totally unobserved by all his predecessors. What poet hath ever taken notice of the leaf, that towards the end of autumn,

> Incessant rustles from the mournful grove,
> Oft startling such as, studious, walk below,
> And slowly circles through the waving air?

Or who, in speaking of a summer evening hath ever mentioned,

> The quail that clamours for his running mate?

Or the following natural image at the same time of the year?

> Wide o'er the thistly lawn, as swells the breeze,
> A whitening shower of vegetable down
> Amusive floats — — — —

In what other poet, do we find the silence and expectation

that precedes an April shower insisted on, as in ver. 165 of
SPRING? Or where,

> The stealing shower is scarce to patter heard,
> By such as wander through the forest walks,
> Beneath th' umbrageous multitude of leaves.

How full, particular and picturesque is this assemblage of circumstances that attend a very keen frost in a night of winter!

> Loud rings the frozen earth, and hard reflects
> A double noise; while at his evening watch
> The village dog deters the nightly thief;
> The heifer lows; the distant water-fall
> Swells in the breeze; and with the hasty tread
> Of traveller, the hollow-sounding plain
> Shakes from afar. – – – –

In no one subject are common writers more confused and un-
meaning, than in their descriptions of rivers, which are generally said only to wind and to murmur, while their qualities
and courses are seldom accurately marked. Examine the
exactness of the ensuing description, and consider what a
perfect idea it communicates to the mind.

> Around th' adjoining brook, that purls along
> The vocal grove, now fretting o'er a rock,
> Now scarcely moving through a reedy pool,
> Now starting to a sudden stream, and now
> Gently diffus'd into a limpid plain;
> A various groupe the herds and flocks compose,
> Rural confusion! – – – –

... Nor do I recollect that any poet hath been struck with the
murmurs of the numberless insects, that swarm abroad at the

noon of a summer's day: as attendants of the evening indeed, they have been mentioned;

> Resounds the living surface of the ground:
> Nor undelightful is the ceaseless hum
> To him who muses through the woods at noon;
> Or drowsy shepherd, as he lies reclin'd
> With half-shut eyes. – – –

But the novelty and nature we admire in the descriptions of Thomson are by no means his only excellencies; he is equally to be praised, for impressing on our minds the effects, which the scene delineated would have on the present spectator or hearer.

Joseph Warton
Essay on the Genius and Writings of Pope (1756)
Text from the third edition (1772)

POMPOSITY IN BLANK VERSE AND ELSEWERE

FROM a desire in the critic, of grafting the spirit of ancient languages upon the English, have proceeded of late several disagreeable instances of pedantry. Among the number, I think we may reckon blank verse. Nothing but the greatest sublimity of subject can render such a measure pleasing; however, we now see it used upon the most trivial occasions; it has particularly found its way into our didactic poetry, and is likely to bring that species of composition into disrepute, for which the English are deservedly famous.

Those who are acquainted with writing know, that our language runs almost naturally into blank verse. The writers of our novels, romances, and all of this class, who have no

notion of stile, naturally hobble into this inharmonious measure. If rhymes, therefore, be more difficult, for that very
reason I would have our poets write in rhyme. Such a restric-
tion upon the thought of a good poet, often lifts and encreases
the vehemence of every sentiment; for fancy, like a fountain,
plays highest by diminishing the aperture. But rhymes, it will
be said, are a remnant of monkish stupidity, an innovation
upon the poetry of the ancients. They are but indifferently
acquainted with antiquity who make the assertion. Rhymes
are probably of older date than either the Greek or Latin
dactyl and spondê. The Celtic, which is allowed to be the
first language spoken in Europe, has ever preserved them, as
we may find in the Edda of Iceland, and the Irish carrols, still
sung among the original inhabitants of that island. Olaus
Wormius gives us some of the Teutonic poetry in this way;
and Pantoppidan, bishop of Bergen, some of the Norwegian.
In short, this jingle of sounds is almost natural to mankind; at
least it is so to our language, if we may judge from many unsuccessful attempts to throw it off.

I should not have employed so much time in opposing this
erroneous innovation, if it were not apt to introduce another
in its train; I mean, a disgusting solemnity of manner into our
poetry: and, as the prose writer has been ever found to follow
the poet, it must consequently banish in both, all that agreeable
trifling, which, if I may so express it, often deceives us into
instruction. The finest sentiment, and the most weighty truth,
may put on a pleasant face; and it is even virtuous to jest when
serious advice must be disgusting. But instead of this, the most
trifling performance among us now assumes all the didactic
stiffness of wisdom. The most diminutive son of fame or of
famine has his *we* and his *us*, his *firstlys* and his *secondlys*, as
methodical as if bound in cow-hide and closed with clasps of
brass. Were these Monthly Reviews and Magazines frothy,
pert, or absurd, they might find some pardon; but to be dull

and dronish is an encroachment on the prerogative of a folio. These things should be considered as pills to purge melancholly; they should be made up in our splenetic climate to be taken as physic, and not so as to be used when we take it.

Oliver Goldsmith

An Enquiry into the Present State of Polite Learning in Europe (1759). Text from second edition (1774)

PAUSES IN VERSE

ABSTRACTING at present from the peculiarity of melody arising from the different pauses, it cannot fail to be observed in general, that they introduce into our verse no slight degree of variety. A number of uniform lines having all the same pause, are extremely fatiguing, which is remarkable in the French versification. This imperfection will be discerned by a fine ear even in the shortest succession, and becomes intolerable in a long poem. Pope excels in the variety of his melody, which if different kinds can be compared, is indeed no less perfect than that of Virgil.

From what is last said, there ought to be one exception: uniformity in the members of a thought demands equal uniformity in the verbal members which express that thought. When therefore resembling objects or things are expressed in a plurality of verse-lines, these lines in their structure ought to be as uniform as possible, and the pauses in particular ought all of them to have the same place. Take the following examples.

> By foreign hands || thy dying eyes were clos'd,
> By foreign hands || thy decent limbs compos'd,
> By foreign hands || thy humble grave adorn'd.

Again:

> Bright as the sun || her eyes the gazers strike,
> And, like the sun, || they shine on all alike.

Speaking of Nature, or the God of Nature:

> Warms in the sun || refreshes in the breeze,
> Glows in the stars || and blossoms in the trees,
> Lives through all life || extends through all extent,
> Spreads undivided || operates unspent.

Pauses will detain us longer than was expected; for the subject is not yet exhausted. It is laid down above, that English Heroic verse admits no more but four capital pauses; and that the capital pause of every line is determined by the sense to be after the fourth, the fifth, the sixth, or seventh syllable. That this doctrine holds true so far as melody alone is concerned, will be testify'd by every good ear. At the same time, I admit, that this rule may be varied where the sense or expression requires a variation, and that so far the melody may justly be sacrificed. Examples accordingly are not unfrequent, in Milton especially, of the capital pause being after the first, the second, or the third syllable. And that this licence may be taken, even gracefully, when it adds vigour to the expression, will be clear from the following example. Pope, in his translation of Homer, describes a rock broke off from a mountain, and hurling to the plain, in the following words.

> From steep to steep the rolling ruin bounds;
> At every shock the crackling wood resounds;
> Still gath'ring force, it smokes; and urg'd amain,
> Whirls, leaps, and thunders down, impetuous to the plain:
> There stops || So Hector. Their whole force he prov'd.
> Resistless when he rag'd; and when he stopt, unmov'd.

In the penult line, the proper place of the musical pause is at the end of the fifth syllable; but it enlivens the expression by its coincidence with that of the sense at the end of the second syllable: the stopping short before the usual pause in the melody, aids the impression that is made by the description of the stone's stopping short; and what is lost to the melody by this artifice is more than compensated by the force that is added to the description.

Henry Home, Lord Kames
Elements of Criticism (1762). Text
from sixth edition (1785)

MEDIAEVALISM AND POETRY IN THE 1760's

William Shenstone to John MacGowan: an extract from a letter,
24 September, 1761

As to the Erse fragments, you judged very rightly, that, amidst the applause they were sure of receiving from the world, they would not fail to afford me a very peculiar satisfaction. I am unfeignedly thankful for the early copy you sent me, and for the ingenious letter which accompanied them. It seems, indeed, from a former version by the same translator, (which Mr. Gray, the poet, received from him, and shewed my friend Percy), that he has taken pretty considerable freedoms in adapting them to the present reader. I do not in the least disapprove of this; knowing by experience, that trivial amendments in these old compositions often render them highly striking, which would be otherwise quite neglected. And surely, under all the infirmities of age, they may be said to have an absolute claim to some indulgencies of this kind. I presume the editor follows the same model of translation in what he is now going to publish. I would wish him particularly attentive to the melody of his cadences, when it may be done without impeachment of his fidelity. The melody of our verse has been perhaps carried to its utmost perfection; that of prose seems to have been more neglected, and to be capable of greater than it has yet attained. It seems to be a very favourable era for the appearance of such irregular poetry. The taste of the age, so far as it regards plan and style, seems to have been carried to its utmost height, as may appear in the works of Akenside, Gray's Odes and Churchyard Verses, and Mason's Monody and Elfrida. The public has seen all that art can do, and they want the more striking efforts of wild, original, enthusiastic genius. It seems to exclaim aloud with the chorus in Julius Cæsar,

'Oh rather than be slaves to these deep learned men,
  Give us our wildness and our woods, our huts and caves again!'

I know not how far you will allow the distinction or the principle on which I build my remark, namely, that the taste of the present age is somewhat higher than its genius. This turn, you see, favours the work the translator has to publish, or has published already. Here is indeed pure original genius! The very quintessence of poetry; a few drops of which, properly managed, are enough to give a flavour to quart-bottles. And yet one or two of these pieces (the first, for instance, together with the second) are undoubtedly as well planned as any ode we find in Horace.

I have perused the Gentle Shepherd with all imaginable pleasure; and here again am indebted to you, sir, for the assistance of your glossary. 'Tis rare to find a poem of this length, where simplicity of sentiment and of language are so very well sustained. The metre is generally musical; and the old Scottish words form an admirable kind of Doric. Good sense, expressed naturally, in a phrase easy, perspicuous, and not wholly void of ornament, seems the talent of Ramsay, whose taste in composition was perhaps more remarkable than his genius; and in whom greater fire and invention would certainly have deprived his readers of the Gentle Shepherd.

And now having thanked you for the Scotch snuff, (better than any I ever tasted before,) I come to ask, whether you have any old Scotch ballads, which you would wish preserved in a neat edition. I have occasioned a friend of mine to publish a fair collection of the best old English and Scotch ballads; a work I have long had much at heart. Mr. Percy, the collector and publisher, is a man of learning, taste, and indefatigable industry; is chaplain to the Earl of Sussex. It so happens, that he has himself a folio collection of this kind of MSS; which has many things truly curious, and from which he selects the best. I am only afraid that his fondness for antiquity should tempt him to admit pieces that have no other sort of merit. However, he has offered me a rejecting power, of which I mean to make considerable use. He is encouraged in his undertaking by Sam. Johnson, Garrick and many persons of note, who lend him such assistance as is within their power. He has brought Mr. Jo. Warton[1] (the poetry professor) to ransack the Oxford libraries; and has resided and employed six amanuenses to transcribe from Pepys's Collection at Cambridge, consisting of five volumes of old ballads in folio. He says justly that it is in the remote parts of the kingdom that he has most reason to expect the curiosities he wants — that in the southern parts fashion and novelty cause such things to be neglected. Accordingly he has settled a correspondence in Wales, in the wilds of Staffordshire and Derbyshire, in the West Indies, in Ireland, and, if he can obtain your assistance, in Scotland, hopes to draw materials from the whole British empire.

William Shenstone

Edinburgh Annual Register, Vol. II (1809), Part II.   Text
from *Letters . . .*, ed. Marjorie Williams (1939)

1. A mistake. Joseph Warton's brother Thomas was Professor of Poetry at Oxford (1757-67).

Art and Literal Truth

But it is not enough in Invention that the Artist should restrain and keep under all the inferior parts of his subject; he must sometimes deviate from vulgar and strict historical truth, in pursuing the grandeur of his design.

How much the great stile exacts from its professors to conceive and represent their subjects in a poetical manner, not confined to mere matter of fact, may be seen in the cartoons of Raffaelle. In all the pictures in which the painter has represented the apostles, he has drawn them with great nobleness; he has given them as much dignity as the human figure is capable of receiving; yet we are expressly told in scripture they had no such respectable appearance; and of St. Paul, in particular, we are told, by himself, that his *bodily* presence was *mean*. Alexander is said to have been of a low stature: a painter ought not so to represent him. Agesilaus was low, lame, and of a mean appearance. None of these defects ought to appear in a piece of which he is the hero. In conformity to custom, I call this part of the art History Painting; it ought to be called Poetical, as in reality it is.

All this is not falsifying any fact; it is taking an allowed poetical licence. A painter of portraits retains the individual likeness; a painter of history shows the man by showing his action. A painter must compensate the natural deficiencies of his art. He has but one sentence to utter, but one moment to exhibit. He cannot, like the poet or historian, expatiate, and impress the mind with great veneration for the character of the hero or saint he represents, though he lets us know at the same time, that the saint was deformed, or the hero lame. The painter has no other means of giving an idea of the dignity of the mind, but by that external appearance which grandeur of thought does generally, though not always, impress on the countenance; and by that correspondence of figure to sentiment and situation, which all men wish, but cannot command. The Painter who may in this one particular attain with ease what others desire in vain, ought to give all that he possibly can, since there are so many circumstances of true greatness that he cannot give at all. He cannot make his hero talk like a great man; he must make him look like one. For which reason, he ought to be well studied in the analysis of those circumstances which constitute dignity of appearance in real life.

As in Invention, so likewise in Expression, care must be taken not to run into particularities. Those expressions alone should be given to the figures which their respective situations generally produce. Nor is this enough; each person should also have that expression which men of his rank generally exhibit. The joy, or the grief of a character of dignity is not to be expressed in the same manner as a similar passion in a vulgar face. Upon this principle, Bernini, perhaps, may be subject to censure. This sculptor, in many respects admirable, has given a very mean expression to his statue of David, who is represented as just going to throw the stone from the sling; and in order to give it the expression of energy, he has made him biting his under lip. This expression is far from being general, and still farther from being dignified. He might have seen it in an instance or two; and he mistook accident for generality.

Sir Joshua Reynolds
'Discourse IV' (1771) from *Seven Discourses
delivered in the Royal Academy* ... (1778)

A REVOLUTION IN GARDENING

BUT the capital stroke, the leading step to all that has followed, was [I believe the first thought was Bridgeman's] the destruction of walls for boundaries, and the invention of fossés – an attempt then deemed so astonishing, that the common people called them Ha! Ha's! to express their surprize at finding a sudden and unperceived check to their walk.

One of the first gardens planted in this simple though still formal style, was my father's at Houghton. It was laid out by Mr. Eyre, an imitator of Bridgman. It contains three-and-twenty acres, then reckoned a considerable portion.

I call a sunk fence the leading step, for these reasons. No sooner was this simple enchantment made, than levelling, mowing and rolling, followed. The contiguous ground of the park without the sunk fence was to be harmonized with the lawn within; and the garden in its turn was to be set free from its prim regularity, that it might assort with the wilder country without. The sunk fence ascertained the specific garden, but that it might not draw too obvious a line of distinction between the neat and the rude, the contiguous out-lying parts came to be included in a kind of general design: and when nature was taken into the plan, under improvements, every step that was made, pointed out new beauties and inspired new ideas. At that moment appeared Kent, painter enough to taste the charms of landscape, bold and opinionative enough to dare and to dictate, and born with a genius to strike out a great system from the twilight of imperfect essays. He leaped the fence, and saw that all nature was a garden. He felt the delicious contrast of hill and valley changing imperceptibly into each other, tasted the beauty of the gentle swell, or concave scoop, and remarked how loose groves crowned an easy eminence with happy ornament, and while they called in the distant view between their graceful stems, removed and extended the perspective by delusive comparison.

Thus the pencil of his imagination bestowed all the arts of landscape on the scenes he handled. The great principles on which he worked were perspective, and light and shade.

Groupes of trees broke too uniform or too extensive a lawn; evergreens and woods were opposed to the glare of the champain, and where the view was less fortunate, or so much exposed as to be beheld at once, he blotted out some parts by thick shades, to divide it into variety, or to make the richest scene more enchanting by reserving it to a farther advance of the spectator's step. Thus selecting favourite objects, and veiling deformities by screens of plantation; sometimes allowing the rudest waste to add its foil to the richest theatre, he realised the compositions of the greatest masters in painting. Where objects were wanting to animate his horizon, his taste as an architect could bestow immediate termination. His buildings, his seats, his temples, were more the works of his pencil than of his compasses. We owe the restoration of Greece and the diffusion of architecture to his skill in landscape.

But of all the beauties he added to the face of this beautiful country, none surpassed his management of water. Adieu to canals, circular basons, and cascades tumbling down marble steps, that last absurd magnificence of Italian and French villas. The forced elevation of cataracts was no more. The gentle stream was taught to serpentize seemingly at its pleasure, and where discontinued by different levels, its course appeared to be concealed by thickets properly interspersed, and glittered again at a distance where it might be supposed naturally to arrive. Its borders were smoothed, but preserved their waving irregularity. A few trees scattered here and there on its edges sprinkled the tame bank that accompanied its meanders; and when it disappeared among the hills, shades descending from the heights leaned towards its progress, and framed the distant point of light under which it was lost, as it turned aside to either hand of the blue horizon.

Thus dealing in none but the colours of nature, and catching its most favourable features, men saw a new creation opening before their eyes. The living landscape was chastened or polished, not transformed. Freedom was given to the forms of trees; they extended their branches unrestricted, and where any eminent oak, or master beech had escaped maiming and survived the forest, bush and bramble was removed, and all its honours were restored to distinguish and shade the plain. Where the united plumage of an ancient wood extended wide its undulating canopy, and stood venerable in its darkness, Kent thinned the foremost ranks, and left but so many detached and scattered trees, as softened the approach of gloom and blended a chequered light with the thus lengthened shadows of the remaining columns.

Horace Walpole, fourth Earl of Orford
'On Modern Gardening' in *Anecdotes of Painting in England* . . ., Vol. IV (printed 1771, published 1780)

BIOGRAPHICAL NOTES

Addison, Joseph (1672–1719), periodical essayist, political journalist, poet and dramatist, first achieved prominence and pleased the Whigs with his poem *The Campaign* (1704) celebrating the battle of Blenheim, and during Whig administrations enjoyed a succession of political appointments. He contributed to Steele's *Tatler* (1709–11), but is chiefly known for his large share of the essays in the *Spectator* (1711–12), which provided its public with literary criticism and a simplified version of contemporary science and philosophy, together with moral discourses, light satire and humorous descriptions and character sketches. He wrote a successful tragedy, *Cato* (1713).

Arbuthnot, John (1667–1735), physician in ordinary to Queen Anne and a writer on medical subjects, was one of a group of Tory wits (with Pope, Swift, Gay and others) known as the 'Scriblerus Club,' to whose satirical projects he contributed. He wrote a number of pamphlets which include *The History of John Bull* (1712) and *The Art of Political Lying* (1712).

Berkeley, George (1685–1753), bishop of Cloyne (1734), a great master of lucid and animated prose, made his most significant contributions to philosophy in his earlier writings, the *New Theory of Vision* (1709), *Principles of Human Knowledge* (1710) and the *Dialogues between Hylas and Philonous* (1713). Notable among his later works are *Alciphron* (1732), a brilliant series of dialogues in which free-thinkers are discomfited, and the curious *Siris* (1743) which combines mystical speculation with discussion of the medicinal virtues of tar-water.

Boswell, James (1740–95), son of a Scottish judge, came to London where he met Johnson (1762) whose friend he remained until the latter's death (1784). He is chiefly known for his great *Life of Samuel Johnson* (1791), preceded by the *Journal of the Tour to the Hebrides* (1785), in which Johnson is the centre of interest. Boswell's talent lay largely in the life-like recapturing of personal incidents and traits of character. His *Journals*, kept in his early twenties and recently edited, are remarkable for their frankness and attempts at self-knowledge.

Brown, Thomas (1663–1704), satirist, journalist and translator, is known chiefly as the author of *Amusements, Serious and Comical* (1700), with its lively and extravagant, if rather coarse, sketches of London life.

Butler, Joseph (1692–1752), bishop of Bristol (1738) and later of Durham (1750), was one of the more important moral philosophers of this period, his theory of conscience being especially notable. His chief works are *Fifteen Sermons* (1726), and the *Analogy of Religion* (1736), a celebrated defence of Christianity against Deism.

Byrom, John (1692–1763), a religious poet and an exponent of short-hand (which he taught in Manchester), is known to us as an attract-ive personality through his *Private Diary and Literary Remains* (1854–57), which give interesting impressions of circles in which William Law and Wesley moved.

Colman, George (1732–94), one of the more able comic dramatists of the middle of the century, and a notable theatrical manager, is chiefly known for *The Jealous Wife* (1761), based on material from Fielding's *Tom Jones*, and *The Clandestine Marriage* (1762), in which Garrick had a share.

Cook, James (1728–79), sea captain and explorer, kept journals of his three famous voyages. From these J. Hawkesworth and others wrote up accounts for publication, but the *Voyage towards the South Pole and Round the World*, edited by J. Douglas (1777), preserves Cook's sensible, unvarnished idiom.

Cooper, Anthony Ashley, third Earl of Shaftesbury (1671–1713), a Deist philosopher, is represented by one work, *Characteristicks of Men, Manners, Opinions, Times* (1711), which includes several earlier writings. He is usually regarded as the founder of the 'moral sense' school, and is important for his emphasis on man's natural feeling, moral and aesthetic, for the good.

Cowper, Mary, Countess (1685–1724), wife of Earl Cowper, the Lord Chancellor, was a lady in waiting to the Princess of Wales. Her diary, a portion of which survives and was published in 1864, describes court life during the first year or two of George I's reign.

Defoe, Daniel (1660?–1731), Whig political journalist and adventurer, novelist, prolific writer on miscellaneous topics, addressed a middle class, dissenting public. His political works include the ironical

Shortest Way with the Dissenters (1702), which led to imprisonment and the pillory, and his periodical, *The Review* (1704–13). His most important novels are *Robinson Crusoe* (1719), *Captain Singleton* (1720), *Moll Flanders* (1722), and *The Fortunate Mistress* (1724). Among his other works are the *Journal of the Plague Year* (1722), the *Tour thro' Great Britain* (1724–7), and *A Plan of the English Commerce* (1728).

Dennis, John (1657–1734), critic and dramatist, and a man of formidable personality, is chiefly known for his hostile relations with Pope. But he has come to be respected as a critic of original opinions. In his *Usefulness of the Stage* (1698) and elsewhere he replied vigorously to Collier's attack on the immorality of the stage, and in his *Grounds of Criticism in Poetry* (1704) he stresses the emotional aspects and the relation of poetry to religion.

Derham, William (1657–1735), clergyman and naturalist, F.R.S. (1702), wrote several works uniting science with theology. *Physico-Theology* (1713) is mainly a descriptive account of the world and its creatures, with continual references to the wisdom of the Creator.

Farquhar, George (1678–1707), a comic dramatist notable for his boisterous humour and naturalness, is at his best in *The Recruiting Officer* (1706) and *The Beaux Stratagem* (1707).

Fielding, Henry (1707–54), one of the greatest and most humane of English novelists, created with *Joseph Andrews* (1742) a new species of comic novel, combining episodic structure in the manner of *Don Quixote* with portrayal of contemporary manners. His other novels are *Jonathan Wild* (1743); *Tom Jones* (1749), commonly regarded as his finest; and *Amelia* (1751), which reaches levels of seriousness not touched in the others. He started life as a comic dramatist, but of his prolific theatrical output only *The Tragedy of Tragedies, or Tom Thumb the Great* (1731) is now known. In his later years he rendered valuable public service as a J.P. for Westminster.

Foote, Samuel (1720–77), a minor comic dramatist, was referred to in his day as 'the English Aristophanes'. *Taste* (1752) is one of a number of light comedies satirizing contemporary follies, but *The Minor* (1760) and *The Maid of Bath* (1771) are regarded as among his better plays.

Garrick, David (1717–79), a great actor notable for many Shakespearian rôles, was a life-long friend of Dr Johnson. Apart from his collaboration with George Colman in *The Clandestine Marriage* (1762), he composed a few quite unimportant comedies.

Gay, John (1685–1732), a poet and dramatist, and friend of Pope and Swift, is best known for *The Beggar's Opera* (1728), the first example of 'ballad opera'. His poems are excellent specimens of Augustan wit and grace.

Gibbon, Edward (1737–94), our greatest historian, was also one of our most brilliant prose writers. His *Decline and Fall of the Roman Empire* (1776–88), a monument to 'Augustan' values for its sympathy with the ancient classical order and contempt for the ages of 'superstition' and 'barbarism' which followed, aroused indignation in some quarters because of its cool, rationalist treatment of the Christian church. His *Miscellaneous Works* were edited after his death by his friend Lord Sheffield (1796), who was responsible for taking materials from his six autobiographical manuscripts and composing them into the 'Memoirs', now better known as Gibbon's *Autobiography*.

Goldsmith, Oliver (1728–74), poet, novelist, dramatist, biographer and essayist, achieved a kind of perfection within limits in several literary *genres*. His best known works are the poems, *The Traveller* (1764) and *The Deserted Village* (1770); *The Vicar of Wakefield* (1766); the two plays, *The Good-natured Man* (1768) and *She Stoops to Conquer* (1773); the biographies of Beau Nash (1762) and Bolingbroke (1770); and the essays known under the title of *The Citizen of the World* (1762). He was a member of Dr. Johnson's circle.

Graves, Richard (1715–1804), country parson, novelist, associate of Shenstone, criticized Methodism and satirized George Whitefield in *The Spiritual Quixote* (1773), a very readable 'novel of the road' and one of a number of Quixote imitations of this period.

Gray, Thomas (1716–71), a poet of small output but of great refinement of feeling and technique, lived the life of a recluse and a scholar at Cambridge. He was a delightful letter-writer, the letter-journal to Wharton containing interesting romantic descriptions of Lake District scenery. A great mediaevalist, in the age of scholars like Thomas Warton and Percy, he left a few interesting essays on mediaeval poetry.

Hearne, Thomas (1678–1735), was an Oxford antiquary and librarian. His diary, published by the Oxford Historical Society (1885–1921), is full of entertaining items, his strong Jacobite views adding to the flavour.

Hervey, John, Baron (1696–1743), immortalized as Pope's 'Sporus', was vice-chamberlain at the court of George II, of which he presented a brilliant but merciless account in his *Memoirs*, edited by J.W. Croker in 1848.

Home, Henry, Lord Kames (1696–1782), minor philosopher and critic, attempted in *Elements of Criticism* (1762) to systematize the whole field of literary and aesthetic theory, in relation to current philosophical and psychological ideas. He made many interesting remarks on Shakespeare's characterization.

Hume, David (1711–76), Scottish philosopher, historian, essayist, was notorious in his day for his sceptical views, especially those expressed in the essay on miracles. Among his chief philosophical works are his *Treatise on Human Nature* (1739–40) and the *Philosophical Essays concerning Human Understanding* (1748), later re-named the *Enquiry concerning Human Understanding*. His excellently written *History of Great Britain* (1754–61), which was long a standard work, places him among the precursors of Gibbon.

Hurd, Richard (1720–1808), bishop of Worcester, was one of those who, in the generation of Gray, Percy and Thomas Warton, helped to develop sympathy for the 'Gothic' in literature. His *Moral and Political Dialogues* (1759), especially the third and fourth dealing with the Elizabethan age, and the *Letters on Chivalry and Romance* (1762), are his contribution to this movement.

Johnson, Samuel (1709–84), critic, poet, essayist, lexicographer, a figure of impressive moral stature, selected by Carlyle as his 'Hero as Man of Letters', lived and worked in comparative obscurity until the *Dictionary* (1755) brought him fame. His poems *London* (1738) and *The Vanity of Human Wishes* (1749) belong to and reflect the years of struggle. The essays in *The Rambler* (1750–52) and his oriental tale *Rasselas* are full of wisdom and weighty, often sombre, moral reflection. A pension of £300 granted in 1762 made his later years comfortable, and with the founding of 'The Club' (later 'The Literary Club') in about 1763, a phase of relaxed social companionship with men like Reynolds, Burke, Goldsmith, Boswell and others began. In 1765 his edition of Shakespeare appeared. In 1773 he visited Scotland and the Hebrides, and published his *Journey* in 1775. His *Lives of the Poets*, the fruits of ripe age, were written at the request of booksellers in 1779–81. Boswell's *Life* is based on intimate knowledge of him during his last twenty-two years.

'Junius', the still unidentified writer of the letters in the *Publick Advertiser* (1769–72), directed some brilliant but malicious invectives against the Duke of Grafton and other public figures.

Law, William (1686–1761), non-juror, 'honoured friend and spiritual director' of the family of Gibbon's father, associate of Wesley and Byrom, wrote controversial works, but is best known for *The Serious Call to a Devout and Holy Life* (1729). Later he wrote some remarkable mystical works under the influence of Boehme.

Lillo, George (1693–1739), dramatist, is important as the exponent of middle-class domestic tragedy. After *The London Merchant* (1731) his most notable play is perhaps *Fatal Curiosity* (1736). His influence abroad on such writers as Diderot and Lessing is quite disproportionate to his slight merit.

Mackenzie, Henry (1745–1831), novelist and periodical essayist, is remembered mainly for *The Man of Feeling* (1771), with its studied cultivation of the sentimental and its 'index to tears'.

Mandeville, Bernard (1670–1733), a sardonic philosopher with an admirably readable and pungent style, shocked his contemporaries with *The Grumbling Hive* (1705), in octosyllabic verse, to which he added the prose *Fable of the Bees* (1714), in which he taught that 'private vices' are 'public benefits'. Berkeley attacked him in *Alciphron*, but Mandeville showed in his *Letter to Dion* (1732) that his analysis was true for this world, 'which a true Christian ought to renounce.'

Montagu, Mrs Elizabeth, *née* Robinson (1720–1800), the wife of Edward Montagu (cousin of Edward Wortley Montagu, husband of Lady Mary) was for nearly fifty years one of London's great hostesses, the epithet 'blue-stocking' being first applied to her circle. A woman of great wit and charm, she was the author of an *Essay on the Genius and Writings of Shakespeare* (1769), a reply to Voltaire's disparagements, and was a vivacious correspondent.

Montagu, Lady Mary Wortley (1689–1762), one of the forceful personalities of her age, a friend and later bitter enemy of Pope, is now known mainly for her letters, those dealing with European and oriental scenes written during the embassy to Constantinople of her husband, Edward Wortley Montagu, being especially vivid and amusing.

Morgann, Maurice (1726–1802), a public official who participated in the peace negotiations with America, is important to literary history for his extraordinary *Essay on the Dramatic Character of Sir John Falstaff* (1777), which was symptomatic of a growing interest in the complexity of Shakespeare's characters, and an early example of the enthusiastic view of his greatness prevalent in the Romantic period.

North, Roger (1653–1734), lawyer and historian, son of Dudley, fourth Baron North, wrote his *Examen* (published posthumously in 1740), to defend Charles II against White Kennett's treatment of him in his *Compleat History of England*, but is more celebrated for the colloquial charm and intelligence shown in his lives of his brothers, Lord Guilford, Sir Dudley North and Dr. John North, which were edited (1740–42) by his son, and also for his *Autobiography*, edited by A. Jessopp (1877).

Piozzi, Hester Lynch, *née* Salusbury (1741–1821), was first married to Henry Thrale, the brewer, and it was at their home in Streatham that Dr Johnson lived almost continually for fifteen years. Her second marriage to Gabriele Piozzi, her relations with whom displeased Johnson, took place in 1784. Among her publications are *Anecdotes of the late Samuel Johnson* (1786) and *Journey through France, Italy and Germany* (1789).

Pitt, William, the elder, Earl of Chatham (1708–78), the 'Great Commoner' and organiser of Britain's astonishing victories in the Seven Years War, was perhaps the greatest parliamentary orator of his day, his most notable speeches being in opposition to the policies of George III's government, especially in relation to America.

Pope, Alexander (1688–1744), a master of satire, comic invention, moralizing and also of more serious kinds of writing in the heroic couplet medium, was the greatest English poet of the eighteenth century. His prose works include contributions to the *Guardian* and to the 'Scriblerian' *Miscellanies*, generous prefaces to the *Iliad* translation and to his edition of Shakespeare (1725), and delightful letters to Swift and other friends.

Reynolds, Sir Joshua (1723–92), the great portrait painter to whom we owe likenesses of many well-known contemporaries, and a member of Dr. Johnson's circle, was the first president of the Royal Academy. His *Discourses* (first collected edition, 1797), full of practical wisdom on the art of painting, are interesting for their emphasis on a generalized 'grand' style.

Richardson, Samuel (1689–1761), a printer, with little education, turned late in life to novel-writing. His three epistolary novels are less read than they deserve because of their prolixity. *Pamela* (1740–41), with its rather unctuous prudential morality, was mocked in the early chapters of *Joseph Andrews* by Fielding, who was probably the author of another skit, *Shamela* (1741). *Clarissa* (1747–48) stands alone in its period as a great tragic masterpiece, and *Sir Charles Grandison* (1753–54) is notable as a study of an exemplary hero. As an explorer of the human heart he has exerted a great influence on European literature.

Robertson, William (1721–93), principal of Edinburgh University and historiographer of Scotland, was one of the forerunners of Gibbon in the art of writing history, and is a neglected prose writer. His chief works are the *History of Scotland* (1759), *History of Charles V* (1769), and *History of America* (1777).

Rogers, Woodes (d. 1732), sea captain and later governor of the Bahamas, wrote an admirably readable *Cruising Voyage round the World* (1712), telling of an expedition against the Spaniards in the South Sea. It contains the celebrated story of Alexander Selkirk, the original of Robinson Crusoe.

Ryder, Sir Dudley (1691–1756), who became Attorney-General and Lord Chief Justice, kept a diary in shorthand of the years 1715–16 (ed. W. Matthews, 1939) which gives an interesting picture of his life as a young nonconformist law student at the Middle Temple.

St John, Henry, Viscount Bolingbroke (1678–1751), chief associate with Harley in opposing the continuance of war with France, supported the Pretender (1715), was attainted, pardoned (1723), and for some years was active in the anti-Walpole party. An admired friend of Swift and Pope, he has failed to maintain his reputation as a great genius with posterity. His *Patriot King* (1749) had an important influence on George III. The remarkable *Letter to William Windham* (1753) has been criticized as a somewhat disingenuous piece of political autobiography.

Shenstone, William (1714–73), a poet and essayist of rather slender talent, was celebrated for his experiments in gardening on his estate, the Leasowes. He was an associate of Percy and other mediaevalists.

Smith, Adam (1723–90), a Scotsman and friend of Hume, began as a moral philosopher, publishing his *Theory of Moral Sentiments* in 1759; but he is chiefly known for his monumental *Wealth of Nations* (1776), a decisive work in the development of classical economic theory.

Smollett, Tobias (1721–71), for some time a surgeon's mate at sea, is best known for his novels, but he also had a busy career as journalist, translator and historian. His novels are characterized by much comic grossness and violence and caricaturing of human nature, but also by the fluent expertness of the style. His best works are *Roderick Random* (1748), *Peregrine Pickle* (1751), *Humphrey Clinker* (1771), and his *Travels in France and Italy* (1766). The note of complaint in his *Travels* earned him the nickname of 'Smelfungus' in Sterne's *Sentimental Journey*.

Spence, Joseph (1699–1768), scholar and critic, a close friend of Pope, is remembered for his gentle qualities, as shown in his kindness to minor poets. His *Anecdotes* (1820) give us much valuable information about Pope and his circle.

Stanhope, Philip Dormer, fourth Earl of Chesterfield (1694–1773), a statesman, was regarded as one of the most polished parliamentary orators of his age, his attack on the Licensing Bill (1737) achieving great celebrity. His literary reputation now rests mainly on his letters to his illegitimate son and godson, with their advice on the art of living.

Steele, Sir Richard (1672–1729), periodical essayist and founder of the

Tatler (1709–11) and other periodicals, dramatist and Whig political pamphleteer, is somewhat over-shadowed by Addison, though some readers prefer him on account of his sincerity and tenderness. As dramatist and critic he tried to reform the manners of the stage, and in the *Spectator* (1711–12) and elsewhere he often used the periodical essay as a vehicle for moral and religious teaching. His charming letters to his second wife, 'Prue', have always given much pleasure.

Sterne, Laurence (1713–68), a country clergyman, achieved immediate fame and immense social success with the publication of the first volumes of his *Tristram Shandy* (1760–67), one of the great comic novels of the world. He was obliged to travel for his health, and *A Sentimental Journey* (1768) is an account, partly factual and partly fanciful, of his personal adventures abroad. Its admirable combination of sentiment and humorous self-awareness has not always been justly appreciated. His *Journal to Eliza*, written (1767) in ill-health and emotional stress to Mrs. Eliza Draper, was first published in 1904.

Swift, Jonathan (1667–1745), a clergyman (mainly in Ireland), is our greatest satirist and political pamphleteer. His early satires, *A Tale of a Tub* (1704) and *The Battle of the Books* (1704) deal extravagantly with pedantries and sectarian absurdities. During the years 1710–13 he was in London at the centre of English political life, supporting the Tories, Harley (Oxford) and St. John (Bolingbroke), in their policy of ending the war, with his periodical *The Examiner* (1711) and such pamphlets as *The Conduct of the Allies* (1712). Exiled in Ireland as Dean of St Patrick's, Dublin (1713), he expressed himself on behalf of the Irish people in pamphlets of great power, *The Drapier's Letters* (1724) and *A Modest Proposal* (1729). During his London period he became associated with Pope and other Tory wits in the 'Scriblerus Club', and *Gulliver's Travels* (1726) had its origin in their early projects. He was also a remarkable minor poet.

Vanbrugh, Sir John (1664–1726), comic dramatist, was also the architect of Blenheim Palace, Castle Howard and other imposing buildings. *The Relapse* (1697), *The Provoked Wife* (1697) and *The Confederacy* (1703) are perhaps his best plays.

Walpole, Horace, fourth Earl of Orford (1717–97), son of Sir Robert

Walpole, was one of the greatest and most prolific of letter-writers, and an amateur in several literary fields. His 'Gothic castle' at Strawberry Hill was an early landmark in the Gothic Revival, his *Castle of Otranto* (1764) was the first Gothic novel, while the *Anecdotes of Painting in England* (1761–71) and *Essay on Gardening* (1771) illustrate other aspects of his connoisseurship of the arts.

Walter, Richard (1716?–85) was chaplain of Anson's ship, *Centurion*, during the celebrated voyage beginning in 1740. His *Voyage round the World* (1748), prepared under Anson's supervision, is outstanding among accounts of voyages.

Ward, Edward (1667–1731), usually known as 'Ned' Ward, a journalist with a strangely colourful style, presents in *The London Spy* (1698–99) a picture of London life which stops at nothing in its presentation of the seamy side.

Warton, Joseph (1722–1800), brother of Thomas Warton, is important in the history of criticism for his *Essay* on Pope (1756, second part 1782), in which he denies him the highest rank among English poets on the grounds that he lacks the 'sublime' and the 'pathetic'.

Wesley, John (1703–91), founder of Methodism and author of a large number of hymns and sermons, published from time to time portions of his *Journal*, a magnificent record of his prodigious activities as a travelling preacher, presenting a varied and animated account of English life over half a century.

White, Gilbert (1720–93), a country parson and naturalist, earned with his *Natural History of Selborne* (1789) a unique position among English writers in this field, by virtue of his remarkable powers of sympathetic observation. This book is a collection of letters written over many years to Thomas Pennant and Daines Barrington.

Wilkes, John (1727–97), a Whig politician and member of the Hellfire Club, was an amusingly scandalous figure of some vivacity and charm. He attacked the Bute administration in *The North Briton* (1762–63), the celebrated No. 45 on the speech from the throne leading to conviction for seditious libel and outlawry. During the Middlesex election period (1768–69) he was supported in his feud with the Government by 'Junius'. Dr Johnson wrote on the other side.

Young, Edward (1683–1765), the poet of *The Complaint or Night Thoughts* (1742–45), which with its sombre rhapsodizings enjoyed a considerable vogue, also wrote *Conjectures on Original Composition* (1759), one of a number of critical writings of this period which are opposed in spirit to neo-classicism.

INDEX OF AUTHORS

ACKNOWLEDGEMENTS

FOR permission to quote extracts from their publications we are indebted to:

Basil Blackwell, publisher of *William Shenstone's Letters* edited by Marjorie Williams; the Clarendon Press, publishers of *The Correspondence of Thomas Gray* edited by P. Toynbee and L. Whibley, and of *The Letters of Laurence Sterne* edited by L. P. Curtis; Messrs Constable, publishers of *Mrs Montagu 'Queen of the Blues' 1762–1800* edited by R. Blunt; the Epworth Press, publishers of *John Wesley's Journal* edited by N. Curnock; Messrs Eyre & Spottiswoode, publishers of *Lord Chesterfield's Letters* edited by Bonamy Dobrée; Messrs William Heinemann, publishers of *Boswell's Column* edited by Margaret Bailey; Messrs Methuen, publishers of *The Diary of Dudley Ryder 1715–1716* edited by William Matthews; the Nonesuch Press, publishers of *Sir John Vanbrugh's Complete Works* edited by Bonamy Dobrée and Geoffrey Webb; and the Yale University Press, publishers of *The Yale Edition of Horace Walpole's Correspondence* edited by W. S. Lewis.